THE MODI EFFECT

Also by Lance Price

The Spin Doctor's Diary
Time and Fate
Where Power Lies

THE MODI EFFECT

INSIDE NARENDRA MODI'S CAMPAIGN TO TRANSFORM INDIA

LANCE PRICE

HODDER & STOUGHTON

First published in Great Britain in 2015 by Hodder & Stoughton
An Hachette UK company

1

A CIP catalogue record for this title is available from the British Library

Hardback ISBN 978 1 473 61089 7
Trade Paperback ISBN 978 1 473 61090 3
Ebook ISBN 978 1 473 61088 0

Typeset in Plantin Light by Hewer Text UK Ltd, Edinburgh

Printed and bound by CPI Group (UK) Ltd, Croydon, CR0 4YY

Hodder & Stoughton policy is to use papers that are natural, renewable and recyclable products and made from wood grown in sustainable forests. The logging and manufacturing processes are expected to conform to the environmental regulations of the country of origin.

Hodder & Stoughton Ltd
Carmelite House
50 Victoria Embankment
London EC4Y 0DZ

www.hodder.co.uk

To James

CONTENTS

CHAPTER ONE
THE OUTSIDER

On 16 May 2014, India's new prime minister, Narendra Modi, entered the record books, after the most extraordinary general election campaign in his country's history. His had been a remarkable victory, not just by the standards of Indian democracy, but worthy of comparison with some of the greatest electoral triumphs anywhere in the world. By virtue of the mandate he had been given, Modi was now one of the most powerful men on the international stage. And yet until very recently he had been a virtual pariah, refused entry to the United States as a religious extremist and frozen out diplomatically by Britain, the European Union and many other western countries.

His in-box was overflowing; he would face enormous challenges if he was to go anywhere near meeting the expectations he had raised on the campaign trail. But just eight weeks after taking office he made time to meet me – a foreigner with no particular expertise in Indian politics, but with a fascination for elections and respect for politicians with the vision and determination to break the mould, defy conventional wisdom and shake off old prejudices.

I have been in and around politics too long to be much in awe of prime ministers and presidents. I have been fortunate enough to meet, chat with, interview, and in one case work for, some of the greats. Tony Blair (my old boss), Margaret

Thatcher, Nelson Mandela, Bill Clinton; they had all overcome their opponents and won elections that had at one time appeared beyond their grasp or that of their parties. All told, I suppose I must have encountered twenty or more heads of government in my career, first as a journalist and then in politics. Almost without exception, whether I agreed with what they stood for or not, I found them fascinating as people. It takes somebody quite exceptional to work their way to the top with all the sacrifices that are required along the way.

Of all of them, Narendra Modi, who I first set eyes on in person in July 2014, is without doubt the most intriguing and the hardest to fathom. To anybody used to British politics, the way things are done in India is at times very familiar and at others a world apart. Trying to compare Modi with prime ministers closer to home is fraught with complications, but the reasons for trying are obvious. He won a thumping victory at the polls and was thrust into the global spotlight where he stood proudly in front of an audience who knew little about him except, perhaps, by reputation. Over the coming months I was to spend several hours in his company as well as meeting many others who had worked with him, or studied him, closely. At the end of it all, I still couldn't be sure I understood him fully, but I was more convinced than ever that he merited scrutiny.

From what I had seen and read, it was clear that if anybody is a full-time, 24/7 politician, it is Narendra Modi. He appears to allow nothing to distract him from the task in hand. He is a teetotal, celibate vegetarian. There are no sports, no hobbies, no family ties. He sleeps only four or five hours a night, and never takes a day off or goes on vacation. When he does do something that isn't directly work-related – as with his daily yoga and meditation routines – it is simply to make him more productive and effective for the rest of the day. I wasn't sure if all that was admirable or slightly disturbing. The only way to find out was to meet him.

I'd been to Delhi several times over the years and wandered around the imposing government buildings, designed a century ago by the British architects Sir Herbert Baker and Sir Edwin Lutyens. But the prime minister's residence at 7 Race Course Road, where I was now sitting, is not on the tourist trail. Unlike 10 Downing Street, where I used to work, or the White House, it can't be seen from the street. India has lost two post-Independence prime ministers, Indira Gandhi and her son Rajiv, to political assassinations, and security is as tight here as around any leader I have met before. There are the usual scanner and body searches, but before you can gain access to the inner sanctum, you must hand over every conceivable electronic device and allow yourself to be driven in a special car to the low building where the PM lives and receives visitors. It is a relatively plain property looking out over some well-tended gardens, where peacocks strut about purposefully far from public view. The toilets, something the building has in common with Downing Street, are rather rudimentary and reminiscent of the lavatories at school or in a small town museum. On the wall outside the building, the plaque still bore the name of the outgoing prime minister, Dr Manmohan Singh. Nobody had yet got round to changing it. Modi said to me later that he hadn't altered anything else either. The paintings on the walls, the furniture, the rugs were all exactly as Dr Singh had left them. 'Honestly, I do not feel I am the PM even today,' he told me. 'Temperamentally, I am a very detached person and it has become increasingly so over the past years.'

The waiting room was spacious, which was just as well as there seemed to be a lot of people with appointments to see him. There was the usual stack of newspapers and magazines, many of them, I noticed, with articles asking where Modi had disappeared to since the election and why there hadn't already been more signs of progress. I chatted politely with the others in the room, including the foreign minister, Mrs Sushma Swaraj. The conversation took an unusual turn when we were joined by a tall man in white robes with the Hindu *tilak*, a red dot and horizontal line, painted on his forehead. He was a holy man and an astrologer and, without prompting, offered some predictions, all of them flattering, for most of us in the room. I would achieve three great things in life, he told me, apparently solely on the basis of how I was sitting and holding my hands. But I was more interested in what he had seen in Mr Modi's future.

Using the suffix 'ji' as a mark of respect, he told me, 'Modiji will be a great leader.' Well that would have come as no surprise to the man then sitting in his reception room just down the corridor. He has no shortage of people to tell him that and he clearly shares the opinion. But the guru's foresight was a lot more precise. Modi would be in power until 2032, with only a short break in opposition. Most of that time he would have an absolute majority in parliament, only once having to work in coalition with other parties.

For all I knew, this holy man's meeting with the prime minister had nothing to do with his astrological skills, but his appearance was a useful reminder to me of something I was becoming increasingly aware of about Indian politics. There is only so far you can go in trying to understand it through the prism of western political norms. Even before I first set eyes on Modi, I knew I would have to strive to take the measure of him according to standards of behaviour and forms of expression that were quite different to what I had been used to elsewhere. What sounds boastful or over the top to a western ear, for example, is often perfectly acceptable in an Indian context. We have got used to mistrusting and denigrating almost everything our leaders try to tell us. That level of cynicism bordering on contempt has not yet polluted the Indian political system to the same degree. Leaders are listened to with respect and the informality of British politics – 'call me Tony', and so on – is all but absent here. I'm not sure I succeeded entirely, but in my conversations with Narendra Modi I did my best to listen politely to what he had to say, and to bite my tongue when the temptation arose to respond with 'oh, come off it', as it sometimes did.

And so while Ronald Reagan was mocked for taking advice from his wife's astrologer, my Indian friends told me nobody in their country would share my surprise that I bumped into one. I know from bitter experience working as a spokesman for Tony Blair that any suggestion a British prime minister (or his wife) had been mixing with some kind of guru would lead to paroxysms of derision in the media. Not so in India. Here mysticism and religion are highly visible threads running through the political fabric. And even concepts that seem at first sight to translate into our way of thinking – like secularism and communalism, to take two highly pertinent examples in Modi's story – have significantly different meanings.

All of which raised another question. Why was I sitting in that waiting room at all? Modi had agreed to give me unprecedented access to help me analyse the campaign that had brought him to power. No other writer, Indian or foreign, was to be allowed the same privilege. Of all the requests for interviews he had received, to agree to mine was, on the face of it, an improbable choice. He arguably deserves credit for having the self-confidence to talk so openly with somebody who is not an ideological soulmate. My politics has always been left of centre and my instincts liberal. It is not hard to find people who readily define Modi as an extremist, a demagogue, even occasionally a fascist. It is fair to say that if I had a vote in the Indian general election of 2014, I would not have cast it for Narendra Modi or his party.

There are a number of reasons why he might have chosen to speak to me, and at such length. A wish to have his success better recognised on the international stage is certainly one. Perhaps a desire to be compared alongside the likes of Tony Blair and Barack Obama as a consummate genius of electoral tactics is another. But I think most important of all was that I came with no prejudices or preconceptions, save perhaps for my liberalism. In India Modi is such a huge figure that everybody has made up his or her mind about him. He is revered and adored by many; loathed and feared by others. There are very few 'don't-knows' in Indian politics today.

The time to meet the object of all those strong emotions had finally arrived. A man in a white uniform appeared, bowed and indicated that I should follow him. The tall double doors at the end of the corridor were opened; at the far end of the room I could see Modi sitting in a hard-backed chair with a small table beside him on which there was a telephone, a glass of water and a pile of papers with his glasses on top. He shook my hand firmly and indicated that I should sit in the other identical chair alongside him. I'd been told that he was aware of, and had perhaps even read, my first book, the diary of my time in Downing Street from 1998 to 2001. It seemed a bit unlikely to me, but as a gift I gave him a copy of my second book on British prime ministers and their relationship to the media. He told me he didn't really read books any more, which was a little disheartening, although his staff quickly interjected to point out that he read a lot of articles and other material online. I wasn't to be left with the impression that the prime minister of India wasn't an intellectual.

This was supposed to be a 'getting to know you' session but, as I suspected it might, it quickly turned into the first of my interviews for this book. Most politicians grasp any opportunity to talk about themselves, and I had never really expected this to be an occasion for small talk. I soon learned that small talk, like many other things, is something Modi just doesn't do. Even as we started discussing politics and the election, I did my best to make the most of my first opportunity to size up Modi the man. He is imposing, there is no doubt about that. Like the best of them, he completely dominates the room. His eyes are sharp and penetrating and I found it very hard to look away from him while making notes or checking something I might want to ask. Sitting beside him you have his complete attention and he seems in no hurry to attend to anything else. I had the same experience when left completely alone for ten minutes with Nelson Mandela when he visited the UK to speak at a Labour Party conference, although in Mandela's case he was more than happy to have a fairly inconsequential chat and I was too in awe to attempt anything else.

Modi is physically commanding also. He's not particularly tall, around 5 feet 7 inches, or 1.70 metres, but he is broad. He once claimed in an election speech to have a 56-inch chest, although I read elsewhere that this is not strictly true, and that 'fifty-six inches is a very cleverly crafted tool to develop Modi's alpha male image'. I'm inclined to believe that interpretation, as I was soon to be offered a very large outpouring of image-building observations, many of them from the horse's mouth. But it didn't strike me as a great idea to start challenging him on his vital statistics within minutes of meeting him.

Modi is always impeccably dressed and takes a lot of trouble over his physical appearance. His grey beard was neatly trimmed and his hair smartly if conventionally cut. He wore one of the long kurta tunics with short sleeves for which he is well-known, white leggings and open-toed sandals. I would discuss his dress sense with him on a later occasion but, right now, he was keen to talk about the book I was hoping to write. Not surprisingly, he had his own opinions about what it ought to contain. 'The global population should know how we smoothly and effectively managed the world's largest election process and also how effectively we have evolved the election process since 1952,' he told me. That was the date of the first post-Independence election, when Jawaharlal Nehru, great grandfather of Modi's opponent in 2014, Rahul Gandhi, won a massive parliamentary majority and became India's first democratically elected prime minister. Nehru, like his daughter Indira Gandhi and her son Rajiv, was leader of the Indian National Congress, better known just as the Congress party. The man sitting next to me was the first non-Congress politician ever to win an absolute majority without needing the support of coalition parties. His Bharatiya Janata Party, or BJP, had a much smaller majority than Congress had enjoyed at the peak of its popularity. Nevertheless, as David Cameron pointed out to him on the day the results were announced, he had just got more votes than any other politician anywhere in the universe.

What Modi had to say about democracy, life, the universe and everything we will get to in good time. What I most wanted to hear from him on that Saturday morning was that I would be free to write his story and analyse how he had secured his victory with complete independence. I was delighted to have been granted unique access to him in this way, but I had to be clear that there were no strings attached. Having read some of the previous books on him, I had the clear impression that he liked his story to be told his way and his way only. He had clearly anticipated the question, and to his credit he said I could write whatever I liked. 'You can criticise me as much as you want.'

Modi has reason to be wary of writers and journalists. Few politicians in India have faced such a barrage of personal attacks as he has done since his very first days as a public figure. If it ever got to him, he is well beyond that now. He didn't always like the questions I asked him during several hours of interviews and he didn't always answer them. But he was generous with his time, unfailingly courteous and appeared content that I should write as fair an assessment of the man and his campaign as I was able to construct.

I'd been warned that he wasn't very confident speaking in English, but he spoke to me almost entirely in perfectly clear and coherent English, only occasionally reverting to his native Gujarati, which my multi-lingual note-taker was able quickly to translate. I didn't feel able to take everything he told me at face value and the reader will soon know when I felt I was being spun. If he had indeed seen my first book, *The Spin Doctor's Diary*, he should have known that it takes one to know one and that I have a very low spin threshold when it comes to the utterances of politicians. He should also have known that I tend to react very forcefully if any government, even one that I worked for and admired, tries to tell me what I can or cannot write.

While I didn't ask Modi about the holy man on that occasion, he clearly does listen to those who claim to be able to see into his future. He later told me the story of meeting another astrologer not long after his first election as chief minister of his home state of Gujarat in 2002. Why, he asked her, had nobody predicted he would get the job? 'She responded by saying that her prediction was that God had the prime minister's position in store for the future. Basically we have a belief in our religion, *Maro Bhagya Vidhata*, which means I am putting myself at the disposition for what God has in store for me. If this is the case why be afraid? I have never worn a bullet-proof jacket.'

My next visit to Delhi, in August, coincided with Indian Independence Day, my first opportunity to see and hear Modi speak in public. By now plenty of people had told me what an extraordinary orator he was. How he could keep a huge crowd in the grip of his hands through his rhetoric. How his speeches, almost all of which he wrote himself after consulting widely, were delivered without notes but with great precision, weaving the personal and the political, the local and the national, the emotional with the policy content. He spoke in Hindi. It is one strand of his nationalist agenda that Indian languages, pre-eminently Hindi, should be favoured over western languages, especially English. Once I had persuaded the rather officious security personnel that my young researcher, Gaurav, had as much right to be in the VIP enclosure as I did, I was able to get a running commentary of the speech's highlights.

Like the rest of the crowd, we had had to get up early to be there. Open-air occasions like this often happen at the start of the day before the heat becomes too oppressive. So, as the sun gathered in intensity behind the ramparts of Delhi's historic Red Fort, Narendra Modi took to the podium for his first Independence Day address. Resplendent in a scarlet and green turban and flowing cream robes, he looked out over the tens of thousands of people who had struggled through the early-morning traffic to see him, pausing before he spoke. He knew that just by standing there he was making history. Not only the first PM with an absolute majority not to owe allegiance to the Nehru-Gandhi dynasty, but also the first man from a lower-caste family born in poverty to lead the nation, and the first to have been born after the country gained its independence.

By now world leaders had started to become used to the idea of the pariah turned prime minister. In any case, this speech wasn't meant for them. At least one attempt had been made on Modi's life during the election campaign and his bodyguards had good reason to urge him to speak behind protective screens. He refused. He wanted to speak directly to the people with as little as possible to separate him off. And they had never seen or heard anything like it. For my part, while I've listened to some great political orators, this was something quite different. The Blairs, Thatchers and Clintons all knew how to woo their audiences. The words of Barack Obama will be quoted for generations to come. But none of them ever engaged a crowd with such fervent, visceral passion as Narendra Modi. If success in politics were just about that, Modi would have no equal in the world today.

Politicians can get into trouble when they try to learn their speeches by heart, although the autocue or teleprompter can be a mixed blessing. It was at the Republican National Convention in Chicago in 1952 that former President Herbert Hoover introduced the world to the device that puts the speaker's words on a screen, supposedly invisible to the audience, and is intended to help make the delivery appear more natural. When Hoover strayed off the script the machine froze, throwing him off his stride. 'This damned thing,' he was heard to mutter, 'I could do better without it.' The teleprompter has never taken off in India, where politicians and the public prefer a bit more passion in their speeches. But on big set-piece occasions, and they don't get any bigger than Independence Day, Indian prime ministers traditionally read from a lengthy text, written with the help of their civil servants and covering all the main issues confronting the government. Not so Narendra Modi.

Everything about his address broke with tradition. He spoke with only a handful of notes in front of him in a language shorn of the usual pomp and grandeur of a formal ceremonial occasion. Where previous prime ministers had talked of India's greatness, he talked of its shame. The nation could send a mission to Mars but it couldn't provide a toilet in every school. Poverty and filthy streets disfigured a country that prided itself on one of the most advanced IT sectors in the world. And above all, the degradation of women, whether through the brutality of countless rapes and sexual assaults, or the inhumanity of female foeticide, brought dishonour on all Indians. Nobody was left in any doubt by the end of his hour-long speech that Narendra Modi was a mould-breaker who meant to do things his own way, a way that was a radical break from the past. 'I am an outsider,' he told them, 'quite isolated from the elite class of this place.'

Claiming outsider status is a familiar gambit among political leaders. It is most effective in those places where disillusionment with the status quo is particularly intense. India in 2014 was just such a place. But nobody walks straight into the corridors of power as a complete outsider, however much they might like to pretend they have. Tony Blair and David Cameron went straight in at the top, becoming prime minister in Britain without any previous experience of ministerial office. But they had at least sat in the House of Commons. Modi took on the job without even having been a member of the Indian parliament, the Lok Sabha. He wasn't exactly an ingénue, however. He was an outsider to Delhi in the sense that Jimmy Carter, Bill Clinton and George W. Bush were outsiders to Washington. He'd governed a large state for twelve years and was no stranger to politics. And Modi's record in Gujarat, on India's west coast, was considerably more controversial than those of the former governors of Georgia, Arkansas or Texas. More than a thousand people died in interreligious violence at the start of his watch, a tragedy that came close to ending his career almost as soon as it had begun.

So to his many critics, Modi isn't enough of an outsider. They believe he should have been excluded from political life once and for all. That even George W. Bush should have considered him enough of an extremist to refuse him a visa said all that needed to be said about him for many western liberals. But on the day the results of the general election were announced, 16 May 2014, Modi had the best of all answers to his critics, a decisive victory delivered by the votes of hundreds of millions of Indian citizens, who knew all about his record and had decided nonetheless that he was the man to take the nation forward.

Just as I would not have voted for him, I never voted for Margaret Thatcher either. But I couldn't help but be impressed by the professionalism and effectiveness of her election campaigns. I was on the inside as director of communications when Tony Blair secured his landslide victory in Britain in 2001. On that occasion we fought with every weapon at our disposal. We battered the Conservative Party into submission and we kicked them when they were down in the hope that they would not be able to recover for a very long time to come.

So I am not squeamish about aggressive election campaigns. In 2014, Modi did exactly the same to the Congress Party. One of Tony Blair's former ministers, Patricia Hewitt, who now chairs the UK India Business Council, called it 'an absolutely model campaign. It had many of the best bits of Blair, Clinton and Obama but with even more modern techniques that even they hadn't dreamed of.' Modi picked up some ideas from campaigns in the west but, as he reminded me, India is a very different kind of country. 'If you take a look at the Tony Blair campaign, it had some very good learnings for us but the scale was much smaller. India is the largest democracy on earth. If you add up the next forty democratic countries you will just about reach the total of the electorate in India. It is this scale that is hard to even imagine.'

Even so, India did inherit the basic structures of its modern parliamentary democracy, and much else besides, from Britain, and that democracy, while far from perfect, has served the country well. As Patrick French, one of the best outside observers of the country, notes, 'Half the people in the world who live in a democracy live in India, and an Indian general election can be like nothing on earth.'

India may have learned parliamentary politics from the west, but the election of 2014 was not merely home-grown, it was an example to political parties across the world of what a determined leader and a disciplined party can achieve. This was India's version of Barack Obama's 'Yes We Can!' but amplified a hundred times over. By its use of innovative technology and social media, its ability to reach parts of the country never touched by a national campaign before, and its capacity for galvanising young people and those normally uninterested in or disillusioned by politics, the Modi campaign was a master-class in modern electoral politics. In many ways it was the right campaign at the right time, and under different circumstances it might not have delivered the clear parliamentary majority that it did. The number of people voting for his BJP more than doubled compared to the previous election in 2009, but for all its success the party fell a long way short of getting Modi a simple majority of the votes cast. Candidates running under the colours of the BJP secured 31%. They were aligned with numerous smaller parties in what is called the National Democratic Alliance (NDA). Between them they pushed the tally up to almost 39%. The once dominant Congress Party could manage only 19% by itself and 23% when its partners in the United Progressive Alliance (UPA) were added in. The first-past-the-post parliamentary system, another hangover from British rule, had served Modi well. The BJP won a higher share of the vote than any single party since 1991, but never before had a 31% tally produced enough MPs to govern alone. Yet Modi was the undisputed winner, and few would argue with the assumption that had it been a genuinely presidential election, rather than a quasi one, he would have won and won handsomely.

The *New York Times* has called an Indian election campaign 'the greatest show on earth.' Hillary Clinton described the supervision of the electoral process across a country of almost 1.3 billion people as a global 'gold standard'. This is not to say that there aren't problems in administering a poll across almost eight thousand towns and 640,000 villages. Bribery, corruption and vote-rigging are no longer endemic, but nor have they been rooted out altogether. Indian democracy has survived and grown stronger over the years, while in neighbouring countries like China it has never had the chance to take root; in others like Pakistan it has proved to be an extremely fragile plant, all too easily trodden underfoot by the military.

As Modi pointed out to me, the eligible electorate in India of 814 million is almost double that of all fifty countries in continental Europe put together (492 million) and comfortably exceeds the combined total for the fifty-six countries in the Americas, north and south, and the Caribbean (645 million). Of those people registered to vote, over 550 million did so in 2014. To achieve a turnout of 66.4% in a country where a quarter of the population live below the poverty line and a similar number can neither read nor write and have little access to the news media is a remarkable achievement in itself. By way of comparison, in the American presidential election of 2012, the figure was 57.5%.

Narendra Modi cannot claim all the credit for this impressive turnout, of course. Enormous efforts were made by the Election Commission of India to raise awareness and register voters ahead of the poll. But the 'Modi Wave', as it became known, undoubtedly contributed to the enthusiasm with which so many people went to the polls, often queuing for hours in order to cast their ballots. The very high turnout among young, first-time voters was a notable feature of the election. And whether Modi created the wave or rode the wave, or a bit of both, he succeeded in reaching the holy grail that has eluded almost every other political leader of our age by inspiring a whole new generation of younger voters not just to listen to him but to vote for him.

One of the many things that makes Modi such a fascinating figure is his ability to weave together and then to articulate so many of India's contradictions and make them appear consistent; to embrace India's future, through its young IT-savvy generation, and its past, embodied in the myths and legends of its cultural heritage. He showed how in that Independence Day address. From the ramparts high above the crowd, and with millions watching and listening at home, he was able to expose India's ugly side while still making Indians feel good about themselves. 'I strongly believe in the words of legends,' he told them. 'I have great faith in the statements made by ascetics, sages and saints.' He went on to quote from his favourite sage, Swami Vivekananda, 'I can see before my eyes Mother India awakening once again.' As he concluded his speech, I could sense that the crowd around me wanted desperately to believe him. But as the former governor of New York, Mario Cuomo, said of all politicians, 'You campaign in poetry, you govern in prose.' To live up to his promises, Modi now had to show the whole of India and the watching world outside that he had as much of an appetite for the prosaic business of getting things done as he did for the razzamatazz of electioneering. The outsider had come inside and he had to make the system work.

As he left the podium at the Red Fort and made his way to the bullet-proof car that was waiting for him, he might have reflected on what had been a momentous twelve months for him personally. A year earlier it was not yet certain that he would even be his party's candidate for prime minister. He had built up a large and fanatical following at the grass roots, but many party elders worried that he was too divisive a figure, with too controversial a past, to be acceptable to the country as a whole. So intense were the feelings he aroused on both sides that it is impossible to understand how he came to fight such a ground-breaking and ultimately successful campaign, without knowing a little about how he came to be such an emotive figure in Indian politics and how he saw off those who hoped to thwart him. The story of Modi's rise from humble beginnings to the office of prime minister is, in any case, a fascinating one. It is interwoven with the complex historical and cultural fabric of India of which he, as a nationalist, is so immensely proud.

I have done my best to make the story accessible to those outside India who want to understand the man and the political environment in which he operates. I hope Indian readers will bear with me if sometimes my explanations seem obvious or unnecessary. There is nothing more irritating than the tourist who spends all his time comparing what he sees to life back home, but I'm afraid a little of that is essential in explaining the whirlwind that hit India with such force in the months leading up to Modi's historic victory. While the western media did, of course, report on the campaign, it was covered with none of the minute detail with which American or British elections are dissected. The lasting memories for even a fairly attentive television viewer in the west would have been of a crushing defeat for the Gandhis, a new prime minister who was supposed to be a bit of a right-wing extremist and, oh, wasn't there something about him selling tea as a boy? A *chai wala*? Yes, that was it.

CHAPTER TWO
CHAI WALA

The name Bharatiya Janata Party translates simply as the Indian People's Party. Its motto is 'country first, party second, self last'. Yet, from the overwhelming volume of photos, images and slogans that drenched the country in the months running up to the general election of 2014, you could have been forgiven for thinking it was now, 'Modi first, Modi second, Modi last'. It was an unashamedly, some might say shamelessly, presidential campaign, and the issue dominating from day one to the announcement of the results on 16 May was Modi. And, in common with all presidential campaigns, his record, his character, and even his upbringing were endlessly raked over. He knew this would happen. It was, as we shall see, a very conscious decision on his part to make it a campaign based almost entirely on his personal capacity to lead the nation in a different direction.

And yet, while making himself the issue, he did his best to maintain that he was a man without personal ambition. 'I am a person who never dreamt of becoming anything,' he told a TV audience as the campaign entered its final stage. 'You should always dream of doing something.' He came from such a poor background, he said, that his mother would have given away free sweets in the village if he had succeeded even in becoming a schoolteacher. 'It's the blessings of people in a democracy that can decide the future of a person. In a democracy, no one can decide his future. Even today, I have dreams of doing things but not one dream of becoming anything.'

Modi is India's great communicator, on a par with Ronald Reagan, but when he does 'self-effacing' he is at his least convincing. He is as egotistical as any politician I have ever met, and his conversation is littered with references to himself in the third person. 'In all corners of the country,' he told me, 'they believed Modi was the only hope and wanted to see him win.' The highly personalised campaign profoundly irritated some of the BJP's grandees. They felt sidelined, which is hardly surprising because they had been. And they believed a myth had been created around Modi, turning him into some kind of all-conquering Superman, able to fly without support. In his defence, much of the hype around him was generated by the genuine passion of his supporters, although he certainly did nothing to discourage it. And when it was all over, he thanked them and the many thousands of party foot soldiers for their help in getting him elected. His most persuasive argument for why it had turned into a 'Vote Modi', rather than 'Vote BJP', campaign was that the country was crying out for leadership. 'Past elections have shown that the Indian culture is such that people have tremendous faith and trust in the individual. People wanted clarity about who the leading person will be and I was seeing this question being asked in every meeting I attended and was hearing vociferous chants, of "Give us a trusted name not a party name".'

Both propositions have the merit of being true. I have no doubt Modi took great satisfaction in hearing his name chanted by vast crowds day in and day out and in seeing his carefully crafted image whichever way he looked. And, in a country cynical about party campaign promises, it also happened to be good politics to promote one man as the vanguard of change. To work, however, it had to be the right man with the right story and a record of achievement that would stand the test of scrutiny during a long and bitter contest. In that sense, the result speaks for itself. The Modi brand did more than survive the campaign, it came out of it stronger, toughened not weakened by the attacks of its detractors. But it was not always obvious that Narendra Modi would be an asset rather than a liability to his party.

His opponents, including some within his own party, thought they could use his unusual and sometimes controversial life story to undermine him, but they never succeeded in doing so. The biggest own goal of the campaign came in January 2014, when one of the Congress Party's leaders decided it was a good idea to refer to Modi's childhood days as a *chai wala*, or tea vendor, in order to humiliate him (see Chapter Nine). The remark rebounded on a party that was already perceived as elitist and run by a family that had never known what it meant to be poor. By contrast, Modi's humble beginnings were an important part of a narrative that used his own transformation through hard work and dedication to tell a story of what India itself could achieve if it chose to do so. His family with no special priviliges, and his refusal to use his position of power to benefit them, was a positive asset on the campaign trail. It showed not only that he understood poverty, but also that he was personally incorruptible. 'In my type of job,' he told me, 'you dedicate yourself to your work. We grew up in a joint family with shared responsibilities, and learnt from each other how to live simply and with very little. My mother even today lives in a small eight foot by eight foot room.'

According to his biographers, when he was six he would help his father sell tea to passengers whenever a train came into the town station. 'After school Narendra would race to his father's tea stall as if working there was the excitement he had been looking forward to all day long and nothing in the world was more fulfilling than serving tea to railway passengers: "I was in the train compartment, the small boy who used to serve tea, and take the money".'

As a rule, Modi chooses his words with extreme care. 'I come from a poor family. I have seen poverty,' he said in his Red Fort speech on Independence Day. It is of no great value to argue, as some do, that poverty is relative and millions of Indians grow up with a lot less to eat and in far worse living conditions than the young Narendra Modi. When he told the country that he detested poverty because he had seen it at first hand, he was telling the truth, and no attempt by his opponents to take that away from him stood the slightest chance of success.

He was born in September 1950 in the small town of Vadnagar in the north of the present-day state of Gujarat. India had gained its independence from Britain just three years previously and Mahatma Gandhi, also a native of Gujarat, had been assassinated the following year, in January 1948. While Gandhi was born into a comfortably off family of India's merchant caste, Modi was an OBC, or 'Other Backward Class'. Officially OBCs are classified as 'socially and educationally backward', but they are far from being the lowest stratum of society, with many castes, including Dalits, previously known better as 'the untouchables', below them. He was the third of six children and the family lived in a three-room, single-storey house built of brick and mud.

The most bizarre publication to have been produced by Modi's supporters during the campaign was a 45-page comic book called *Bal Narendra – Childhood Stories of Narendra Modi*. It was never officially endorsed and soon went out of print, but nevertheless it caused quite a stir with its catalogue of larger-than-life deeds of heroism and selflessness by the fearless young boy. By this account he really was too good to be true. He rescues a drowning boy and a trapped bird, swims in crocodile-infested waters, stands up to school bullies, dutifully attends the local temple and cares daily for his siblings and parents. His mother must have adored him. 'He was a perfectionist and liked his clothes clean and crispy. So he would always fold them carefully once they were dry,' according to one caption. Gandhi described salt as 'the only condiment of the poor', and much of the media choose to take the comic book's claims with a very large pinch of the Mahatma's favourite additive. The publication did, however, encourage journalists to visit Vadnagar and see how the young Modi was actually remembered by those who knew him; the *Times of India* turned up some fascinating insights.

'Modi's childhood friends are certain that he was destined to make history,' the paper reported. 'Once when we were returning from school, we met an astrologer and showed our palms to him,' according to Nagji Desai, now a local leader of the Congress Party. 'We were all keen to know what the future held in store for us. While the astrologer did not say anything great for us, he told Narendrabhai that he would either become a revered saint or a big political leader. We even started poking fun at Narendrabhai by calling him *rajneta* (politician).' Another school friend, using the same suffix, *bhai* ('brother'), as a mark of respect, told the paper, 'Narendrabhai would also read our palms and rue the fact that we had such a bleak future while he was destined to move around in big cars.'

As for the crocodile-infested waters, the *Times of India* says they disappeared from the lake close to where Modi was born decades ago. But they were still there when he was a boy.

When asked about swimming with them, Modi denied that by doing so he was misbehaving. 'I was brave, not naughty. There was a pond in my village and I loved to swim in that pond. I even had to wash my clothes there. So one day I picked up a crocodile baby and took it home. Later on I even took it to school and my teachers were very upset.' Most of the time, however, it seems his teachers were satisfied with his behaviour and work record. He was not an exceptional student, but in those days he was a voracious reader. There was early evidence of the theatrical side that has stood him in such good stead in his subsequent political career. Prahlad Patel, who was his Sanskrit teacher, told one interviewer he was 'only an average student. But he showed keen interest in debates and theatre. I set up the debating club at the school, and I remember Narendra was among the regular students in the club.'

Although he would eventually complete a master's degree in political science through a correspondence course at Gujarat University at the age of 33, school failed to keep the attention of a boy who was clearly restless and searching for his role in life. His oldest brother, Sombhai Modi, told the magazine *The Caravan*: 'Narendra always wanted to do something different. Something more than what we did on a daily routine at home and school.' Modi would later join the National Cadet Corps (NCC), but the organisation which gave his life its true purpose and helped define him, for better or worse, for the rest of his life was the Rashtriya Swayamsevak Sangh. The RSS had a greater impact than anything else on the character of the man and on the politics of the candidate for prime minister more than forty years later. It is worth putting Modi's life-story on hold briefly in order to understand it better.

To anybody unfamiliar with Indian politics and Hindu culture, the RSS can be hard to relate to, but it is impossible to comprehend Modi without first getting to grips with the organisation. Its own website is not much help. Describing the 'Sangh Parivar', as its members prefer to call it, it says that, 'A unique phenomenon in the history of Bharat [India] in the twentieth century is the birth and unceasing growth of the Rashtriya Swayamsevak Sangh (RSS). The Sangh's sphere of influence has been spreading far and wide like the radiance of a many splendored diamond.' In 2014 it spread to the prime minister's office in Delhi, although just how much Modi is still guided by its leaders today remains a contentious question and one that he is apparently happy to leave unresolved.

Many of his ministers and closest supporters, who owe allegiance to the RSS themselves, see no reason to fear its influence. Others who view the organisation from the outside are considerably less sanguine. The literal translation of its name is the 'National Volunteer Organisation', and the RSS calls itself a movement for those who want to make 'social work their life's mission'. The epithets it attracts from those outside its ranks range from 'extreme Hindu nationalist' to 'fascist'. One thing they all agree on is that the RSS isn't kidding when it talks about its 'unceasing growth'. Although it doesn't publish figures and there is no formal registration process, estimates for its membership range from between two and six million people. Even at the lowest end, that makes it the second largest political movement in the world after the Chinese Communist party.

The word 'political' is not inappropriate, despite the fact that most of its supporters are far more comfortable helping out in their communities than engaging in ideological debate. They perform countless good deeds and do a vast amount of work helping the poorest in society, often ignorant of the organisation's history and heedless of the fact that its leadership is so closely entwined in BJP politics. The RSS was founded in 1925 with the aim of uniting Hindus and opposing British imperialism. Many of its early leaders were impatient with the passive resistance espoused by Mahatma Gandhi and, not long after Independence was finally won, the RSS was banned for a year as a direct consequence of Gandhi's assassination by one of its former adherents, Nathuram Godse. The organisation was acquitted of any involvement in the murder and Godse had left because he thought it wasn't militant enough.

The 'fascist' tag made more sense in the mid-twentieth century than it does today. While it is purely coincidental that the swastika is an ancient Hindu symbol (it is a familiar emblem in Buddhist and Jain culture, too, and was used by the ancient Greeks and Celts), during the Second World War some of the RSS's leading lights expressed open admiration for Hitler and his dreams of racial purity. Even today, the uniform worn when RSS members come together every morning at a *shakha*, or meeting, to perform exercises and recite nationalist slogans, often while wielding a long stick, is closely modelled on that worn by Mussolini's Blackshirts. In more recent times, however, the RSS leadership has involved itself in democratic politics and bitterly resents any attempt to tarnish the organisation by associating it with fascism. In 1980 it played a key role in establishing the BJP as a vehicle for translating its beliefs into action, and it continues to think of itself as the guardian of Hindu nationalist belief and the ideological conscience of the party. Officially the BJP is independent of the RSS and open to all Indians, but the importance of the Sangh's vast network of members cannot be overestimated. It provided many thousands of the foot soldiers who worked tirelessly at the grassroots level to secure the election of Modi and his government (see Chapter Twelve).

Perhaps the most useful, though incomplete, comparison is with the trade union movement in many western democracies. While the unions can cause embarrassment to leaders of the Labour Party in Britain or the Democrats in the United States, for example, especially when they are perceived to be influencing policy, their support is still vital at election time. And, just as with the unions, many outside the ranks of the RSS view it as being a bit of a dinosaur, rather old-fashioned and even irrelevant in the modern world. Worse than that, it is often portrayed as not merely supporting Hindu values, but as being anti-Muslim and anti-Christian. Indeed anti anybody who doesn't believe that all of India should be Hindu. Its defenders, like the journalist Swaminathan Gurumurthy, take a very different view. He believes the RSS has been subjected to endless ignorant abuse and needs to be more objectively assessed. He put it for me like this: 'The RSS is at best an effort to protect Hinduism'. In his opinion, Hindu civilisation would be at risk of extinction without it. 'In the world of organised religions and peoples, no unorganised culture or civilisation, or even religion, will survive', he said.

The question as to what degree Narendra Modi still subscribes to the philosophy of the organisation he grew up with took on a new significance when he became prime minister. But the question was not a new one. Another reason why his life story is so important is in order to shed some light on whether India is now governed by a man still committed to an ideology that many of his non-Hindu citizens feel excludes them, or whether he has put it aside in his pursuit of economic development. At the age of 51, Modi assumed the highest office in his home state, and he soon showed the first signs that he might be ready to distance himself from the ideological dictates of the Sangh. He presented himself as a thrusting chief minister trying to modernise Gujarat's economy and his own image. But conserving traditional values rather than modernity was the *raison d'être* of the RSS and during this period Modi developed something of a hot and cold relationship with its leadership. As he conceded himself to a recent biographer, 'There are several senior leaders of the Sangh who are very fond of me. And there would be some who are less fond.' The second group clearly felt he was getting too self-important. But he never burned his boats with them and, crucially, when it mattered most in 2013 and 2014, the RSS top brass were among his strongest supporters, convinced that only he could lead the BJP to victory.

To get a balanced and informed assessment of the RSS and its influence on Modi and the BJP today, I visited the veteran BBC commentator, Mark Tully, at his home in central Delhi. Tully has been observing and writing about Indian politics since the late 1960s; during all that time he has been trying to translate its intricacies for a western audience. One reason, he told me, why it's wrong to think of the RSS as a fascist organisation these days is that it is intrinsically hostile to any kind of authoritarian leadership. 'There is no Mussolini in the RSS and there never has been. There's no Hitler in them, although some people are glibly calling Modi Hitler. It's always been a reasonably corporate type of leadership and suspicious of anybody who becomes too big, too important, too well known. And that's why some of them have been suspicious of Modi. Some of them would admit that there is unease that Modi is running away with the show.' As for what they stand for, Tully says the tenets of Hindu nationalism, known as Hindutva, can't be compared to the extreme nationalism we associate with far-right movements in the west. 'It is much more to do with culture and a belief that all of Indian culture is Hindu.'

Tully is the first to agree, however, that many liberal Hindus, including many of his neighbours in the more comfortable districts of the capital, don't see it that way. To them Hindutva is not an inclusive ideology but one that stirs up hatred against anybody who refuses to accept its precepts.

During the general election campaign, the BJP did its best to avoid any discussion of Hindutva. When it looked as if they were all but certain to win, however, the debate over what relevance it has to the India of today intensified, even if Modi himself refused to get involved. Ashutosh Varshney, director of the India Initiative at Brown University in Providence, Rhode Island, added an academic perspective. He wrote that, 'Anyone who has read the basic texts of Hindu nationalism knows that three ideas constitute the thematic core of Hindu nationalist ideology. First, Hindus are the primary, or exclusive, owners of the Indian nation. India is a Hindu *rashtra* (nation). Second, two minorities – the Christians and especially the Muslims – have a profoundly ambivalent relationship with India. As Savarkar wrote in *Hindutva*, a classic text of Hindu nationalism, Muslims and Christians can call India their *pitribhumi* (fatherland), but India is not their *punyabhumi* (holy land).' Most parties carry with them some controversial ideological baggage, so we should not be surprised that Narendra Modi is as reluctant to talk about Hindutva as Labour leaders are to discuss the Marxist and socialist texts that were worshipped by many of their founding fathers.

Fortunately, not all BJP leaders are so reticent. The party HQ, close to Delhi's government district, is a world away from the calm efficiency of the prime minister's residence. The waiting area here is a crowded room, close to the street, where all manner of people hoping for a meeting jostle for attention. The offices beyond are contained in a sprawl of low-level buildings with a constant swirl of comings and goings and an air of purposeful, if somewhat chaotic, activity. I went there for the first time to see the party's official spokesman, Prakash Javadekar. It was his job to deal with the many and varied demands of the media, so his life was lived very much in the here and now. He clearly thought the party had better things to talk about, but he was more than ready to give me his thoughts on Hindutva, insisting that it posed no threat to minority religions in the country today. 'It is a way of life in India, how Indians live,' he told me. 'It has nothing to do with theocracy, nothing to do with any one religion. Hindutva is a bigger concept. Hindu is a religion, Muslim or Islam is a religion, Christianity is a religion. But Hindutva is an identity, a cultural civilisation, an ethos of India which is shared by everybody. Because Muslims or Christians here have not come from outside, they are Indians. They share the same history, same ancestors, so there is no issue.' The party's manifesto in 2014 repeated its support for the concept of 'one nation, one people and one culture'. Those who see nothing wrong with this formulation point out that most Muslims and Christians in the country are the descendants of people who converted from Hinduism, hoping, in vain as it turned out, to improve their status in society by embracing Islam or Christianity.

As the party's most recent historian, Kingshuk Nag, explained, 'Many found this theory of the BJP abhorrent because it seemed to convey that India was mono-cultural.' Or as Tully puts it, 'They say, "It's OK, you can be Muslim, but you have to realise that you come originally from Hindu stock." Obviously the Muslims don't like it. They think, "What you're really saying is that I'm not a Muslim at all, I'm a Hindu".'

Time then to resume Modi's life story where we left off. He was just eight years old when he attended his first RSS meeting and took the oath to become a *bal swayamsevak* or child volunteer. It seems fair to assume that the doctrinal niceties of who was and was not a Hindu were not uppermost in his mind at the time. But signing up to the RSS was no childhood whim. Nor was it just the Indian equivalent of joining the Boy Scouts. He embraced its rigours of 'renunciation, dedication and hard work' with such enthusiasm and conviction that he became estranged even from his own flesh and blood. It is no exaggeration to say that for much of his adult life the RSS and Hindu nationalism have been his family. On a personal level, Modi has never been known to deviate from the way of life that full-time RSS volunteers and propagandists, known as *pracharaks*, are expected to adopt, including that trio of supposed virtues: vegetarianism, teetotalism and celibacy.

As a teenager, Modi remained wedded to traditional teachings that placed such an emphasis on self-denial and the service of others. He even considered entering the priesthood. It came as something of a shock to him, therefore, when in common with most Indian parents, Modi's mother and father arranged first an engagement and then a marriage for him. It was only when he came to file his papers as a candidate for the general election that Modi finally confirmed publicly that the wedding had taken place and he was, in fact, still married to a woman by the name of Jashodaben. Even now, Modi refuses to discuss the marriage, but his brother Sombhai says it was 'only a formal ritual' and was never consummated. Rather than follow his parents' wishes, the teenage Modi left home and started the first of many long periods of nomadic wandering across all parts of India, starting off with the Himalayas. 'Mother and all of us were very worried for him,' Sombhai recalled. 'We had no idea where he had disappeared to. Then, two years later, he just turned up one day.' But when his parents tried to bring him together again with his wife, he packed his bag once more and disappeared. By his own account, 'I could fit all my belongings in a small bundle. I kept wandering for forty/forty-five years and I spent over forty years begging for food.'

This was the non-political side of an RSS volunteer, seeking spiritual understanding, spreading the word, helping out in communities, and putting 'self last'. In Britain, candidates who have never known a career outside politics are treated with suspicion, and every once in a while some prominent MP or another will take time off, usually little more than a week or two, to 'listen to the people'. Forty years would seem to be taking that to extremes, but it belies the idea that Modi was convinced from an early age that it was his destiny to drive around in big cars.

It's hard to escape the conclusion that there has to be a bit of spin in play at this stage in his story. He left home at the age of seventeen, and thirty-five years later he was already chief minister, having previously worked as a BJP organiser in both Gujarat and Delhi. The chief minister's residence might have been his first permanent home, and his wanderings and subsequent political work certainly kept him on the move, but it is stretching things more than a little to claim to have been begging for food for forty years or more. Even if we allow for a bit of embellishment, however, it is undoubtedly the case that Modi came to elected politics relatively late in life and that he did so having seen a great deal of the country he would go on to govern, and not from the windows of a speeding motorcade.

Over this lengthy period of time, Modi proved beyond doubt his dedication to the cause and his capacity for self-sacrifice and hard work. Over time that commitment graduated from the mainly social and community work of the RSS to the political sphere and to the BJP itself. It was here that he showed his true calling as he honed his skills as a party back-room man, skills that he says later helped him plan and execute his own election. 'Until 1978 I was behind the curtains but over the years I was picking up skills that were required and this made me a master organiser. This meant I had a strong understanding of what worked and how to plan.' While as yet he had no place on the national stage, party workers and RSS volunteers from all over the country got to know him or to hear of his reputation, and these people would later be key to his takeover of the leadership.

'Behind the curtains' he might have been, but at one stage he very nearly ended up behind bars. When, following a long period of political unrest, Indira Gandhi suspended democracy in 1975 and declared an Emergency, enabling her to rule by decree, tens of thousands of opposition leaders and activists were imprisoned and the RSS was again banned. Modi narrowly avoided going to jail himself and took to wearing elaborate disguises as he travelled around distributing clandestine propaganda and helping to organise peaceful protests demanding the restoration of democracy. Inevitably it hardened his contempt for Mrs Gandhi and her Congress Party, but it also brought him into contact with activists from other parties outside the narrow world of the Sangh. Writing about his memories of this period on his blog, Modi said: 'At that time I was a twenty-five-year-old youngster who had recently started working for the RSS but what I witnessed during those dark days remains forever engrained in my memory. Who can forget the manner in which personal freedom was brutally trampled over?' That period in his life, he told me, made him more of a democrat. 'I was lucky to work with socialist leaders. I was lucky to work with Islamic organisations, with liberal organisations – so many people. That period was a good period to mould me. Because of that and the democratic values that I found, it became part of my DNA. Yes, that was one of the best experiences that I had. I became aware; I understood the constitution, I understood the rights, because before that I was living in a different world.' The Emergency, which lasted for twenty-one months between 1975 and 1977, was the lowest point in Indira Gandhi's career and it taught Modi a great deal about political protest and the essential safeguards of democracy. It pained him greatly that at the lowest point in his own career, a quarter of a century later in 2002, he was accused of being a demagogue and of encouraging violent anti-democratic behaviour.

The events in question – the Gujarat riots – occurred very soon after he finally came out from 'behind the curtains' and was catapulted into political leadership himself. They put him at odds with all his allies from his time as an underground defender of democracy: the left, the Muslims and the liberals. They branded him indelibly as an extremist in the eyes of many and led to his exclusion from the United States for allegedly violating religious freedoms. They were the biggest single impediment to his ambition to become prime minister. And, worst of all, they resulted in the deaths of well over a thousand of the people he was in office to protect. For Modi the candidate to succeed in 2014, he would have to live down one thing above all: Godhra.

CHAPTER THREE
CHIEF MINISTER

Fortunately for Narendra Modi, the western media don't have a vote in Indian elections and few of those who do are much influenced by what they read in foreign publications. The UK's pro-business, free-market magazine *The Economist* found much to admire in his platform of development and economic liberalisation and yet it advised its readers in India not to vote for him. Why? Because, it wrote, he was dangerously divisive. 'By refusing to put Muslim fears to rest, Mr Modi feeds them. By clinging to the anti-Muslim vote, he nurtures it.' The paper concluded that 'it would be wrong for a man who has thrived on division to become prime minister of a country as fissile as India . . . He should be judged on his record – which is that of a man who is still associated with sectarian hatred. There is nothing modern, honest or fair about that. India deserves better.' The editorial board of the *New York Times* took a similar line, concluding that 'India is a country with multiple religions, more than a dozen major languages and numerous ethnic groups and tribes. Mr Modi cannot hope to lead it effectively if he inspires fear and antipathy among many of its people.'

The paper claimed that 'his rise to power is deeply troubling to many Indians, especially the country's 138 million Muslims and its many other minorities. They worry he would exacerbate sectarian tensions that have subsided somewhat in the last decade.' Both publications examined his achievements as chief minister of Gujarat, but felt that whatever successes he had chalked up in boosting his state's economic development, they could not wipe the slate clean of the horrific events of February and March 2002, just a few months after he took office.

Modi's first taste of power came not through the ballot box, but by appointment. In 1998 the country's first stable BJP-led government took office in Delhi under the reformist and relatively moderate Atal Bihari Vajpayee. Although it was reliant on a clutch of smaller parties for a majority in parliament, the Vajpayee government survived for over six years. It might have lasted longer, in the view of Vajpayee himself, but for Narendra Modi. Vajpayee was forced to turn to Modi, and later to defend him against his own better judgement, because the politics of the time were very different to how they look today. The BJP was more used to electoral defeats than victories and sorely lacked people with the gift of political alchemy.

Towards the end of the twentieth century the BJP was not the disciplined and united party that came to power in 2014. At the risk of over-simplifying some very complex political and personal relationships, it is clear there was a divide between those perceived to be moderates, led by Vajpayee, and the hardliners who looked towards the party president, L. K. Advani; divisions that would surface from time to time in public. Advani, more than twenty years older than Modi and the grandest of the party's grandees, would go on to play a hugely significant role in his future career, and not always a supportive one. At this time, however, Modi was seen to be a disciple of Advani and in sympathy with his more fundamentalist take on Hindu politics. But in Gujarat at the time the rivalries were more to do with personalities than ideologies. Basically, Modi's face didn't fit and – despite having friends in high places – he was effectively excluded from his home state for several years.

By 1994, however, the Gujarat party was in such disarray that Advani was able to insist that Modi should be allowed to return to help organise the forthcoming state elections. Modi was quick to repay the trust that had been placed in him. The result, a two-thirds majority for the BJP, was a triumph that only added to his already growing reputation as a back-room genius. In the short term, however, it didn't do him much good as the personality clashes, compounded by a healthy dose of jealousy at his mounting popularity, saw him banished once more, this time to the north-west of the country where he continued to show great organisational prowess. Those skills were too valuable to do without for long, and he was called back to Gujarat again to help the BJP to another victory in 1998, an achievement that this time earned him a major promotion as general secretary in charge of organisation for the national party.

The Gujarat government was then battered not so much by the old rivalries, although they had not gone away, but by natural disasters. First a cyclone, then floods and then a catastrophic earthquake hit the state. There were allegations of corruption and nepotism levelled at the chief minister, Keshubhai Patel, and these, combined with Patel's inept handling of the disaster relief after the earthquake, led Vajpayee to demand his resignation. To fill the vacancy, and to try to avert electoral disaster, the prime minister – on the advice of L. K. Advani – turned once again to Modi. This time it wasn't for a job 'behind the curtains' but very much in front of them. On 4 October 2001, with the world still reeling from the aftermath of 9/11, Modi was made leader of the Gujarat party and interim chief minister, even though he wasn't a member of the state assembly. In global terms, a man nobody had heard of was appointed to a post nobody was interested in, at a time of unprecedented international crisis. Less than five months later, however, Gujarat and Narendra Modi would be hitting the headlines for all the wrong reasons.

On the morning of 27 February 2002, a train carrying over two thousand passengers pulled into the station at Godhra in the east of the state. Most were Hindu pilgrims returning from the bitterly contested holy city of Ayodhya in Uttar Pradesh. Ayodhya is the most sensitive of all religious venues in India. It was the site of the Babri Masjid mosque, built in 1527 on the orders of the first Mughal emperor, Zahir-ud-din Muhammad Babur. Many Hindus believe Ayodhya was the birthplace of the Hindu god Ram, who gave his name to the *Ramayana* epic, and that a Hindu temple on the same spot was demolished so the mosque could be constructed. Recent archaeological evidence suggests that there was a Buddhist temple even before that. The centuries-old conflict over Ayodhya had been reignited in 1992 when the mosque was destroyed by a rampaging mob after a march to the site led by nationalist leaders including L. K. Advani. So the people on board the train that made its way towards the Godhra station were not just any passengers. As it slowed down they could see out of the windows a large crowd of angry Muslims. Soon afterwards burning rags were thrown into one of the compartments. Unable to escape, fifty-nine people, including twenty-six women and twelve children, were burned to death.

The attack was horrific, but what followed was on a far bigger and bloodier scale. Over days of rioting across Gujarat, more than a thousand people were killed in inter-racial violence, the overwhelming majority of them Muslims. The reverberations of the attacks continue to be felt across Indian politics even today. Modi has consistently maintained that he did everything in his power to contain the rioting and was even-handed in his efforts to help the victims and their families. His critics have accused him of everything from indifference to the embattled Muslim communities to complicity in the violence itself. Sonia Gandhi referred to Modi as '*Maut Ka Saudagar*' or a 'merchant of death' while campaigning in Gujarat five years after the rioting, and the allegation resurfaced intermittently during the 2014 campaign. The Congress Party clung to the hope that by reminding people of the ethnic violence they could unite Muslims, Christians and liberal Hindus against him, so denying him a majority in the country. Modi's response was not to cower in the face of the verbal attacks but to do his best to turn them around, accusing Sonia Gandhi and her party of besmirching not just his reputation but that of all Gujaratis. That Congress manifestly failed to consolidate the opposition to Modi is clear from the results, both in Gujarat state elections and later at the general election. Muslims make up around 15% of the Indian electorate. In 2014 Congress managed only 19% overall when the final votes were counted up.

The case against Modi relies on a wealth of first-hand contemporaneous evidence from those who were caught up in or witnessed the massacres, much of it collated by the New York-based Human Rights Watch in its report of May 2002 titled 'We Have No Orders To Save You'. The report declared that 'Human Rights Watch's findings, and those of numerous Indian human rights and civil liberties organisations, and most of the Indian press indicate that the attacks on Muslims throughout the state were planned, well in advance of the Godhra incident, and organised with extensive police participation and in close cooperation with officials of the Bharatiya

Janata Party (BJP) state government.' It went on to say that 'The attacks on Muslims are part of a concerted campaign of Hindu nationalist organisations to promote and exploit communal tensions to further the BJP's political rule – a movement that is supported at the local level by militant groups that operate with impunity and under the patronage of the state.' The report's dramatic title came from the authors' findings that 'Panicked phone calls made to the police, fire brigades, and even ambulance services generally proved futile. Many witnesses testified that their calls either went unanswered or that they were met with responses such as: "We don't have any orders to save you", or "We cannot help you, we have orders from above".' This report, and others like it, led directly to the decision by the United States to deny Modi a visa in 2005 and bar him from the country for the best part of a decade. Modi fell foul of the US Immigration and Nationality Act, which states that anybody who has been 'responsible for, or directly carried out, at any time, particularly severe violations of religious freedom' cannot enter the country. Despite a request from the government in Delhi to review the decision, the administration of George W. Bush refused to relent.

Modi did visit Britain in 2003 and addressed a meeting at the Wembley Conference Centre where he spoke about investment opportunities in Gujarat. He was besieged by thousands of mainly Muslim protestors waving placards calling him a murderer and demanding that he be arrested, in the same way former Chilean dictator, General Augusto Pinochet, detained in London in 1998, had been. The British government said that while it understood the concerns expressed, there were no grounds to refuse him a visa. There was not any question of him meeting ministers, however. In a statement the Home Office said, 'We are aware he's visiting the UK. He is not visiting at Her Majesty's government's invitation nor does the government plan to have any contact with him when he's here.' Ministers were conscious of the feeling in the Muslim community and many, like the foreign secretary, Jack Straw, had large Gujarati Muslim populations in their constituencies, but they decided not to follow the Americans down the road of excluding him altogether. 'We were under intense domestic pressure to do something,' Straw told me, 'and some of the demands were to ban Narendra Modi's entry to the UK altogether. I recall a lot of reluctance in government to a ban, and I agreed with that, so this diplomatic quarantine was seen as a reasonable compromise.' In practice it meant that Modi would be unable to meet any ministers or senior officials for nine years. A similar informal boycott was adopted by the European Union. A planned return visit to Britain in 2005, during which human rights groups threatened to redouble their efforts to get him arrested, was cancelled on security grounds.

Modi and his supporters have consistently accused western governments of ignoring the facts as they see them and of being too ready to listen instead to human rights organisations. They insist no actual evidence has ever been produced linking him to any wrongdoing and say that, on the contrary, he couldn't have done more to stop the marauding mobs without police and military support from outside the state, which he asked for but which was not forthcoming. Some politicians, including members of both the BJP and Congress, were convicted and jailed for their involvement in the rioting, but despite protracted legal proceedings, no case against Modi has ever been proved. It went all the way to the Supreme Court, which set up a Special Investigations Team, or SIT, to sift all the available evidence. Modi spent many hours giving his own testimony to the SIT enquiry. When its report was finally made public in February 2012, it concluded that, while his answers to some of their questions 'possibly indicates his discriminatory attitude', 'no criminal case is made out against Narendra Modi'. It said that while the rioting was in progress, 'Law and order review meetings were held by Modi and all the things was done [sic] to control the situation . . . the army was called on time to contain the communal violence'. The report found there was no basis for the allegation that Modi had instructed senior police officers 'to allow Hindus to vent their anger'. As a result most of the domestic media coverage concluded that he had been given 'a clean chit'. But the findings did not satisfy all his critics. India is no different to Britain, the United States or anywhere else in this respect. Not even a lengthy judicial enquiry can be expected to lay everybody's doubts to rest. Some alleged that the SIT had 'looked the other way'. Others said that in his evidence, Modi had 'pulled every trick in the book: selective facts, evasion, amnesia, outright lies and rhetoric'. What mattered for his future political prospects, however, was that he could now say that all the allegations had been thoroughly investigated and he had been exonerated.

Modi is usually reluctant to talk about his emotions, but in a blog written the day after the SIT report came out he said that the events of 2002 had 'pained me deeply'. The blog went on to say that 'as if all the suffering was not enough, I was also accused of the death and misery of my own loved ones, my Gujarati brothers and sisters. Can you imagine the inner turmoil and shock of being blamed for the very events that have shattered you? The Gujarat government had responded to the violence more swiftly and decisively than ever done before in any previous riots in the country. Yesterday's judgement culminated a process of unprecedented scrutiny closely monitored by the highest court of the land, the Honourable

Supreme Court of India. Gujarat's twelve years of trial by the fire have finally drawn to an end. I feel liberated and at peace.' When, later in the year, the Supreme Court used the SIT report to rule out further action against him, Modi was more succinct. He tweeted simply, 'God is great.'

There are, however, as the former BBC correspondent Mark Tully points out, 'no full stops in India'. Modi's trials and tribulations over Godhra were not yet at an end. One of the complainants, whose husband had died in the rioting, challenged the findings of the report, and hearings continued almost until polling day, until on 11 April 2014, the Supreme Court rejected her attempt to overturn the 'clean chit'. Even then, Rahul Gandhi called the ruling 'politically expedient' and 'too premature'. Nevertheless, despite continuing allegations that evidence went missing and that witnesses were intimidated into withdrawing their affidavits, Modi can justifiably assert that the highest court in the land has found no grounds to prosecute him. It is one subject that he refused to engage with in my interviews with him. 'Regarding Godhra, I have said enough and you can read the reports and the Supreme Court judgment for yourself,' he told me. His reluctance to be drawn is no doubt motivated in part by the fact that when he has talked to interviewers about his reaction to the riots his answers have often provoked yet more outrage. The charge that has lingered longest against him is his alleged insensitivity towards the Muslim victims on those rare occasions when he has expressed a view.

It was this, above all, that exercised the *New York Times* editorial board. 'When Reuters asked him earlier this year if he regretted the killings in 2002,' they reminded their readers, 'he said if "someone else is driving a car and we're sitting behind, even then if a puppy comes under the wheel, will it be painful or not? Of course it is".' That incendiary response created a political uproar and demands for an apology.' No doubt conscious that an apology would be interpreted as tantamount to an admission of culpability, Modi refused. Speaking of himself in the third person, as he likes to do, he said, 'If Narendra Modi committed such a crime, then he should be hanged, that is my upfront demand, but if people are attacking me with criticism for political purposes without considering my effort of saving people's lives, then I don't have an answer for them.'

Back in 2002, in the immediate aftermath of the rioting, it was Modi's political life that hung in the balance. Modi gave his opponents within the party their chance when he offered his resignation to the BJP general executive committee. Prime minister Vajpayee's first instinct was to accept it, but he was dissuaded from doing so by the hardliners, led once more by L. K. Advani, who argued that the right response was to hold new state elections and let the people decide. In the short term it seemed like a smart political move. When the elections were held in December, the BJP won comfortably, taking 127 of the 182 seats in the state assembly. But nationally the aftermath of Godhra continued to damage the party's image, and after Vajpayee lost the general election of 2004 he told a TV interviewer, 'The impact of the Gujarat riots was felt nationwide. This was unexpected and hurt us badly. Modi should have been removed after the incident.'

Instead Modi started twelve years of unbroken rule in the state, which came to an end only when he exchanged the chief minister's residence for that of the prime minister at 7 Race Course Road, Delhi. The move wouldn't have been possible if the people of India, or enough of them to give him a parliamentary majority, hadn't been ready to set aside the tragic events of 2002 and judge Modi by other criteria. Their willingness to do so was reinforced by the fact that from 2002 to 2014, Gujarat was almost completely free of inter-communal or religious violence. The state became known instead for its economic development, and the 'Gujarat Model' entered the lexicon, synonymous with dramatic improvements in the state's electricity and water supplies and huge investment in better roads and infrastructure projects. This in turn brought massive inward investment by both national and international companies, all of it trumpeted with great fanfare at the biennial 'Vibrant Gujarat' business jamborees, at which the lead soloist was Narendra Modi. He was able to boast that between 2004 and 2012 Gujarat's economy had grown at 10.1%, compared to the national average of 7.6%. Although the state accounts for about 5% of India's population and 6% of its land area, it contributes around 16% of the country's industrial production. Statistics are always helpful, but in politics it is the personal experience of individual voters that counts. The electrification of all 18,000 villages in the state and dramatic improvements in irrigation not only pushed up agricultural production at the fastest rate in India, but also made possible significant improvements in health care and helped make the streets safer, especially for women.

Not surprisingly, the BJP's political opponents warned that these facts and figures shouldn't be taken at face value. They claimed that many of the improvements were under way even before Modi took the helm, and that the state had a lot of natural advantages going for it, including large tracts of government-owned land available for development and, most important of all, a population that had always had a reputation for hard work and business acumen. What's more, they said, not all the available statistics put Gujarat in such a good light, with education spending below the national average, and figures for infant and maternal mortality that remained disturbingly high.

It is true that Gujarat has a more dynamic, go-getting feel about it than many places in India that I've visited. There are a multitude of small and large businesses and the sheer size of the state and the better-than-average roads and other infrastructure must make it an attractive place for inward investment. There are some very fancy hotels in the largest city, Ahmedabad, and one look around the lobby or the restaurant shows just how many businesspeople from outside India are there to exploit the opportunities it has to offer. One place you won't find them, however, is in the bar. Gujarat has long been one of India's 'dry' states, where the sale of alcohol is not permitted. In 2012 the *Times of India* declared Ahmedabad 'the best of India's mega-cities, edging out Pune, Delhi and Mumbai in a very close contest.'

The nearby state capital of Gandhinagar, where Modi was based as chief minister and from where he ran his general election campaign, is also comparatively easy to get around and apparently prosperous. But while they have rather more of a buzz about them than many Indian cities, it would be an exaggeration to say that Gujarat is somehow a state apart. And it is worth noting that Bangalore, capital of the southern state of Karnataka, has established itself at the centre of India's equivalent of Silicon Valley. IT jobs have not been created in Gujarat in the same way, partly because Modi's government there didn't give the same priority to improving English-language skills. So, on balance, most commentators would probably agree with the assessment of *India Today* magazine that while 'Gujarat is not yet the perfect state that supporters of Modi would have us believe, nor is it as broken as . . . others suggest.'

Even Britain's *Economist*, while refusing to endorse him, acknowledged that 'Mr Modi's performance as chief minister of Gujarat shows that he is set on economic development and can make it happen.' Business leaders in the state certainly think so, which is why they have supported him with such enthusiasm. And they point out that all this economic activity benefited Gujarat's Muslim community as much as the Hindus. In political terms this was translated into the BJP's election mantra of '*Sabka Saath, Sabka Vikas*', which translates as, 'Together with all, development for all'. Piyush Goyal, who was made energy minister in the Modi administration, was one of the politicians closest to him and was responsible for overseeing the party's advertising. He told me this inclusive language was possible only because of Modi's proven record in Gujarat, although he acknowledged that not everybody in the country was yet convinced. 'I believe it will take a few more years for this message to show results. In future, people will judge us on our work.'

Modi has never been shy about shouting his successes from the rooftops and he employed some of the best PR and advertising agencies available to ensure that everybody got the message about the Gujarat Model and what it could do for India as a whole. Any politician with his eye on the main prize would do the same thing, although inevitably it has contributed to the accusation that there is a lot of spin associated with the Gujarat Model. Modi's answer is always the same: Don't take my word for it, ask the people. When he first became chief minister, he says, 'People would come to me and say, we are not asking for anything big. But at least provide us electricity during dinner-time so that we don't have to eat in the dark . . . Today Gujarat has electricity all around the year. This cannot be proved through marketing. When people switch on their bulb and see light, it is then that they believe that Modi has provided electricity.' Piyush Goyal puts it succinctly in marketing-speak, 'We had a good product to market to the people. If the perfume doesn't smell good, it will not sell however hard you try.'

Like Piyush Goyal, Smriti Irani is one of Modi's younger and most telegenic ministers. A former actress, she was appointed as human resource development minister at the age of just thirty-eight. Unlike Piyush Goyal she hasn't always been a Modi fan. Along with Atal Bihari Vajpayee, she held him responsible for the BJP's defeat in the general election of 2004. After failing in her personal bid to become an MP at that time, she went much further than her party leader, threatening to fast to the death unless Modi resigned. He didn't, and clearly nor did she. Today she blames the media for what she calls her *faux pas*. 'I was twenty-seven at the time,' she told me, 'and I didn't understand that the media's influence is so strong that it can change public perception.' She is grateful to him for showing forgiveness. 'To take even detractors along, to position them in places like the HRD ministry, speaks a lot about him as a leader.' In return she became one of his most loyal and articulate defenders.

The razzamatazz and the clever marketing should not be allowed, she said, to distract from the real success of the 2014 election campaign, a success that owed nothing to religion-based politics. 'I have a surname called Irani. Nobody knows what religion I practise. I have always said that when Modi said make good roads, did on any of the roads he write that only a Hindu can walk on these? When he said we are giving villages 24/7 electricity, did he anywhere say that this electricity should only go to Hindu homes? He did not. He spoke about the need to deliver these essentials to every citizen irrespective of their religion or the region they reside in.'

It is clear that, directly or indirectly, the events surrounding Godhra and Modi's reaction to them were still significant by the time he was running for prime minister. Whether it was part of his calculations or not, Modi's refusal to say sorry for the anti-Muslim violence of 2002 shored up his political support among the hardliners of the BJP and its parent organisation, the RSS. One of those intimately involved in the election planning, who didn't want to be quoted by name, told me that the strategy towards Muslim voters was 'just to make sure they didn't become aggressive towards him.' When I asked him if they had ever thought they could win many Muslim votes he laughed. 'Do you think that is possible? Many is a very subjective word. In a population of 150 million Muslims, if one million voted for him that is still many.' But there was no deliberate attempt to win over Muslims. 'Addressing town hall meetings of Muslims, or seeing muftis or Muslim scholars, that would have been seen as counter-productive because you would lose more votes than you would win.' At the same time, according to the same adviser, 'Modi knows that a hardliner cannot rule today's India.' In 2014, with the support of the hard right already secured, Modi's task was to reach out to a much wider swathe of the electorate, unimpressed or uninterested in 'communal' politics rooted in religion.

Eradicating, or at the very least neutralising, his reputation for religious extremism was central to Modi's campaign for political advancement from 2002 onwards. The strategy he adopted was not to lay the ghosts of Godhra and its aftermath to rest, something that was beyond his power, but instead to let them fade into history as he focused on economic development. As he told me, 'Since 2002 the opposition has continued to talk about communal issues and divisive politics and in return I have only talked about development for all.

Which is why from 2002 to 2012 I have won every single election in the state of Gujarat.' He points with pride to the constituency of Jamnagar on the west coast, a town that is 90% Muslim. In municipal elections in 2013, all 24 of the BJP's candidates, who were themselves Muslims, won, sweeping aside Congress, which had dominated the area politically since Independence.

It would be ridiculous to suggest that Modi took up the development cause merely to expunge the memory of Godhra. He gets justifiably irritated when anybody suggests as much. He told one biographer to 'Look at the records and see what I had done for the first one hundred days after becoming chief minister – that is before Godhra, and then compare it with what I did after that and what I am doing even now. You will find that Modi is doing the same thing. The image that has been built that I went into a reactive mode because of Godhra is wrong.' He pointed out that his first business summit was in February 2002, with the British as a partner. 'The Godhra incident happened after that. It is not that I started something new after that to change my image.'

His image did change, however, and he put an enormous amount of effort into ensuring that it did. If it hadn't and he had allowed himself to be irrevocably defined as a religious extremist or worse, then all the predictions that he would one day become prime minister and drive around in big cars would have come to nothing. And the closer he got to his chosen time for making the move to national leadership, the more urgent became the need to burnish an image that was to his own liking and make it so dominant in the public's imagination that he could no longer be defined by his enemies. It was a task he set about with all the single-mindedness and determination for which he was now renowned.

CHAPTER FOUR

BEHIND THE MASK

The sentiments are familiar to anybody who followed the 2014 campaign, however casually. They were expressed so often they became the soundtrack of the election, impossible to ignore. 'In Narendra Modi, India has a politician with most required qualities to change the tide. It is not any exaggeration to say that, after his experience and experimentation with Gujarat, he probably has the answers to all the problems that the nation is facing today. He is not only the best choice but perhaps the only choice to lead the country.' Except those words were not part of the carefully scripted BJP communications strategy following Modi's selection as the party's candidate for prime minister. They had popped up on Facebook four years earlier, at 18.01 on 20 October 2010, under the heading 'Narendra Modi as Prime Minister? Why Not?'

The art of using social media for short, pithy messages had yet to be developed by the Modi fanbase. The posting ran to a lengthy 4,428 words, a not-so-mini manifesto for a man it describes variously as 'unique', 'incorruptible', 'unshakable' and yet 'humble'. In short, 'an icon'. Clearly these were not the casual musings of a grateful, though anonymous, citizen of Gujarat. They were the first hint of the brilliantly organised and breath-takingly successful campaign that was to come, marrying one man, Modi, with one job, prime minister of India.

While nobody has claimed authorship of the post, it – and others like it – were being closely monitored at the BJP's media office in Delhi by Arvind Gupta, head of information technology. 'Across digital media, whether it was Facebook or Twitter or blogs, people were getting together. I call them the New Age Volunteers. They weren't part of the party, they didn't have to worry about whether they had permission from anybody to do something.' Was it really so spontaneous, I asked him, or was somebody, somewhere, giving it all a bit of a push? 'There could have been a bit of a push,' he conceded, 'but an unstructured push. There was no one person guiding it.' And so far as the team working on social media was concerned, the posts were very welcome. At the highest level the party might still have been a long way from deciding on their candidate for prime minister, but as individuals they had already made up their minds. 'We all hoped that he would be the candidate. We knew he was the man,' said one.

There seems little doubt that Modi shared their opinion, but he had no choice but to keep his head down. Publicly, at least, the only thing on his mind was doing a good job as chief minister of his state. In fact he was engaged in a massive campaign of self-promotion and recruiting new talent to help him do it. With the party not yet ready to endorse him, and with other contenders still weighing up their chances, he needed a clandestine team that would report to him personally. It suited him very well to see the online volunteer army grow in numbers and in strength, and if he didn't give them a bit of a push himself, he certainly didn't discourage others from doing so. But he also needed professional support.

He set about gathering around him a small group of talented individuals who would become part of his inner circle, where many remain to this day. They were almost all young men excited by the idea of being at the vanguard of a movement the like of which India had never seen before. Some were given desks in or close to the chief minister's own office; others came from the worlds of advertising and PR and were recruited to work only part-time. Most of the new recruits came from distinctly non-political backgrounds. They carried no ideological baggage and were attracted not by party politics, which usually involves years of gradual rising through ranks, just as Modi had done, but by the opportunity to work as part of a closely knit team around a man who was already being talked of as a potential prime minister. Among them was Dr Hiren Joshi, an electronics engineer turned academic, and Prashant Kishor, a former public health expert with the United Nations. At a more junior level, Dr Nirav Shah had been a dentist while Yash Gandhi was a student. Each had caught Modi's attention in the course of various public engagements and was recruited for his talent and ability to get things done rather than for his politics.

In addition to his highly valued senior civil servants, Modi had long-standing political advisers like Parag Shah and Parindu Bhagat, popularly known as Kakubhai, and he continued to rely heavily on their inputs. But simultaneously he was putting in place a complex web of supporting players. Some of these, including Bhagat's son Maulik, used their own existing businesses to produce TV ads and support social media campaigns. Others set up new private companies, like 'New Hope Infotainment Limited', to push the Modi message. At the same time professional PR agencies were employed by the Gujarat government to improve the image of the state, and with it, of course, the image of its chief minister. It all made it very hard for either the official Election Commission or enquiring journalists to keep track of what was going on.

Sreenivasan Jain, a critical commentator on the NDTV network, summed it up by saying, 'The Modi spin machine appears to use a mix of official, quasi-official and private players, with fragmented responsibilities, a structure that allows for grey areas of accounting and accountability.' It was a mix Modi came to rely upon and deploy right up until the day he became prime minister.

Manish Bardia, a publicity agent and film-maker, first worked for Narendra Modi soon after his appointment as chief minister in 2001. I met him at his office in Ahmedabad and he told me that Modi had appreciated the need for professional PR very early on. 'At the beginning, back in 2001, no political people were using advertising agencies apart from in election campaigns. It was unusual. He said he wanted a fresh approach to communication.' Ask Bill Clinton what is the key to success in politics and he says 'never stop communicating', which is exactly the Modi approach according to Bardia. 'As I understand it, for other politicians it is for two or three months every five years, but for him his entire five years is like a campaign. He has always worked like that. I would say even before you get your election result he would be on the next thing.' Modi was using the internet as a campaign tool long before most politicians in India had learned how to log on, and when Bardia suggested he should have his own YouTube channel, Modi's reply was, 'I want it in two days.' Two weeks later it had secured a million hits.

Manish Bardia's association with 'Brand Modi' has been good for business. His company has worked for some of the country's top corporations and even for India's ambitious space programme, but his eyes lit up when he talked about his most famous client. Behind his desk stood two plaster models. On the left was Barack Obama; on the right Narendra Modi.

When Bardia took them off the shelf their heads moved from side to side in a very Indian, but distinctly un-American, way. 'After Obama's election I went to the US and I saw these things in a merchandising store and I quite liked them. So I bought a few pieces and tried making one for Modiji. It worked out fine so he said, OK, you can use them.' To Bardia it was just one more example of Modi's willingness to embrace new ideas, especially those that help project him and his work.

Manish Bardia is best known for another, less high-tech, contribution to political campaigning, the Modi mask. It was first used in the 2007 state election and gained nationwide coverage in the media. This is no two-dimensional cardboard cut-out of the kind used the world over, more often to mock politicians than to promote them. And the idea was Modi's own. 'Yes it was his idea. One day someone called from the chief minister's office. They showed me some examples of Hillary Clinton and her masks. They were caricatures and I was surprised that he would want them made for him. But he said, "No, I don't want this." He said "I want a real replica of Narendra Modi". So it was 3D. I checked up in India and nobody had done such a thing here, so all night until four a.m. I checked on the internet the methods to measure the face. I called up next morning and said I would require a minimum of one or two hours of his time. Could he spare that much time? I was told he would manage.'

Modi patiently sat while his face was measured and photographed using 3D digital equipment. Bardia went away with the measurements but Modi was impatient to see the results. 'After a week he called and asked what had happened. I said yes it's ready, I am sending you a visual. He saw the visual and said it's good but there are some mistakes, some things need to be corrected. "My eyes are not looking right", he said. In three days again he called and asked did something happen? So then I showed him the actual bust.' Modi approved and some sample latex masks were made from the mould. At first Bardia heard nothing and was worried they hadn't gone down well. But after two weeks Modi called again and said he wanted five thousand of the masks delivered in ten days. Modi's closest confidantes are selected for their 'can do' attitude, but on this occasion the answer was 'no can do.' Bardia said they might be able to turn out a hundred, or at most a hundred and fifty, a day. These were duly delivered to schedule but again there was silence. 'Then one day I saw a newspaper filled with the images,' he recalled. Every BJP candidate had been told to turn up to file their nomination papers for the election surrounded by ten slightly spooky-looking Narendra Modi lookalikes.

The mask episode reveals not only Modi's extraordinary attention to detail but also his early recognition that his own image was a crucial selling point for his party and its candidates. On the face of it, pun intended, it also looks like a rather extreme form of political vanity, something that worried even the mask's creator. 'We thought like that. In fact I once asked him, doesn't it look like too much of yourself?' said Bardia. 'He said "no, people should know my face. If they don't know my face how would they know about me? And if they don't know me how would they know that I work for them?"' Modi masks reappeared at rallies across the country in the general election campaign although, this time around, the cost of the 3D version was prohibitive given the number required, so most were of a more conventional cardboard variety. Even these provoked criticism from Modi's opponents that his was a 'one-man band' led by a showman. For good measure, Congress alleged that Modi was wearing a 'pseudo mask of development' to hide his real, much more ugly face of religious intolerance.

It is a familiar charge in Indian politics. Shekhar Gupta, who was editor in chief of the *Indian Express* for almost twenty years, recalled that the same accusation was made against Atal Bihari Vajpayee, the previous BJP prime minister, implying that his moderate face was just a mask for the hardline politics of Hindu nationalism and the RSS. Vajpayee had no choice but to deny it at the time, but when he lost power in 2004, blaming, in part, Narendra Modi, he told Shekhar Gupta that the accusation had been true and that regrettably what he represented was not the real BJP. Gupta recalled the story to make a more original point. In his view Modi is the first prime minister in Indian history to exactly resemble his own mask. 'Americans would put it as, the man you see is the man you get. In India, in the BJP's current context, it is, the man you see on the mask is the man you get as your leader.' Gupta believes that man is unapologetically from the nationalist Hindu right-wing tradition but that he is now as 'inclusive, conciliatory, forward-looking and modern' as his speeches suggest.

Whether in his heart Modi has indeed moved on from the more hard-line interpretations of Hindutva ideology is impossible to judge for certain. It may be that only he knows the answer. Outwardly, however, he eschews any comment that could lead to him being accused of extremism. What Hindutva means to him personally is a subject he is reluctant to discuss, but he did tell one biographer, Nilanjan Mukhopadhay, that he should 'Forget the literal meaning – in essence it means well-being of all without any distinctions of sect, or of one geographical area.' It is worth noting that almost all of the young professionals he gathered around him as he prepared for the 2012 Gujarat election believe his transformation was already complete by then, and some admit frankly that they wouldn't have joined the team if they thought otherwise. According to one, 'He has worn the mask so much he has become the mask.' And while Modi's private, spiritual time has always remained strictly out of bounds, these men have had more of an opportunity to see behind the mask than most, and they remain among his consistently loyal supporters. Yes, they concede, an array of public relations and marketing techniques were employed to promote Modi, but not to distract attention from the real man, rather to counter what they saw as the media myths about him.

If they could finally lay to rest what they perceived to be those 'media myths' in 2012, it would liberate their man to launch his bid for national power in 2014 on his own terms. One of those recruited at this time, who asked not to be quoted by name, said that the general election of 2014 was always on the agenda. 'Yeah, from the very first day. We used to discuss that the Gujarat election is just a bump in the way. So I believe that he was seriously thinking about this in mid-2011. He would have not called me just for the Gujarat election.' Nevertheless it was a 'bump' that had to be surmounted comfortably. Another close adviser throughout this period described it as 'the semi-final'. If you don't win that, you can forget about the big game. And it was never a one-way bet. 'The Gujarat election was a far bigger challenge than the national election,' in the assessment of one of those who was close to Modi throughout both. 'He needed a very decisive mandate. Unless he were to win that election and win it convincingly there would be no question of him even being considered for the prime ministership. And he was facing an anti-incumbency factor, a very tough battle.' So tough, according to this aide that, unusually for him, Modi feared he might not make it. 'He would talk openly about how he had these big battles to fight. Against Congress, against people in his own party and then in the general election.'

Modi may have had a rare 'wobble' in private, but in public he remained as confident as ever. His carefully crafted media image doesn't allow for any trace of weakness. He regards journalists as almost invariably predisposed to look for the worst in people, and he is not necessarily far wrong. He can sometimes takes his suspicion of the profession too far, even in the eyes of his advisers. Journalists working for the western media have been consistently harder to persuade of Modi's supposed transformation than many of those working in India itself, but his team were delighted to see their man on the cover of *Time* in May 2012, albeit only in the South Asia edition. The magazine found 'Modi in makeover mode: an act of self-purification, humility and bridge building in a state that is still traumatised by the Hindu-led anti-Muslim massacres of ten years ago and the flawed investigations in their wake.'

Modi immediately picked up on a mistake in the article, which was later corrected, exaggerating the number of people killed. He wanted his staff to launch a public attack on the magazine for shoddy journalism and had to be patiently talked down and convinced that being on the cover of *Time* with the caption 'Modi Means Business' was good news not bad, even with the question mark after the subheading, 'but can he lead India?' He was eventually persuaded that all most people would remember was the praise for his development policies and the description of him as a firm, 'no-nonsense leader' capable of steering India out of a 'mire of chronic corruption and inefficiency'.

Modi had not always enjoyed a friendly relationship with the business community. After the Gujarat riots, the

Confederation of Indian Industry had given him a very frosty reception. Many of those attending a get-to-know-you meeting with Modi in Delhi clearly felt the rioting had caused great economic as well as human damage to the state and their business interests. Several leading industrialists had spoken out against him, much to his fury. Characteristically, however, he fought back, and with the support of wealthy friends in the corporate world, including Gautam Adani and Karsan Patel, he assiduously rebuilt his reputation, until within five years he was something close to the businessman's darling.

The single most dramatic example of his pro-business approach bearing fruit had come in October 2008 when Tata Motors, a subsidiary of the vast Tata Group, announced that it was moving its no-frills 'Nano' car project to Gujarat and away from West Bengal, where worker disputes and other problems had been bedevilling production. Modi had told his officials to move heaven and earth to get the Tata deal; when they succeeded, he cheekily wrote to West Bengal's left-leaning political leaders suggesting that they might like to adopt his 'right-wing route' to development, if they wanted to see more industry and jobs in their state. It was certainly a coup, and one that gained Modi valuable national publicity. Just ahead of the 2012 elections, the Associated Chambers of Commerce and Industry of India (ASSOCHAM) reported that Gujarat had 'emerged as the most preferred investment destination out of the twenty emerging industrial states in India.'

As the elections approached, Modi received a boost of another kind, this time on the diplomatic front. The British high commissioner in Delhi, Sir James Bevan, had become convinced that it was time to bring the chief minister's pariah status to an end. He recommended lifting the ban to the foreign secretary, William Hague, and got the green light to go ahead with a meeting that he knew would be seen as highly symbolic. The United States was not yet ready to reopen relations, but the Foreign Office announced London was going it alone, 'in line with the British government's stated objective of improving bilateral relations with India.' On the morning of Monday 22 October, Bevan travelled to the chief minister's office in Gandhinagar and spent fifty minutes in talks with Modi, followed by a well-publicised photograph of the two men smiling and shaking hands. The high commissioner described the meeting as 'open, positive and constructive', and said they had discussed ways to 'develop cooperation between the UK and Gujarat across a very broad range of fields, including education, science and innovation, energy and climate change.' Godhra was not completely forgotten. Bevan said the British government still wished 'to ensure justice for the families of three British citizens who were killed in the 2002 riots', but Modi was back in the fold, at least so far as Britain was concerned.

Among those who had been urging the UK government to change its position – after the Supreme Court had found no evidence to hold against him – was Patricia Hewitt. As Tony Blair's industry secretary, she had been the last British minister to visit Gujarat before the diplomatic embargo was imposed. She knew from personal experience that the wounds from Godhra had not fully healed as she had many Gujarati families living in her Leicester constituency, some of whom had lost loved ones in the violence. After leaving the House of Commons she became chair of the UK India Business Council, and met Modi soon after Bevan. She became an admirer of his development policies and said of the riots, 'Personally I don't think he was culpable.' Even before Britain, Sweden and Denmark had already allowed relations to be discreetly reopened, but it would take the representatives of other European Union countries a few more weeks before they followed suit by inviting him to an unpublicised lunch at the German ambassador's residence in early January. The host, Michael Steiner, said, 'We are now in a new phase. This respect from us towards India is what the people of India expect from us.' It would take US Ambassador Nancy Powell over a year before she met Modi in February 2014 to indicate that her country was also ready to end its boycott.

Modi went into his third state assembly election with the auguries looking highly favourable, but in this campaign, as in every other he has ever fought, he was not content to rely on a good tail-wind to push him over the finishing line. Modi had other objectives than simply retaining power as chief minister. The beginnings of a gradual diplomatic thaw showed that foreign governments recognised it was likely he could be standing for higher office in a matter of months, but nothing was in the bag and he now needed the maximum momentum possible to carry him on to the next stage in his career. He also wanted to trial some of the messages and techniques that he would go on to use to such good effect in the general election. The Gujarat campaign themes were thus very much a dry run for 2014. The positive appeal was a mixture of 'development' and Modi's strong approach to leadership. At the same time, the party highlighted the suffering caused by runaway price inflation and rampant corruption, both of which it attributed to the failures of the Congress-led government in Delhi. But it was the use of new high-tech campaigning methods that Modi was most keen to try out. Traditional rallies and public meetings were not set aside, and Modi criss-crossed the state with as much energy as ever. Already, however, he and the team of young, technologically astute men he had gathered around him were looking at ways of reaching parts of the electorate that conventional campaigning might otherwise miss.

His website, which was given a smart brush-up in time for the elections, promised a campaign that would be 'very special because it marked a paradigm shift in the way technology was perceived and utilised in any election campaign in the history of India.' He started by launching his own state-wide television channel 'NaMo Gujarat' to add to his YouTube channel. 'NaMo', as a short form for his name, seemed to catch on, although some couldn't resist pointing out that in Gujarati *namo* means 'to bow down'. The channel would broadcast all his speeches and rallies and promote his somewhat exaggerated message that 'Gujarat is unanimous for the formation of a BJP government.' His Facebook and Twitter accounts went into overdrive, and he became the first politician in India to target young voters by taking part in a Google+ Hangout discussion. An estimated half a million people at home and abroad clicked on to the event, helpfully raising both his national and international profile in the process.

Most radical of all was the use of the so-called 'Pepper's Ghost Illusion', or at least a very twenty-first-century version of it. John Henry Pepper was a British chemist, who in Queen Victoria's day used glass and mirrors to make an object or person in one room appear as if by magic in another. His first success was for a production of Charles Dickens's *The Haunted Man* on the London stage on Christmas Eve 1862. A century and a half later, in 2008, Queen Victoria's great-great-great-grandson, Prince Charles, used a system based on Pepper's Ghost to deliver a speech to a green energy conference in Abu Dhabi from his home in Highgrove in the Gloucestershire countryside. The point was to highlight the carbon emissions that would have been involved if he had flown out to make the speech in person. So Modi was not the first man in his sixties with thinning hair, a distinctly formal manner and old-fashioned values to make use of the hologram technology more usually associated with the stage shows of pop stars on tour. Indeed, other high-profile figures like Vice President Al Gore, David Beckham and Sir Richard Branson had also used the technique; but for Narendra Modi it wasn't sufficient to repeat somebody else's trick, and concern for the environment was far from his mind as he sent a fleet of relay trucks out to different sites across Gujarat on 18 November 2012.

If others had shown a little bit more imagination, the 3D rally would not now be associated forever with Modi. The latest incarnation of Pepper's Ghost was designed by a German innovator, Uwe Mass, and a demonstration model was shipped from London by his company, Musion. As potential prime ministerial candidates of the future, both L. K. Advani and Rahul Gandhi were approached but failed to spot the potential. It was the film director Mani Shankar who suggested trying Modi. Senthil Kumar, one of the team who flew out to pitch to him, was instantly impressed, according to an interview he gave to Rediff News. 'I had no idea what he was like in person. When I met him, I liked the way he carried himself. There was an aura about him. He looked like a divine personality. The way he dressed, the way he spoke, the way he walked – everything about him impressed me. His body language was that of a leader, and he looked like a giant. He greeted each and every one of us personally and asked whether we were comfortable and had food. It was only when he was assured that we had all eaten and were fine that he asked if we could get down to work.' Shankar and Kumar started filming and asked Modi to talk about whatever he liked. 'What amazed us was the subject of his speech,' said Kumar. 'He had spent time learning about holograms and spoke about the technology for about twenty-five minutes. After he spoke, we showed him what he said in hologram so that he could get an idea how it worked. He was happy and said we shall use it in the assembly election.'

According to one man close to the project, Modi was more than just impressed. He was convinced it could win him the election, so much so that he swore everybody to secrecy until four days before it was due to go public. The first outing was relatively modest, with just four locations. 'I'm delivering this speech in 3D to show you that India is not being left behind, that we are world leaders in technology,' Modi said. It was a claim that was marred somewhat by technical hitches on the night, and at times during his forty-minute speech the sound was inaudible. The cost was put at over £150,000, and some commentators argued that it was 'morally reprehensible' to spend so much money on a 3D speech in a country with such widespread poverty, but most of the media lapped it up. Modi was undeterred by any criticism and insisted on a dramatic expansion of the project. On 12 December a speech delivered from his residence in Gandhinagar was beamed live to fifty-three different locations in twenty-six cities simultaneously, earning him a citation in the *Guinness Book of World Records* for 'the most simultaneous broadcasts of a Pepper's Ghost Illusion.'

The scene was set for an election that could have only one result, a victory for the BJP, but a variety of outcomes. The outcome Modi wanted, an unstoppable momentum towards an assault on national power, would require just a little bit of good old-fashioned spin. The pre-election opinion polls, as well as some of the predictions made by Modi's own advisers, had pointed to as many as 125 seats for the BJP in a state assembly of 182. In the end they won 119, still a highly credible result, but with undercurrents that caused one of his personal number-crunchers more than a little concern. 'If you look at the results, despite him doing phenomenally well in terms of his campaign, and we did some of the newest possible things, we won 119 seats out of 182. If you take out the five big cities of Gujarat, actually Congress and the BJP had an equal number. In rural Gujarat the Congress put up a very spirited fight.'

But election day was no occasion to give credit to the opposition or to concede that Modi might have done better. In his victory speech, Modi said the heroes of the day were the 60 million people of Gujarat. Those in the crowd, and the millions more watching on TV, were quick to notice that whatever he said about the state's electors, he didn't say it in their language. Rather than speaking in Gujarati, as he normally did, Modi was speaking in Hindi so he could be understood across most of India. He merely smiled when the ecstatic crowd started to chant 'PM, PM' and 'Delhi, Delhi'. He gave those speculating about his future intentions plenty to chew on when he said, 'By serving Gujarat, I serve India. The results of the Gujarat elections have proved that the voters in the country know what is right and what is wrong.' Those still looking for the elusive apology for the massacres of 2002 were intrigued to hear him say, 'If I have made any mistakes, forgive me. Give me your blessings so I make no mistakes in future,' although he didn't elaborate on what those mistakes might have been. In words that were already redundant by the time he uttered them, the now thrice-elected chief minister said, 'Political pundits can discuss Modi all they want.' Which is just as well, because they were already doing exactly that.

CHAPTER FIVE
THE BIG MO

As the year 2013 began, Narendra Modi was treading carefully. His clear victory in his third Gujarat state election and the assiduous efforts of his supporters to raise his profile in both the traditional and social media meant he was now a well-known public figure across India. He'd proved his ability to win popular support, confounded his critics and established his credentials as a politician of national stature. To his rapidly growing fanbase both within and outside the BJP, he was not merely the favourite, but the only possible candidate to lead the party into the general election in eighteen months' time. Modi had that much-sought-after 'big Mo', the momentum to carry him forward and upwards. But he knew his party and its leadership well and was aware that what seemed obvious to the many was not so clear-cut for the few.

The BJP had lost two elections in a row but the prospects for 2014 appeared bright. The Congress-led government had never looked more vulnerable. During its first term, as it sought to liberalise and grow the economy like never before, it had enjoyed widespread popularity. At times it looked as if the unassuming prime minister, Dr Manmohan Singh, could walk on water. Now it was rudderless, tired and battered after being hit by a succession of corruption scandals and political failures. Every opposition party in a democracy everywhere in the world likes to claim that 'it's time for a change', but political cliché or not, there was ample evidence that – across India – change was exactly what people were looking for. If the BJP was the party best placed to benefit from this mood, why put the likelihood of victory at risk by selecting a controversial and potentially divisive candidate like Narendra Modi?

Most Indian governments are coalitions, and there was a well-grounded fear that some smaller parties would desert the BJP if they chose Modi, making it harder to construct a majority in parliament after the elections. And if Congress managed to win back liberal Hindus and hold on to its support base among religious minorities, then the prospect of winning enough seats to form a stable government would recede still further. Better, perhaps, to play safe and go for a more consensual, if less exciting, candidate. Modi, after all, had no experience at the national level and had never been elected to parliament, and there were highly respected, battle-hardened party leaders in Delhi quite capable and more than ready to be the BJP standard-bearer. Foremost among them was L. K. Advani, Modi's long-time mentor, who had served as both deputy prime minister and leader of the opposition. That Advani, once the party's nationalist hard-man, could now be seen as the unifying alternative to Modi was extraordinary in itself. But he was also in his mid-eighties and had led the party to defeat in the last general election, making him even less credible in the eyes of Modi's supporters. And yet, while Advani never pushed his own candidacy publicly any more than Modi did (that was not the BJP way of doing things), those who wanted to keep his hat in the ring could argue that his qualities were still needed, given that the political landscape looked so different this time around. Advani, who had once been a crucial part of Modi's political life-support system, was now the biggest threat to his hopes of keeping his ambitions alive.

After a decade in office, the Congress-led government was widely perceived not to have delivered on its promises and was associated indelibly in the minds of many Indians with corruption, incompetence and weak leadership. Zoya Hasan retired as professor of social sciences at Delhi's Jawaharlal Nehru University just as Modi was making his ascent on power. She has closely examined the ebbs and flows in the fortunes of both Congress and the BJP. In 2014, she told me, 'People wanted the Congress out.' In her judgement, those who most hoped to see the back of the party were 'the corporate sector, the media, the middle classes, upper castes and so on', but overall people were 'pretty disgusted with indecisive leadership, dual power centres and policy paralysis.' And while she said corruption was nothing new in India and 'corruption and India are synonymous, so to speak', it was the high level of what she called 'mega-corruption' that was so damaging. 'Not that Congress is the only corrupt party but it had been in government for ten years and there had no doubt been a significant increase in corruption.'

The list of scams and scandals associated with the administration was bewildering in its length and complexity. Match-fixing allegations against leading members of the Indian cricket team damaged the country's international reputation, but it was scandals that robbed the public exchequer of hundreds of millions of pounds that fatally damaged the government. The multiplicity of allegations of fraudulent financial deals around the 2010 Commonwealth Games in Delhi was described in the *Times of India* as 'by far the biggest and most blatant exercise in corruption in independent India's history.' The list of criminal charges arising from the scams ran to sixty pages, with the most high-profile of the accused being a Congress MP, Suresh Kalmadi, who chaired the games organising committee. The way the games had been tarnished was a national embarrassment, but the corruption was just the tip of a vast iceberg. Hardly a month went by without the public hearing of new allegations implicating people in high office or positions of authority in public life. Some were more strictly about incompetence and bad judgement than graft, but they all got lumped together under the heading of 'scams'. There were scandals over the allocation of mobile phone licences, the auctioning of coal stocks, the purchase of helicopters, trucks and other equipment for the armed services, the distribution of state-owned apartments and much more besides.

Manish Tewari was the information and broadcasting minister in the Congress-led government. He is also a successful barrister and decided not to stand in the 2014 elections for health reasons. When I met him at his law offices in Delhi he was frank about the damage done by all the corruption allegations. He may now be out of high office, but he hasn't lost the politician's touch. If defeat could be blamed solely on overzealous investigators and corrupt ministers, especially if they were members of coalition parties and not Congress itself, then by the same token Modi deserves little credit for his victory. 'Even with somebody else leading the BJP, the result would not have been materially different,' he told me. 'The elections were actually lost by November 2010.' It was then that the story about the sale of the 2G mobile phone spectrum licences broke, with India's comptroller and auditor general (CAG) putting the cost to the public purse at almost two thousand billion rupees (close to £20 billion). Tewari says that figure was 'a very sensational number', thrown into the public domain by a CAG who had started behaving like an activist. It was, he said, later 'conclusively demolished' by a parliamentary committee, but by then the damage had been done. The telecoms minister responsible, Andimuthu Raja, was from one of the Congress Party's coalition partners, the DMK. He was accused not only of misallocating the licences, but also of taking personal kickbacks. He was forced to resign and was arrested, charged with corruption and sent to jail. It wasn't just the career of A. Raja, as he is known, that was destroyed. The reputation of the government as a whole was indelibly tarnished. As Dr Singh's former media adviser, Harish Khare, put it, 'The "2G scam" became emblematic of a perceived flaw in the UPA arrangement: a regional political party demanding a licence to loot in exchange for its support, and a weak Prime Minister unwilling and unable to throw the thieves out.'

Two years later, the CAG published another report with a still more eye-watering price tag for the public finances. 'Coalgate' had the potential to inflict even greater political damage, as some believed it led right to the door of the prime minister. From 2004 to 2009, the government had sold off the right to mine huge deposits of coal. But instead of auctioning them to the highest bidder, as originally intended, allocations were made in a decidedly opaque manner following recommendations from an inter-ministerial committee headed by the coal minister. And the man who held that position, among his other responsibilities, was none other than the prime minister himself, Dr Singh. In many cases his committee had decided to give away the mining rights for free, and the lucky recipients were shown to include companies led by individuals with close links to the government. The CAG claimed the result was a massive windfall for private companies, some of which hadn't even bothered to turn up to the committee in person to make their case for securing the rights.

The government challenged the figures and said its main concern had been to increase coal production and to keep down energy prices, but few were convinced. Their argument that the coal had no value to the state as it hadn't yet been mined seemed absurd. Nor did it help them much to point out that allocations had been going on in much the same way under the previous government led by the BJP. Confident that there was no evidence that he'd sought to benefit personally from the allocations, Dr Singh offered to resign if he was ever found guilty of corruption. But the halo that had hovered for years over his turban in the eyes of his many disciples – among the better off in India, corporate leaders, economists and the international financial community – was looking decidedly tarnished.

Such was the scale of the abuse of public money that, had the media run a story about a major project that had been completed without a bribe being paid or a contract forged or a ministerial oversight, people would have refused to believe it. And yet it wasn't always obvious that the BJP opposition would reap the political benefit from the public's disgust at what had been going on. In common with other scandal-hit democracies, the UK included, India might easily have turned against the political class as a whole, on the grounds that they were all just as bad as each other. At first it was figures from outside the conventional political arena who took up the anti-corruption crusade and captured the public imagination.

Going without food is a peculiarly Indian way of seeking to bring about political change. Mahatma Gandhi's fasts and hunger strikes were hugely successful, at least in so far as they brought international attention to his demands for independence and democracy. Anna Hazare has sometimes been likened to Gandhi in his pursuit of his own campaigns to clean up that hard-won democracy. Thanks to the internet and India's vibrant media, Hazare, who was born ten years before the British finally relinquished control of the country, was able to spread the word further and faster than the mahatma ever could. When he began an indefinite fast in April 2011 to demand an effective system of ombudsmen to root out corruption, he received support from all corners of the country. Within five days the government was forced to set up a committee charged with drafting new legislation to establish an independent citizens' ombudsman, known as the Jan Lokpal. A year later, frustrated at the slow progress, Hazare started another fast-unto-death that he called India's 'second struggle for Independence'. India, he said, was not safe in the hands of Congress or the BJP and he raised the prospect of a new grassroot political movement designed to put 'good people' into parliament at the next election. It would take another two and a half years until, in December 2013, the Lokpal Bill was passed into law.

One man who clearly thought of himself as an example of the good people was an early supporter of Anna Hazare's campaign, a former civil servant turned social activist by the name of Arvind Kejriwal. He first started exposing alleged scams while still employed as a tax inspector by the Indian Revenue Service. Kejriwal is no stranger to the hunger strike, but his preference is for more practical methods of bringing about reform. While Hazare showed no interest in running for office himself and was suspicious of all politicians, Kejriwal believed in taking on both Congress and the BJP where he felt he could most hurt them, at the ballot box. Kejriwal's decision to set up a political party of his own, the Aam Aadmi Party (AAP), or Common Man's Party, was a step too far for the veteran campaigner. 'I am going on the path of agitations and he has formed a political party,'

Hazare told a news conference. 'This country has gained freedom and many other things through public unrest and agitation and not through political parties.'

Another man who, initially at least, believed that neither of the big parties was the solution to the corruption problem was India's most famous yoga guru, known as Baba Ramdev. He became a household name, at least in those households that possessed a television, a decade ago, when his morning yoga shows attracted a vast audience of people keen to get fit without straying too far from their living rooms. His charismatic televangelism for both yoga and meditation earned him international recognition and a very healthy income as well. When he held a rally in Delhi in early 2011, and was joined on stage by both Anna Hazare and Arvind Kejriwal, over a hundred thousand people turned up to hear him. Given his undoubted popularity, and the simple appeal of his demand for an end to corruption and the return of so-called 'black money' stashed away by India's super-rich in foreign banks, ministers were forced to take note. So much so that when he flew into Delhi in his private plane at the beginning of June after threatening to start his own hunger strike, no fewer than four government ministers were at the airport to meet him. The delegation was led by the finance minister, Pranab Mukherjee, and included telecoms minister Kapil Sibal, parliamentary affairs minister Pawan Kumar Bansal, tourism minister Subodh Kant Sahay and the cabinet secretary K.M. Chandrashekhar. Wiser heads within Congress could see this for the overreaction it was, but nobody could be in any doubt that there were big dividends to be paid to any politician or party that could credibly claim the anti-corruption mantle.

Another guru with a massive personal following was also in search of a leader who could set India back on the right path.

Sri Sri Ravi Shankar led the vast Art of Living Foundation, based in Bangalore but now active in over 150 countries worldwide. Not to be confused with the musician who made the sitar famous, Ravi Shankar heads a movement with over 100,000 active volunteers in India and claims to have 'touched the lives of over 370 million people.' His mission to restore human values to the lives of individuals and in government made him a natural supporter of the anti-corruption movement. With his many programmes to promote happiness, relieve stress and alleviate poverty, among many others, he was able to communicate with his supporters from a position of trust, something most politicians would give their eye teeth for. He wasn't yet ready to endorse any potential new leader, but like Baba Ramdev he would soon make his preference very clear (see Chapter Eight). But while he insisted there were good people in all parties and that his campaign was 'spiritual not political', it was Congress that was most clearly identified with corruption in the public's mind, and his intervention helped reinforce the idea that it wasn't just opposition politicians who were outraged by the many scams and allegations.

Anti-corruption protests were not unique to India at this time. People were taking to the streets all over the globe to condemn what they saw as corrupt governments or financial institutions. In the Arab world and the former Soviet bloc, leaders had been forced out of office, while all across Europe, North America and Latin America huge crowds had demonstrated or joined the 'occupy' movements. But while ministers in Delhi were not alone in being subject to the anger of their citizens, according to Professor Zoya Hasan, 'the anti-corruption movement was badly mishandled by the government. For a start, they underestimated it. Underestimated the force of the movement, underestimated its popularity, underestimated the disgust it was able to bring to the public domain. Disgust with politicians who were seen to be more corrupt than, say, the corporate sector or the bureaucrats. The success of the Anna Hazare movement was the way in which it was able to pin it on politicians and on Congress in particular.'

Sitting in the prime minister's office in Delhi throughout all this turmoil was a man who nobody accused of being personally corrupt, but who few believed had what it took to clean up the system. Dr Manmohan Singh, the first Sikh to hold the office, became prime minister against most people's expectations in 2004, when the Congress Party leader Sonia Gandhi decided against taking the job herself. Both her husband, Rajiv, and her mother-in-law, Indira, had been assassinated, but Sonia had said before that she would follow her 'inner voice' if the opportunity came her way. That voice told her she should decline, and by heeding it she also showed herself to be a shrewd politician. Had she, the Italian-born widow of a former PM, assumed the top job, the controversy would have been a massive distraction from the work the government wanted to get on with. Mrs Gandhi had been famously unwilling to enter politics at all until she was press-ganged into it by the Congress Party, which had long since translated Henry Ford's 'any colour so long as it's black' into 'any leader so long as it's a Gandhi'.

Singh, the man she chose for the job, was first and foremost an economist rather than a politician. His dream was to open up and liberalise India's economy but, while he wanted to see the country get rich, there has never been any suggestion that he hoped to seek any financial benefit for himself. He drove one of the cheapest cars on the market and was said to insist on going home every lunch-time to eat with his wife of fifty years. Other world leaders, as well as the media at home and abroad, spoke eloquently of his integrity, decency and good manners. Unfortunately, he himself never spoke eloquently about anything. He was understated to the point of monasticism. He almost never talked to the media or held a news conference, and a book by his former spokesman quoted his wife as saying he 'swallows everything, doesn't spit anything out.' Britain's *The Economist*, which was sympathetic towards him, said that while 'the prime minister's personal honesty is not in doubt . . . he refused to confront corrupt underlings', and never once considered threatening resignation to force better behaviour on others. If India was looking for somebody to lead the fight against corruption from a position of power, then the search was still on.

If Manmohan Singh had been better able to articulate his government's successes, the Congress Party might have been in a less vulnerable state. Instead people were left wondering why a country that was led by a supposedly gifted economist was suffering from sluggish growth and runaway price rises. Worse still was the perception, which Singh did little to counter, that he was prime minister in name only. The most damaging charge in the book by his spokesman, Sanjaya Baru, was that he was trapped in a 'politically fatal combination of responsibility without power'. Sonia Gandhi might have turned down the job, according to this interpretation, but she still liked to make all the big decisions. When he wasn't at home with the mother of his children, he was at work waiting for the matriarch of his party to tell him what to do next. As the BJP leadership looked towards the 2014 poll, it is hardly surprising that many felt the election was theirs for the taking, whoever their candidate might be. Arun Shourie, himself a well-respected journalist and economist and a former BJP minister with a long history in the party, told me that it felt as if Congress was handing them the election on a plate and 'Manmohan Singh was the chief election agent.'

Despite being tipped as a possible finance minister, Shourie was passed over for a job in Modi's first government, so he felt freer to talk openly about the tussles that had gone on behind the scenes over who should be the party's candidate for prime minister. He describes the BJP as 'diffuse', every bit as much in need of strong leadership as the country itself. 'There were a few persons in Delhi who had appropriated these powers for themselves and they said they were the party.' Shourie's assessment was confirmed to me off the record by some of those now holding high office. They recognised his view that the leadership, such as it was, comprised 'persons who were just jostling against each other. Their mass base was six journalists each, that's all. They weren't leaders who had risen in a province and so had roots. They were Delhi's stateless leaders.'

Modi, by contrast, is careful never to criticise the party elders, either in public or in private. 'There is a galaxy of leaders who are equally competent,' he insists. Of men like L. K. Advani he says, 'These are people who held Modi's hand to make him walk,' adding for good measure, 'I am a worker of the party. We are a team.' Nevertheless, he is proud of the deep roots he has put down over the years; not just in Gujarat, but across India, in his long years as an activist and organiser, first with the RSS and then with the BJP. His many grassroot supporters didn't have a vote in the selection of the candidate, but their voices were impossible to ignore on social media and were passed up through the party's internal networks.

If Advani was going to hold back the wave of support for Modi's candidacy, it had to be on the basis of something other than a popularity test. He couldn't put his own case for selection in person, but there were others who could. His old friend K. N. Govindacharya told *Headlines Today* that 'Given the testing times being faced by the country – both economically and culturally – I believe we need an experienced hand as PM. I feel that L. K. Advani should be the prime minister.' Modi, he suggested, should gain experience as a cabinet minister first. 'Running a country with so much diversity and contradictions needs a much more flexible leader. Being a PM involves a lot of skills which Modiji has not exhibited so far.' The BJP national council had just been held in Delhi and Modi had been given a standing ovation by party workers. For his part, Advani had allowed himself a dig at the exuberant claims being made for the so-called Gujarat model of economic development. It had already been successful, he told the meeting, and Modi had 'only made it a better state'. Speaking just after the council concluded, Govindacharya was almost certainly reflecting Advani's own views when he implied that Modi was in too much of a hurry. 'Politics is a skill of patience. I feel that an atmosphere of impatience is being created which is not good for Modi or the country.'

Certainly Modi's move from chief minister to prime minister designate was moving at a pace that suggested he was indeed impatient, or at the very least that others were impatient on his behalf. In March 2013 he was named as a member of the party's top decision-making body, the BJP parliamentary board. Then, in June, the national executive named him as chair of the general election campaign committee. The meeting took place in the same venue in Goa where Modi's resignation after the riots of 2002 had been rejected. On that occasion Advani had been his most vocal supporter. This time around he stayed away on health grounds, but he followed the proceedings carefully and the following day resigned all his party positions in protest at

Modi's elevation. His resignation letter said that, 'For some time I have been finding it difficult to reconcile either with the current functioning of the party or the direction in which it is going. Most of the leaders are now just concerned with their personal agendas.' Now it was Advani's turn to have his resignation rejected. The head of the RSS, Mohan Bhagwat, asked him to reconsider. After being told that his 'sage advice' and 'guidance' were needed more than ever before, Advani relented. The prediction that Modi's elevation would cause tensions with the BJP's partners proved true a week later when the Janata Dal United (JDU) Party, which was in government in Bihar state in the east of the country, brought to an end its seventeen-year-old electoral alliance.

There was no love lost between Narendra Modi and the JDU leader, Nitish Kumar, who also had a reputation as a proactive, development-minded chief minister. At around 11.00 a.m. on Sunday, June 16, Modi was having a meeting with a few of his trusted aides at his residence when he was passed a note informing him that Kumar was withdrawing from the alliance. It was big news and the others around the table expected the meeting to be abruptly curtailed. Instead Modi just nodded, put the note to one side, and continued as if nothing had happened.

Modi's *sang froid* may have impressed his team, but political divisions always make the blood of journalists and commentators rush and are usually bad news for the party concerned. Media coverage of the 'disarray' in the BJP over the summer raised questions over whether the opposition was in danger of throwing away its best opportunity of power in a generation. As Modi set about putting the election structure in place, while harrying Congress over its failures as best he could, he wasn't alone in thinking that the BJP could only concentrate its fire on the government properly once it was able to unite around its own prime ministerial candidate. Advani's supporters insisted there was no need to hurry, but in August the RSS called on the party to get on with it and threw its support behind Modi. Advani had one last jibe at Modi, chastising him for attacking Manmohan Singh on Indian Independence Day, which is usually kept free of party politics, but by now it was obvious to just about everybody else that Modi was unstoppable. On 12 September Advani was said still to be digging in his heels, worried that an early announcement would shift attention from the weakness of Congress and onto Modi's controversial personality. The following day the BJP parliamentary board formally announced that Narendra Modi would indeed be their candidate for prime minister. Although Advani was a member of the board, he refused to attend, telling the party president, Rajnath Singh, by letter, of his 'anguish as [sic] also my disappointment over your style of functioning.'

Piyush Goyal, a long-time Modi supporter, told me that the decision was inevitable. 'Only a handful at the top were nurturing their ambition to become leader. The rank and file had no doubt in their minds.' When I asked Modi himself about how he felt when he got the news, he was back in that detachment mode that is impossible to challenge, however hard it is to accept at face value. 'It was Mr Rajnath Singh who called me first and broke the news. It was not a surprise. Since my win in the state elections in Gujarat in 2012 I was clear that I would be one of the candidates under consideration. But I never really thought about it or ever tried to lobby within the party to be nominated as the prime ministerial candidate. Nor was I really curious as to whether I or someone else would be nominated.'

If he really wasn't curious, then he was alone among the politically conscious people of India. And, once he was in place, what now made them curious was how his erstwhile rival would react. It may be that Advani could draw on the same capacity for detachment that Modi claims to have learned from his years with the RSS. A few days later he appeared to signal that he was ready to accept the result, when he described Modi as 'my friend' and praised his work in bringing electricity across Gujarat. You didn't have to be the Indian equivalent of a Kremlinologist, however, to notice the crucial qualifier as he went on to say that the party had chosen Modi and 'if that fructifies . . . then we will repeat all the good work that we have done in BJP-ruled states across the country.'

Arun Shourie is as good a reader of the political undercurrents as you could hope to find and the qualified 'if' was not lost on him. 'Even after Modi was selected some of them thought that he would stumble and they might become prime minister,' he told me. Then, with a laugh, he went on: 'In India people believe in astrology so hope never dies.'

CHAPTER SIX

THE MODI OPERANDI

If you were to ask any politics student, at least in Europe or North America, to name the birthplace of democracy, they would almost certainly answer 'Ancient Greece'. That is, if they had paid any attention at all to what they had been taught. It was the Athenians, according to this historical view, who had come up with democracy as a means of countering the absolute rule of tyrants around 2,600 years ago. Even the word, *demokratia*, is Greek. Relatively recent archaeological evidence, however, suggests that it is time to set aside this western-centric assumption. In his epic *The Life and Death of Democracy*, John Keane tells us that 'The lamp of assembly-based democracy was first lit in the "East", in lands that geographically correspond to contemporary Syria, Iraq and Iran. The custom of popular self-government was later transported eastwards, towards the Indian subcontinent, where sometime after 1500 BCE, in the early Vedic period, republics governed by assemblies became common.'

So much for the idea that it was the benevolent British who first bequeathed India democracy as a last act of generosity before leaving the country to fend for itself. Narendra Modi has good reason to speak with pride about his country's democratic system. It has served him well. 'The DNA of democracy is ingrained in the Indian people and you can never separate it out even from the most illiterate of the citizens,' he told me.

'Never assume that just because someone is illiterate they do not understand democracy, and ultimately this is what makes India.' What made him prime minister was his ability to marshal a campaign that was able to reach more of the Indian people than ever before at election time. My attempts to understand from him how he had done it were inevitably influenced by my own experience of successful campaigns that I'd either worked on or witnessed in Britain and the United States. Here we fall all too easily into the language of military conflicts. There's a 'war book' setting out the main battle lines; we have 'attack units' charged with producing the ammunition to fire at the other side, and a system of command and control that makes sure that what the party's top brass want is put into effect by the foot soldiers out on the streets.

Much of this language has found its way into the Indian political system. There are 'war rooms' at state and constituency levels and the parties fire salvos at each other directed by powerful figures who go by the title 'war room in charge'. Part of Modi's appeal was the offer of strong leadership, and it seemed to me that he was a man who liked to lead from the front and who expected those working for him to produce results and produce them quickly. He was surely the commander in chief, the most senior general leading his troops into battle. So how, I asked him, had he exercised command and control over his own campaign?

Wrong question.

'Why talk about leadership styles like command and control at all?' he replied. 'Command and control sounds so much like a leader in the armed forces as compared to a leader who has a heart. In my opinion a leader is one who has the heart to embrace all. As a leader my philosophy is that you have to be available to shake the hand of your fellow beings as a human and not as an army person. The army commander role, while necessary, is a very different role. This does not mean that a leader has to please everyone, however you must have the belief in your own conviction. People will disagree, but as a leader you must first yourself have the conviction that your intentions are right and only then can you truly convince other people. You have to light a lamp to drive darkness away. It is only through a power of conviction that lamps get lit and light spreads.'

Being seen as a conviction politician is clearly part and parcel of strong leadership, and several of Modi's inner team described him to me as India's Margaret Thatcher. There are some grounds for making the comparison. Both were nationalists on the political right who came from modest backgrounds and rose to lead their parties through hard work and single-minded determination. But he preferred to call in the aid of a leader who could hardly have been more different to the Iron Lady. 'Firmness comes out of commitment and not out of strong control or arrogance. There is a vast difference between the two, and yet a thin line that separates these two characteristics. Mahatma Gandhi was never seen as a command and control leader but was always regarded as a very firm and strong leader because he never compromised with his convictions.' And yet the mahatma never had to lead an effort to convince over eight hundred million people to go to the polls and to vote for him when they got there.

Of the dozens of men (and they were almost all men) I spoke to about their roles in the campaign, none could describe the overall structure in terms that would be familiar to an election strategist in London, Washington or Canberra, for example. They may have had their 'war rooms', but there was no 'war book' setting out in detail who did what and laying out the campaign strategy for all to follow. But nobody seemed to think it mattered. They all knew what they had been expected to do, but doubted if anybody – not even Modi himself – knew the full picture. It was his drive, energy and, yes, conviction that kept it all together and gave it direction. His decision-making was swift and his instructions, usually delivered in person or over the phone, were clear, according to those in his inner circle. And it was his extraordinary memory that prevented anything from being overlooked. 'If in the morning he gave you ten things to do,' said one, 'he would remember all ten. You couldn't get away with doing only nine.' From the first morning meeting at the Gujarat chief minister's office in Gandhinagar until he returned there late at night after a day's campaigning, Modi would be issuing instructions, gathering information and monitoring events across the country by phone, email and frequently the WhatsApp function on his mobile. According to somebody who saw him every day: 'There was nobody looking over his shoulder. Nobody but him knew who he'd been speaking to.'

The best description for the structure that wasn't really a structure was to call it an 'ecosystem', one in which all the different organisms were interlinked and often interdependent but had lives of their own. It wasn't entirely without form. There were three distinct components, each with their own roles to play: the RSS, the BJP itself and the army of new volunteers. The first two were disciplined and had long-established methods of operation. The third was more fluid and made up its own rules as it went along, and was all the more effective for that.

At the top, the leading figures of all three parts of the ecosystem had the ear of Modi. They were joined by others who provided a link to the professionals employed to support the campaign and to the officials who still had the responsibility of looking after Modi as chief minister. Thus a relatively small group of people could determine who should do what further down the line and try to ensure that the different limbs worked so far as possible as one body without falling over each other. It didn't matter whether on paper they were the people with the most senior positions in each sphere; these were the men he trusted most. It wasn't a closed circle. Others could speak to Modi as and when they needed to, but these men had pivotal roles. Within the BJP it was Amit Shah, his closest political ally and a controversial former minister in the Gujarat government. Piyush Goyal, a member of the upper house of parliament, was party treasurer and had responsibility for the campaign advertising. Ram Lal, the RSS general secretary in charge of organisation, dealt with the cadres on the ground. Ram Madhav was the link person with the RSS leadership. Representing the volunteer groups, the most influential person was Prashant Kishor, who was now running an organisation called Citizens for Accountable Governance, or the CAG. From the Gujarat government secretariat, Modi depended greatly on the sagacity and experience of the chief principal secretary, Kuniyal Kailasanathan, or 'K.K.' as he is known.

Just outside this inner core there were others – again all of them men – who Modi would turn to on a regular basis. Arun Jaitley was one of the party's most confident and eloquent spokespeople. Dr Hiren Joshi handled Modi's personal interactions on social media. Sanjay Bhavsar had responsibility for managing his schedule. A.K. Sharma, another of the senior Gujarat bureaucrats, contributed to his speeches, while G.C. Murmu looked after legal affairs. Bharat Lal, the state of Gujarat's resident commissioner in Delhi, acted as Modi's eyes and ears in the capital while the campaign was being run from Gandhinagar. Among the professionals for whom

Modi's door was always open were Manoj Ladwa, a Gujarati-born London lawyer, who spent several weeks in India working closely with the core team, and Rajesh Jain, a Mumbai-based internet entrepreneur.

At the very top of the campaign, therefore, all the various stakeholders were represented and through their proximity to Modi their representatives held the structure together. The further down you went into the ecosystem, however, the more the different components would operate independently. At the next level – that of the twenty-nine states and seven union territories – there was still a high degree of cooperation and coordination. But at the lower strata, towards the grass roots, the different elements generally operated largely in isolation, either by choice or on instructions from above.

To understand the role of the RSS – the 'Sangh' – in the campaign, I went to visit Ram Madhav. He had recently taken over as national general secretary of the BJP, but before his promotion he was in charge of election management for the RSS, which he too describes as the party's 'ideological parent'. The *Sarsanghchalak,* or 'Supreme Leader', of the RSS, Mohan Bhagwat, had known Modi almost all his life. They had played marbles together as children. This bond had helped overcome the doubts of others at the top of the RSS about Modi's candidature. It was Ram Madhav's job to help ensure that the same level of trust spread down through the rest of the organisation. He told me that in 2014 the RSS activists were more involved than they had ever been before in an election campaign. By his assessment, around a million people attended the morning meetings, known as *shakhas*, for an hour every day in fifty thousand towns and villages across the country. They were all encouraged to take the message about the need for a change of government back to their families and friends, increasing the reach of the Sangh via word of mouth to something like thirty million potential voters. In addition there are more than forty separate organisations affiliated to the RSS, including India's largest trade unions, the Bharitya Kisan Sangh (BKS) or Indian Farmers' Union and the Bharitya Mazdoor Sangh (BMS) or Indian Labourers' Union, with a combined membership of more than 16 million, and other groups for women, university students and so on. To try to protect its thin veneer of political independence, the RSS told its volunteers that they should urge people to vote for 'change at the helm' rather than for the BJP or Modi specifically, but in practice it made little difference.

One RSS worker with a gift for simile described their way of working to *The Caravan* magazine. '"The instructions given are: never go to the BJP office, don't hold the BJP flag, don't be seen on the BJP stage, don't use Modi's name in pamphlets etc." He held up his palm to make the point. "You see this hand? You can only see the palm lines and it is clean. The millions of micro-organisms will only be visible under a microscope. Similarly, the Sangh workers are invisible, but always at work."'

According to Ram Madhav, all those millions of people associated with the Sangh were motivated to get involved for two main reasons. 'They all saw that this was an important turning point for our nation,' he said, but equally they had one of their own as the agent for change. 'Naturally because of his very long association with the RSS, the cadres do value that identification with Mr Modi.' Significantly, though, even a man so closely wedded to the Sangh as Madhav recognises that in his twelve years in Gujarat, focusing above all on economic development, Modi had 'outgrown' his RSS roots. 'He became a sort of icon for development and good governance, so for an average RSS man he symbolises both; he's our man in the sense that he comes from our rank and file, but also he's the real development man.'

The senior television journalist Rahul Kanwal saw many RSS people out working for Modi while filming constituency reports for *Headlines Today*. 'There are a lot of misnomers about the RSS,' he told me, 'but those guys are very, very committed, far more than workers from any other political formation. They felt they had to do this for India. They felt that the country was going in the wrong direction, that the Congress had taken the country to the dogs and they felt that Modi would be the guy to set it right, and so they went out of their way to work for him.'

Sitting in his cubicle in the *Headlines Today* newsroom, Kanwal admitted that the media didn't always do justice to what motivated the cadres. 'The RSS worker ordinarily doesn't like to get involved in politics. Because the mandate of the RSS, unlike the television notion of what the RSS stands for, is actually far deeper than just going out and campaigning. They are a social organisation and they do a lot of work on the ground, especially in the tribal areas and the poorer areas. That's their primary mandate. Politics is just one small part of what they do. For them it's not that important and they think it's something where everybody gets corrupted so they don't like to devote much time and energy in politics. But for the first time, they functioned as the party cadre on the ground. They would go to small tea stalls and speak to workers, speak to villagers, for days on end. Because the party doesn't have the machinery to campaign 24/7. A leader will come, he will make a speech, he will go away and then the villagers are back to doing what they do usually. But the RSS worker lives in those villages.'

If the RSS was at the ideological heart of the ecosystem, the political brain was the party itself. Here, inevitably, there was more of a conventional structure, with specific responsibilities delegated to more or less clearly defined constituent parts. Under the party president, Rajnath Singh, there was the Central Election Committee, which he chaired himself once Modi became the candidate. It comprised most of the leading politicians and met whenever their collective expertise was required. Beneath it were twenty new committees set up by Modi, with the most important being the Election Information Campaign Committee, or EICC, chaired by the party treasurer Piyush Goyal. The EICC would often meet at Goyal's home, not far from the party headquarters in Delhi. 'I had to build a temporary extension to the house,' he told me, as he showed me around. 'We had to fit in another twelve to fifteen workers.' It was part of Goyal's job description to keep a close eye on everything the party was doing. 'I knew more of what was going on than most people because I held the cheque book.'

Some of the key decisions about the public face of the campaign, its advertising, slogans and posters, were taken around the table in his garden. Goyal resembles Modi in his desire to keep in touch with as many people as he can and has three telephones close by him at any one time. 'I don't like to leave things hanging,' he told me. And were decisions sometimes held back until Modi had given his approval? 'No. He trusts people to get on with the tasks they have been given.'

One of the first things Goyal did was to commission a public opinion survey by a team of professionals from the United States. It analysed the views of some 127,000 respondents, making it one of the largest surveys ever conducted across India. Goyal believes it paid off the investment a hundred times over, although its top-line conclusions were hardly a revelation. 'The nation was very angry about high prices and corruption.' More valuable intelligence came from the regional breakdowns, which showed that certain issues, like unemployment or women's security, played more or less strongly in different parts of the country, helping the party to target its messaging to better effect. Modi read the results, although he told me he was something of a sceptic about professional polling. 'I do not completely believe in these election pre-polls or surveys. I use my own methods, and most of these deal directly with the common man. For instance, if someone is manufacturing and selling soap I ask the person to call all his distributors and ask what are people feeling and saying. I do not ask them for any analysis but all I seek is the raw data from which I draw my own analysis. It is not that we reject professional surveys, but in a diverse country like India what we depend on is my own and the party's analysis.'

Aside from the special election committee structure, the BJP is organised on a cellular basis with forty-five national cells reporting to party HQ. Not all played an active part in the election. Although in the context of Hindu politics, the Cow Protection Cell carries a greater political and cultural significance than its name might at first suggest, it was rarely called upon. Similarly, the Weavers' Cell and the Naturopathy Cell were largely left in peace. But others were working overtime, in particular those responsible for IT, communications and the media. And here, at least, there was a little bit of command and control. Under Prakash Javadekar, the BJP's official spokesman, the media team tried to ensure the party was speaking with one voice. 'I used to coordinate our state spokesmen, our panellists, whoever would appear on TV or radio. We did it every day so the message and the stand we are taking will be one throughout the country. So everybody says the same thing and doesn't deviate from the stand of the party.'

Opinions differ as to how effective the party's contribution was. One professional consultant, who reported directly to Modi's team in Gujarat and not to the party HQ in Delhi, remembered a revealing conversation with Modi himself. Speaking off the record he said, 'I told him the party should do this, the party should work on that, but he said that in life you should always try to create new structures. If you try to repair old structures they will always remain creaky. So my brief was not to work for the party. It was a sort of presidential campaign'. And rightly so, according to Arun Shourie who, despite being a former BJP minister, is dismissive of the party's contribution. 'There was no party,' he said. 'It was Modi who energised the workers. It was just him and the workers with no intermediate layers. So Modi did a wise thing of bypassing the party and running an almost independent campaign.'

That independent campaign, unconstrained by the disciplines imposed either by the RSS or the party, had been building momentum for more than three years. Insofar as it had leaders at all, they were among the young men he had started to gather around him from 2011 onwards. Their brief was to use all the opportunities available on social media and the internet to create a buzz around the idea of a Modi candidacy, and to so dominate the discussion that nobody else could get much of a look-in. 'He was very clear about what he wanted,' said one of those who discussed the opportunities in detail with him. 'He was very clear that in the online world, it's all about branded content. When I do a Google search, both good and bad comes up about the guy. But it always depends on the frequency of the usage of the news, what comes at the top. He was pretty sorted that if there were multiple platforms talking about things he believed in, then when people searched for Modi, those things would pop up.' And the more independent the sources of that information were, the more credibility they were likely to have.

One of the most effective outfits to set about delivering this goal was Citizens for Accountable Governance, which went public in June 2013. At first it was ostensibly a non-party political pressure group dreamed up, according to its website, 'when a group of [a] few individuals consisting of a fresh Graduate, a Lawyer, an Entrepreneur, a Software Engineer and two Investment bankers began to discuss the nation's current state at a restaurant's coffee table.' They were 'a group of young and enthusiastic individuals with hope in their hearts and a dream in their eyes'. That was part of the story, certainly, but not the whole story. The fuller picture started to emerge in October, when the *Times of India* ran a profile of Prashant Kishor under the headline, 'Meet the most trusted strategist in the Narendra Modi organisation.' The article described Kishor as 'a 35-year-old public health specialist, statistics whiz and a former UN mission chief in Africa [who] has been working with Mr Modi since December 2011.' It revealed that he worked without pay at the chief minister's official residence in Gandhinagar and reported directly to him. CAG, it said, was his brainchild and had emerged 'as India's first effective political action committee (PAC), an instrument that has transformed the US campaign landscape but is yet to take root in India.'

According to one of those around the coffee table, CAG wasn't actually Kishor's idea, but when they approached him he quickly saw the value of it and took it under his wing. His proximity to Modi immediately gave the organisation the authority it needed to become the most influential newcomer within the ecosystem. Modi's support for the CAG was evident from the fact that he agreed to spend more than eight hours at two events organised by the group, a 'Young Indian Leaders' Conclave' and another for college students. Kishor acknowledged that the façade of independence didn't last long. 'We would like to believe we are an independent body,' he told me, 'but ultimately we were called Modi's back-room boys. Because I was managing it, it became obvious that it was Modi's team.' CAG also became known as the special projects team, available to take on those things that the party couldn't do. And in the process to recruit the kind of people for whom conventional party politics held little appeal. 'On-the-ground campaigning was left to the party,' said Kishor, 'but everything around him was supposed to be built by us. Our focus was building the Modi phenomenon.'

Around the same time, two of the so-called professional 'poster boys' of India's dotcom boom were busy putting their skills and experience at Modi's disposal from the country's IT capital, Bangalore. Having spent some time studying and working in the United States, B.G. Mahesh returned to India and, in 2006, set up Greynium Information Technologies. He was drawn into working with Modi by a fellow entrepreneur, Rajesh Jain. Between them they would provide much of the technical brainpower behind the online campaign. Jain was the more overtly political of the two and was the founder of Niti Digital. Niti, which stood for New Initiatives for Transforming India, declared its vision to be 'changing minds to change people's votes to bringing political change to bringing about the right policies for India's development.' What it lacked in grammatical style it made up for in the resources available and the creative imagination of its founders. It would eventually have almost a dozen different websites working simultaneously to advance Modi's development agenda and recruit volunteers to go out and change all those minds and votes. Niti Central, launched in August 2012, was its news and information portal, dedicated to providing a constant stream of stories and discussion to counter what it believed to be the anti-Modi bias of the traditional media. It was overtly political and quickly became a one-stop source for people who wanted news and views that were 'bold and right'.

The following summer, Niti Central hosted a new platform, India 272+, as a practical tool for translating support for Modi's ideas into votes at the ballot box. Brainstorming for the idea began soon after Modi's hat-trick win in Gujarat at the end of 2012, but they could go public only when it was clear they had their chosen candidate in place. Two hundred and seventy-two were the number of seats the BJP and its allies would have to win to have a majority in the lower house of parliament, the Lok Sabha. The + at the end was Modi's own suggestion. He didn't just want to reach the winning line, he wanted to pass it comfortably. As long ago as May 2011, Rajesh Jain had written a paper for the party in which he argued that the BJP had to raise its sights and 'change from trying to win 175 seats to winning 250–275'. The party, he wrote, 'needs to stop worrying about trying to get new allies because none will come, and even if they do, there is no guarantee they will stay after the elections.' The only strategy that could succeed was to 'switch focus from maximising allies to maximising seats.' It was a liberating and, back then, a radical suggestion. By 2013, its time had come. Shashi Shekhar, Niti Digital's CEO, said anything less would mean going 'back to the Nineties with a fragmented Lok Sabha, allies that you had to depend on and all kinds of coalition pressures making it much more difficult to bring change.' At the time of the public launch, 272 seats 'looked like a wildly impossible goal, so the idea was that it would motivate people.'

With Modi's blessing and the support of Piyush Goyal and other senior leaders, Mission 272+ became a party objective also. Niti Digital was plugged into the party network, with Rajesh Jain sitting on Goyal's EICC by dint of being convenor of the 'Friends of BJP' cell, but it wasn't under the party's authority. That, said Shekhar, meant 'it had the flexibility to respond with a lot of speed and nimbleness, without being bogged down by ten people approving a simple tweet. You could do things here that the party might have to think a hundred times about doing or not doing.' The object of Mission 272+ was not unlike that of the RSS, but by other means and on a far smaller scale. Sign up volunteers and ask them to pass the message on to their friends and family. Because this was the internet, it could be turned into an online game. Through the NaMoNumber.com dashboard, volunteers could compete with each other for the number of sign-ups. Every valid name needed a voter ID and a mobile number to go with it, and so the database of people who could be contacted by text grew at the same time. In the great scheme of things, Mission 272+ reached only a million or so volunteers, but in terms of changing perceptions about Modi and his chances of outright victory it contributed more than the raw numbers might suggest.

As part of the extensive online campaign (see Chapter Ten), Niti Digital hosted a series of dialogues to provide a platform for people with very specific concerns or objectives. As an example of what they achieved, Dr Pranav Desai and his wife, who were both disabled, ran a campaigning forum called 'Empowering the Specially Abled'. The group pointed up the flaws in proposed legislation put forward by Rahul Gandhi and helped turn what Congress believed was one of its winning cards into an issue the BJP could successfully use to its advantage. Some groups were run from outside India by so-called

NRIs, Non-Resident Indians. By feeling engaged in the campaign, even from as far away as America's west coast, the NRIs were able to contribute ideas, money – and in some cases actual votes, if they felt sufficiently motivated, as some did, to take leave from their jobs and travel home to join the queues at the polling booths.

Elsewhere in the ecosystem, there were dozens of other volunteer groups that had sprung up in support of Modi's candidacy. Among the largest was the NaMo Brigade, made up mainly of IT professionals, college students and young, often self-employed, entrepreneurs. The brigade was launched in the south of the country but soon spread nationwide. It was entirely self-funded, and organised events from bicycle rallies to voter awareness campaigns. Other volunteers set up their own websites linking Modi with values or issues that could work to his advantage electorally. Many closely mirrored his pre-campaign strategy, of first creating a vacuum and then presenting Modi as the leader to fill it. The Mera Bharosa ('My Trust') website helpfully reminded people that 'Democracy in Greek means rule of the people,' while going on to assert that under Manmohan Singh, 'today's democratically elected government in India and its governing style has never been so distant from what people want or represent.'

As soon as Modi was named as the BJP candidate, the site was reborn as Modi Bharosa ('Trust Modi'), claiming 'There's only one person who can bring about change and alter the fate of our country. Narendra Modi.' No party leader in India had ever had such an array of organisations and structures in place ready to support their bid for power. Now the moment had arrived to put them all to the test.

CHAPTER SEVEN
I, MODI

When party president Rajnath Singh called a news conference on Friday 13 September 2013 and announced that the BJP parliamentary board had unanimously chosen Narendra Modi to be its prime ministerial candidate, the hopes and expectations of Modi's many supporters had finally been realised. All the preparatory work, the elegantly designed websites and steadily growing databases had not been in vain. The fiction that they could have been deployed in support of any other candidate was quietly forgotten. Like the supposedly reluctant Roman emperor Claudius, who went on to be worshipped as a god, Modi had been forced to bide his time, but he could now take his place in the spotlight.

The idea that Friday the 13th is an unlucky date is a peculiarly western superstition, but the fortunes of Modi's rivals in both his own ranks and, more importantly, the Congress Party took a nosedive. A little bit of Indian superstition may have helped force the timing. Some in the BJP and the RSS were said to have wanted to avoid the two-week run-up to the Hindu festival of Maha Navratri in early October, supposedly an inauspicious time to begin anything of importance. Modi likes to say that his destiny lies in the hands of the gods, but now the destiny of the party had been placed into his. Any hope his opponents might have clung to that the BJP would hesitate and adopt a safer pair of hands was dashed.

Modi had never for a moment contemplated a 'safety first' campaign, one that would have relied on disillusionment with the Congress-led government to hand him power by default. Now he had the opportunity to set in motion the campaign he'd always wanted, one designed not just to win, but to win big, by dominating the agenda and sweeping the country with the political equivalent of shock and awe. At the news conference he promised '*nayi soch, nai ummeed*' (new thinking, new hope), the first of many catchy slogans he would unveil in the months to come. In his own mind, Modi told me, he had divided the campaign into three phases. The first, 'the preparatory period', was now over. The second, from September to early December, would focus on the upcoming legislative assembly elections in four key states, including Delhi, while planning the detail of the national campaign to come soon after, and all the while continuing to do the job to which he'd already been elected. 'I was still the chief minister of Gujarat and was running the campaign from there. Saturdays and Sundays would be for attending to my chief minister's job, while the other five days of the week were for inviting various people from the different states and discussing and understanding the political scenarios.' At the same time he sent some of his advisers on an undercover mission around the country. 'I sent five or six of my trusted people to the different states so I could get a first-hand idea of the situation on the ground. They did not declare that they represented me, so as to avoid any biases while they collected the information. These intelligence inputs were crucial to the design of my messages to the people. The way I thought about it was that my campaign had to be national but my appeal had to be local to the people.'

India got a taste of what was to come with Modi's first big speech two days later in Rewari, south-west of Delhi in the state of Haryana. At a rally for ex-servicemen, he spoke of his personal connections with the area, his pride in the contribution made by the military since India's Independence, and asserted that the country would only be secure once there was an 'efficient, patriotic government dedicated to the safety of every Indian citizen in Delhi.' It was a blend of local and national appeal that would become the hallmark of all his big speeches.

Modi used the opportunity to establish himself as the Delhi outsider from humble beginnings, a theme he would return to frequently in future. He told them that, as a child, 'I used to serve tea and snacks to the soldiers', and he even dreamt of becoming one. The first time he ever saw a post office was when he went to send off for the army prospectus. It cost two rupees but he 'belonged to a poor family and never got to see even two rupees at once'. His school friends contributed to the cost and a teacher helped him fill in the form when it arrived. But when he told his father he needed money to go and take the entrance exam for army school, 'my father said, son, this we cannot afford. You complete your studies at the village itself. That dream of mine was shattered.' He didn't need to contrast his childhood with the privileged upbringing of Rahul Gandhi and his family, his message was clear enough.

The speech was unusual in one respect: it touched directly on the question of religion, something he would try to avoid for most of the campaign. Again without mentioning Congress by name, he spoke of 'those who are trying to break society in bits and pieces under the umbrella of secularism for the sake of vote bank politics.' Once again his meaning wasn't lost. The BJP had long accused Congress of pandering to religious minorities in order to 'bank' their votes. By contrast, Modi based his appeal not on what he would do for any particular religious group, caste or section of society, but on what he would do for India as a whole. What better example of that, he asked, than the armed forces where Hindus and Muslims had historically fought side by side and 'the way they have respect for all creeds, the way all of them are working together just to serve the mother nation.'

The Rewari speech was significant, too, for the way in which it was disseminated well beyond the thousands in the crowd. It was tweeted live and his followers on social media were advised that they could watch the speech again on Modi's own YouTube channel. The text was available in full in Hindi and English on his website, www.narendramodi.in, and the attacks on Congress were given prominence on the Niti Central news pages, where a live audio feed was made available to internet users. Even before he spoke, the BJP announced another innovation. People could listen to the speech as it happened by calling a special number, 022-45014501. The mobile numbers of everybody who did call in were duly stored and automatically subscribed to Modi's SMS and tweets. It was part of a conscious effort to use social media to force the newspapers, TV and radio to take notice of every speech and to cover them in a way that reflected the priorities of the campaign. In the view of Shashi Shekhar of Niti Digital, this was the single biggest contribution that social media platforms like his were able to make. 'This was the first campaign where every speech was a media event. Every speech he made was being streamed live and, thanks to Twitter, every word he uttered was being broadcast. This forced the media to get on the bandwagon.'

By contrast Rahul Gandhi's first rally following Modi's emergence as the BJP standard-bearer was widely written up as a disappointment. He chose to speak in Baran in the state of Rajasthan, something of a BJP stronghold, and so got some credit for taking his campaign onto enemy territory. The sweltering heat no doubt contributed to the evident wish of many in the crowd to get away as soon as he'd finished speaking, but Congress will have been more worried that the speech failed to resonate across the country in the same way that Modi's had done. Coming so soon after Modi's first outing, it was inevitable that direct comparisons would be drawn, and *India Today* was not alone in noting that 'barring one or two occasions, Rahul Gandhi failed to connect with the crowd the way Modi did in Haryana on Sunday.'

On one level Modi and Gandhi were still dancing around each other, with neither prepared to refer to his opponent by name. Although India's powerful Election Commission had strict rules that forbade personal attacks, they came into effect only when the election schedule had been announced, and this had not yet happened. For different reasons, neither side was likely to benefit from getting into a personal scrap at this stage. And in a crucial respect it was, and would remain, an unequal contest between the two men. Narendra Modi was now officially the BJP candidate for prime minister. Congress hadn't said who would head the government if they were to win – and they never did. The party could justifiably argue that it was simply reverting to tradition. The practice of declaring who would be PM if they won was only a recent innovation. But there were personal and political forces at play also. It was perceived to be a forlorn attempt to protect Gandhi from the fallout if the party lost, and many people within Congress as well as in the wider public were by now convinced that Gandhi had no real appetite for the job. Either way, it crippled the Congress campaign. Harish Khare, the former journalist who had worked as media adviser to

Manmohan Singh, described it as the 'lacuna at the heart of the Congress strategy . . . depriving the campaign – conceptually, intellectually and organisationally – of a focus. Yet the Opposition, especially Modi, has been allowed to target-practise on a sitting duck'. Modi would refer to Gandhi disparagingly as 'the prince', suggesting that the younger leader thought he had some right by birth to inherit the crown. The word Modi actually used was *'shehzada'*, which carried with it an even more scornful note as it often denotes a spoiled brat. Shehzada can also be a Muslim name and Khare believed Modi deliberately intended to place a subliminal connection in the voters' minds. He pointed out that 'the use of Muslim names has long been part of his demagogic repertoire, with a very subtle invitation to his audience to equate his political rivals with "them" (the Muslims)'. Congress protested that the use of the word was 'undignified'. What really troubled them, however, was that it was devastatingly effective.

Both the professional survey conducted by the BJP and the private soundings taken by Modi's undercover advisers who toured the country had revealed a demand for strong leadership. When the BJP offered Modi as the answer to that demand, Congress appeared to lack anybody with the confidence to stand up and challenge him. When Modi is asked to recall some of his personal highpoints of the election, they are almost all occasions when his popularity was evident from the size of the crowds or the intensity of their reaction. One that stood out was an occasion when Modi wasn't even present. The legendary batsman Sachin Tendulkar played his last test match for India against the West Indies at Mumbai's Wankhede Stadium on 14–16 November 2013. Modi doesn't have the time – or apparently the inclination – to watch much cricket, but it was the political significance of the event that he remembers. 'Rahul Gandhi went to see the match and as soon as he walked into the stadium the entire crowd started chanting "Modi, Modi". You would have expected people to be chanting "Rahul, Rahul", but it was the Modi chant that was happening. This was a surprise even to me, and goes to show how viral a campaign can be when people take it upon themselves that they want change and see hope in a new leader.'

There is no reason to suspect that the reaction of the crowd of cricket fans had been in any way stage-managed. And already Modi's own rallies were taking on an extraordinary momentum. Where once people had to be paid to attend political meetings, now they were willing to buy admission tickets to see him speak. The determination of so many people to go to great lengths to witness Modi in person was more than amply demonstrated at the end of October at Patna in the state of Bihar. Sanjay Singh, who planned to cover the event for the *First Post* news site, had received an early call from a friend to advise him to get up and start walking, as, 'There is no public transport and there is an emerging human sea on the roads.' As he pushed through the crowds, he listened to conversations around him and quickly came to the conclusion that this wasn't like most political rallies he'd covered where people were bussed in and given food, drink and even money as an incentive to attend. For the most part there seemed to be genuine enthusiasm for Modi, 'although some others had equally strong passion against him'.

When he got to the Maurya Hotel, close to the Gandhi Maidan park where Modi was due that afternoon, he was invited up to meet the BJP president, Rajnath Singh, in his suite. Looking out over the venue, with the banks of the River Ganges beyond, Singh predicted that it would be the biggest political rally the country had ever seen. But Patna was to be remembered for other reasons. At 9.30 a.m. a bomb exploded in a public toilet at the town's train station. Over the course of the morning, another six devices exploded at different locations, including inside the park itself. Six people were killed and another eighty-five injured.

When Modi landed at the nearby airport, he was told that while the crowds had not been deterred by the violence, the rally would have to be called off. He recounted for me what went through his mind. 'Despite the bombings, over a million people had assembled and I was touched that even amidst the danger of injuries and deaths so many people were willing to risk hearing me speak. I therefore said I would speak at the rally despite so many of my people advising me against it. I believed speaking at Patna was my moral duty and I spoke for a full sixty-five minutes. This is the least I could do to show leadership from the forefront for the people of a state rocked by such violence and yet risking their life to come and hear me. I was told later that there were more bombs found at the venue.' One of these was close to the podium where Modi had stood.

Before he took to the microphone, there were announcements over the speaker system referring only to 'tyre blasts and fire crackers' and appealing for calm. With the proceedings once again being transmitted live, the organisers wanted to avoid panic but were equally determined not to let the violence distract from what Modi had planned to say. He made no direct reference to the bombs although, 'I had to make the point that it was not about Hindus fighting against Muslims any more but was our joint fight against issues like poverty.' He prefaced his speech with comments in two local languages, Bhojpuri and Maithili, provoking cheers from the crowd, many of whom were young and had never attended a political rally before. He talked again about his poor upbringing and made the first specific reference in the campaign to his childhood days as a *chai wala*. 'Congress leaders don't know what poverty and hunger are. I used to sell tea on trains. I know how difficult it is to get onto trains and make a living.'

Sanjay Singh reported that, despite the bombs, 'the rally continued as if nothing had happened.' After the crowds had dispersed, Singh was back in the hotel. 'At 5.15 as I file this story, another blast has gone off in Gandhi Maidan. The noise was loud. From where I sit, on the fifth floor of the Maurya Hotel convention room, I can see the fire and smoke.' Singh concluded that the size of the rally and the response of the crowd 'would surely unnerve Modi's political rivals,' while noting that 'The rally was, if nothing else, a security failure.'

After he left the ground, Modi tweeted his reaction to what had happened, saying, 'Blasts in Patna are deeply saddening and unfortunate. Condolences with families of deceased and prayers with injured. I appeal for peace and calm.' One of his local party officials tweeted that they had raised concerns about security in writing with the state government, 'Yet necessary arrangements were not made. This is criminal negligence.' The chief minister, Nitish Kumar, denied that there had been any security lapses and said there had been no intelligence warnings of a risk to the event. There was a political undercurrent to the row as it was Kumar's party, the JDU, which had abandoned its long-standing alliance with the BJP when Modi was selected, claiming he was a divisive leader who didn't have the confidence of Muslims (see Chapter Five). Journalists reported seeing very few Muslims in the crowd, despite what they had been told were efforts by the BJP to encourage them to attend. Ten people were charged in connection with the bombings, all of them Muslims, alleged by the National Investigation Agency to have 'conspired to target and attack Narendra Modi, the BJP's PM candidate, who they thought would be inimical to their interests if he was to become PM of the country.' At the time of writing, the case had not yet come to trial.

The Patna rally had been overladen with danger. The decision to go ahead, despite the possibility that there were further bombs in the park, was taken by politicians who judged that the risk of causing panic by calling it off was even greater. In the event political violence, if that is what it was, was not allowed to disrupt the election and nothing remotely comparable was to happen again on the campaign trail. When I discussed it afterwards with Modi, I was interested too in how he had responded as a man rather than as a politician. He told me that his own personal safety had never been a concern. 'I really never thought about this and nor do I worry about my safety. I believe your life is pre-decided and so why worry?' It occurred to me that if he had been a family man, with a wife and children, he might have thought about them before putting himself in danger. For the first and only time in our discussions he seemed briefly lost for words. 'Perhaps, but I have never had them so how can I know?' he replied after a long pause, before adding, 'But I have a mother. I have brothers.'

Modi is never comfortable talking about deeply personal matters, least of all affairs of the heart. And the Indian media is far more reluctant than, say, their British counterparts, to ask questions about a leader's private feelings. That Modi is unmarried is rarely considered worthy of note. The position of women in Indian society, on the other hand, is a live political issue and one that Modi refers to frequently. The subject came up again in the context of an intriguing saga that appeared on the internet on the same day the test match crowd was yelling Modi's name. Two investigative news websites, www.cobrapost.com and www.gulail.com, broke a story that was instantly dubbed 'Snoopgate'. At its heart were 267 audio recordings that had been handed over to the Central Bureau of Investigation (CBI). The websites claimed that the recordings contained telephone conversations in August 2009 in which Modi's most trusted colleague, Amit Shah, then Gujarat's home minister, could be heard ordering the surveillance of a young woman architect whom the journalists christened 'Madhuri' to protect her identity. On the tapes of the alleged conversations, which were posted online, Shah could be heard asking for the surveillance to be carried out at the behest of someone referred to only as 'Saheb' (sir), which was claimed to be a reference to his boss, Narendra Modi.

According to www.gulail.com, 'The tapes indicate that for at least over a month the Gujarat police apparatus used its sweeping powers to rigorously monitor every private moment, every personal conversation and every daily movement of Madhuri . . . Strict orders were given to closely observe and profile those who met her. Shah was particularly interested in knowing the men she was meeting and whether she was alone or with some man when she checked into a hotel in Ahmedabad. Her phones and those of her family and friends were tapped. Every bit of information was conveyed to Shah in real time, who in turn claimed to be relaying it to his Saheb.'

At first the BJP seemed unsure how to react, but the following day party president, Rajnath Singh, said the allegations were without foundation. 'We had already said much earlier that we apprehend that the dirty tricks wing of the Congress will make such baseless allegations against Modi as the elections draw near.' Singh went on to reveal that 'the girl's father has also given a statement that he had asked Modi, with whom he had family relations, for security for his daughter. The head of the government is responsible for ensuring the safety and security of the people. Modi was only performing his *dharma* [duty].' The BJP had got its act together and hoped to close down the story by getting the father to say he had been the one to initiate the trailing of his daughter, but Singh's statement also served to confirm that the surveillance had indeed taken place and that the 'Saheb' was Modi.

Snoopgate was one subject on which Modi refused to answer any of my questions. Whatever had really gone on, the fact is that in terms of its impact on the campaign, Snoopgate was the dog that didn't bark, or if it did then not very loudly. The central issue was one of privacy and that was effectively answered once the woman's family stated that the surveillance had been undertaken at their request. Congress did their best to exploit the story by fielding an array of senior female MPs who insisted there were still many unanswered questions in the affair, but with little success.

They tried again in March 2014 when Congress spokeswoman Shobha Oza targeted female voters, saying, 'I would like to ask the women, the daughters, the wives and the mothers of this country whether they would like to have in their households a person like Modi, who is known for his anti-women attitude. Modi, who is yet to answer for Snoopgate.' Then, just days before the end of the campaign, the woman at the centre of the allegations filed a petition to the Supreme Court saying she and her father were 'thankful to the Gujarat government' for accepting 'a personal request' to ensure her safety. Any further investigation, she said, would invade her privacy. Snoopgate, which several of Modi's advisers had briefly feared could do him significant damage, had done nothing of the kind.

CHAPTER EIGHT
IRON MAN 2

'With Modi,' according to one of his aides, 'everything has to be the biggest, the boldest or the best.' Another said simply, 'He's about big. That's how he made his cult image.' The media love superlatives and breaking records is always a good way to get yourself noticed, a point never lost on the young whizz-kids of Team Modi, who were encouraged by him always to think outside the box. In most cases he likes those superlatives to be all about himself, but occasionally he is willing to take second billing alongside one of his heroes. At first sight, Sardar Vallabhbhai Patel is an unlikely hero for a BJP leader whose avowed ambition is to create a 'Congress-free India'. Patel was home minister and deputy prime minister in the first Congress government of Jawaharlal Nehru, Rahul Gandhi's great-grandfather, and it was Patel who banned the RSS after the assassination of Mahatma Gandhi. But Modi didn't admire him for the party he belonged to or the company he kept. Patel was known as India's 'Iron Man', and he was a Gujarati. He is credited with the extraordinary feat of persuading the princes, maharajas and other hereditary leaders of over five hundred different territories to throw in their lot with the newly independent India. It wasn't an entirely peaceful process, but it was a success, and India's territorial integrity today is largely down to the Herculean efforts of Sardar Patel. On a personal level, Patel was an orthodox

Hindu and proud of it. This, among other things, led to some lively confrontations with Nehru, who had a vision of a secular nation in which religion would not be allowed to define identity. Thus, by honouring a Hindu, nationalist Gujarati whose mantra was unity, Modi was scarcely going off-message.

On the last day of October, Modi and L. K. Advani came together on the river island of Sadhu Bet near Vadodara in Gujarat to lay the foundation stone to a statue of Patel on the 138th anniversary of his birth. Inevitably this would be no ordinary monument, but the largest statue in the world at 182 metres, or 597 feet. Designed by the American digital artist Joe Menna, when completed it will contain the world's fastest elevators to take visitors to the top. When he first unveiled the idea back in 2010, Modi boasted that it would be almost twice as high as the Statue of Liberty and five times taller than Christ the Redeemer in Rio de Janeiro. 'It will be a unique memorial which will also have a museum depicting the life of Sardar Patel, research centre for subjects like good governance and agriculture technology, which were close to Sardar's heart.' By the time the foundation stone was being laid, a memorial garden and an underground aquarium had been added to the plans. Prime Minister Manmohan Singh tried to sprinkle just a few drops of rain on Modi's parade by saying he was proud Patel had been a Congress man, but Modi slapped him down, saying the statue was for everyone and 'we should not divide our legacy.'

The timing of the inauguration was, of course, highly political, and unity across the political divide had nothing to do with it. Modi wanted the whole country talking about him, so he ordered a national appeal for iron to go towards the project. Every village would be asked to contribute old farming implements, tools or other waste metal for shipment to Gujarat. A coordination committee was set up by Rajnath Singh to oversee the collection of all this iron – although whether all, or indeed much, of it would actually become part of the statue was questionable. For such a huge edifice, only the strongest and most durable materials would be usable, but the rest could be melted down and used in related construction work. And, in any case, according to the committee chairman, Om Prakash Dhankar, the nationwide collection wasn't just about any old iron. District-level committees would be established in every part of the country charged with raising awareness of the project. This would be done 'through pamphlets in regional languages. They will also conduct essay and painting competitions around the theme. There will be folk song programmes to involve the youth.' The real purpose of it all, conceded Dhankar, 'is not so much to collect iron, but create that emotional unity among the villages for a national cause.' A cause associated in everybody's minds with none other than Narendra Modi.

People were invited to sign a petition calling for good governance and to contribute ideas for how this could be achieved. It was intended to be, naturally, the largest petition ever signed in the world. To be sure that the project achieved the maximum possible impact, the back-room boys of the Citizens for Accountable Governance were called in to assist. The CAG was officially announced as a National Movement Partner for the project, and quickly set about recruiting ten thousand volunteers to push it forward. They organised seminars and public discussions about how best to use Patel's memory to promote unity, but their boldest idea was a 'Run for Unity', which duly took place on 15 December, the 63rd anniversary of Patel's death. At nearly eleven hundred different locations, runners came together to cover distances of five, fifteen or twenty-one kilometres simultaneously. It was, according to the organisers, far and away 'the largest mass run of its kind in the world.' As he prepared to drop the flag to set off the run, Modi said, 'Sardar Patel devoted his life to unify the nation. He integrated the common people in the freedom struggle and made efforts to rid the nation of the colonial mind-set. He undid the mind-set of divisiveness and united the nation.' Heaven forbid that anybody should wonder who might do the same in 2014. 'Please do not view it from the prism of politics,' pleaded candidate Modi.

There was no other prism through which to view the other big news that same week, the fall-out from the state assembly election results. The BJP had good reason to be pleased. In four out of five of the elections they had emerged as the largest party and in three, Rajasthan, Madhya Pradesh and Chhattisgarh, they had comfortable majorities. Only in Mizoram, India's second least populous state in the far north-east, where the BJP was traditionally weak, did Congress secure a substantial victory. The main attention, however, was on the Delhi Legislative Assembly. Congress, which had been defending forty-three seats, were reduced to a miserable eight; their chief minister, Sheila Dikshit, duly resigned, telling reporters, 'We are idiots, right?' The BJP were the largest party by a whisker, in terms of seats won, with thirty-one, but the big news was that the Aam Aadmi Party (AAP), of the anti-corruption campaigner Arvind Kejriwal, had won twenty-eight seats in the first election they had ever contested. Kejriwal had beaten Mrs Dikshit in her own constituency in New Delhi.

As the largest party, the BJP were invited to form a government, but declined on the grounds that they could not command a majority. It proved to be a very shrewd move. Delhi's lieutenant governor, Najeeb Jung, then turned to

Arvind Kejriwal. Although Kejriwal had said he would not work with either of the other parties, the AAP couldn't govern if the BJP and Congress united against them. So he wrote to both parties asking them to clarify their stand on a variety of issues. The BJP response was to accuse Kejriwal of trying to find excuses to run away from the responsibilities of government, but the Congress party was more positive. Kejriwal carried out a widespread consultation exercise across the city before agreeing to form an administration with outside support from Congress. On 28 December he was duly sworn in as chief minister. He called it a 'tryst with destiny' and quickly announced a hotline for people to report accusations of bribery or corruption, instructing his ministers 'to never be conceited or arrogant.'

As 2013 drew to a close, Kejriwal was both the flavour of the month and the media's darling, two attributes that seasoned politicians know can have a very short shelf-life. The *Times of India* commented with commendable prescience, 'For Kejriwal, the real challenge – of governance – begins now. He has changed the rules of the game, playing the role of an outsider with consummate political savvy. Whether his "movement" can go national will depend on how wisely he runs Delhi.' Within a very short space of time the media were talking not about the wisdom of Kejriwal's governance but of the 'anarchy' that had infected the city's administration. He seemed to want to be in power and opposition at the same time. Never before, for example, had the country seen a chief minister and his cabinet colleagues taking to the streets to demand the suspension of police officers who had allegedly failed in their duties.

Then, just forty-nine days after he had been sworn into office, Arvind Kejriwal resigned. The *Times of India's* question mark over his leadership qualities had proved to be well positioned and the paper noted that the 'AAP's dream run from being a rank outsider to forming the Delhi government in a little over a year came to an end on a rainy, cold Friday evening with Kejriwal announcing that he would rather sacrifice the CM's chair a thousand times than compromise on fighting graft.' The party had been defeated in a vote on its anti-corruption bill by the combined votes of Congress and the BJP. It looked to outside observers very much as if he had engineered his own defeat in order to launch his general election campaign with a strong 'plague on both your houses' message. But the media darling was now damaged goods. 'Wracked by several controversies, the short-lived AAP government never settled down', wrote the *Times of India*, 'and while populist decisions to slash power tariffs and deliver free water are seen to have consolidated its support, AAP's commitment to governance has also been questioned.' The following month, Kejriwal announced his intention to take on Narendra Modi head-to-head in the constituency of Varanasi and promised a 'political earthquake'.

Modi was unmoved. He decided never to mention Arvind Kejriwal by name between then and polling day. He certainly wasn't willing to cede to the AAP leader the mantle of the anti-corruption candidate, but he also showed himself to be much the superior political tactician. 'My silence is my strength,' he told me. 'Narendra Modi knows the strength of silence. You should know that in the grand scheme of things, Kejriwal was nothing but a small single city leader. He was getting far more coverage than he deserved as compared to other more established opposition party leaders. So why spend time even ignoring someone? It was therefore not even worth my time to ignore Kejriwal. Kejriwal was elevated by a select group of vested media interests fuelled by the Congress to target Narendra Modi and try and save the Congress. Keep in mind he was not even a member of parliament; had lasted only forty-nine days as CM, and had won less than 1% of the national vote.'

Kejriwal was losing not only friends in the media, but also influential allies. The yoga guru Baba Ramdev, who had shared platforms with the AAP leader, now came out for Modi instead. He accused his former associate of losing control and said, 'I feel that people had a lot of expectations that he will do something good and reform politics, but people are now calling the AAP the Arajak Aadmi Party.' No longer the 'Common Man's Party', then, but the 'Anarchist Man's Party'. Modi, on the other hand, 'agrees with us on the issues of black money, corruption and change in the prevailing system. Hence, we are supporting him.' Ramdev proved a very on-message convert. He accused Rahul Gandhi of being 'confused from head to toe', and asked, 'How can you expect vision from a man who is confusion personified?'

In March, Modi shared a platform in Delhi with Ramdev at a yoga festival that the organisers said was being broadcast live to 600 locations across the country. The televangelist guru might not have had a following to match that of the RSS, but his Bharat Swabhiman Trust claimed to have followers in 638,765 villages. The Election Commission would later order an investigation into whether money owned by this and other trusts controlled by Ramdev had been improperly used to fund political campaigning, but it was Ramdev's endorsement rather than his money that meant most to Modi. There is no way of knowing how many voters decided to follow his advice and back Modi on polling day, but the BJP was fulsome in its praise for him once the results were in. The new party president, Amit Shah, said Ramdev 'contributed significantly to the formation of the Narendra Modi government at the centre.'

The other high-profile yogi, the leader of Art of Living, Sri Sri Ravi Shankar, had come to much the same conclusion. Although he had been part of the anti-corruption movement with Kejriwal, in January 2014 he declared that the AAP wasn't ready for power. 'It's like giving keys to a driver with a learner's licence to drive the vehicle in difficult terrain. Hence it is better to wait some more time to analyse its performance. Time is not ripe yet for AAP to form a government at the centre.' Shankar said he had 'no opinion' of Rahul Gandhi, as he'd never met him, while Modi, who he'd met a couple of times, 'appears to be a good man'. Helpfully he also said that coalition governments had proved a failure and 'a single party with a majority' was needed this time. And at this time, of course, there was only one party with any chance of achieving that. A couple of months later he would make his endorsement of the BJP clearer still. Referring to the Hindu goddess of wealth, love and prosperity, he said, 'Lakshmi always rides on the lotus.' By now few people in India could fail to be aware that the lotus flower was the symbol of the BJP.

While Shankar's praise for the 'good man' Modi was welcome, far more valuable was his announcement of a new mission, which he called 'Vote for Better India'. Its aim was to enlist 120 million young people and ensure that they registered to vote. Art of Living's volunteers were to spread out across three hundred or more constituencies, giving talks, holding meetings and distributing a 'happiness survey'. This was a clever form of indirect marketing, designed to lead people towards a vote for the BJP. With questions like number 7, 'Have you been seriously affected by a) Corruption, b)

Price Rises?' it steered respondents in the right direction while asking them to volunteer 'for a better India' and to pledge to vote 'for the right candidate for a strong and stable government'. Those conducting the survey were told to introduce themselves along the lines of, 'Hi! I am Janil. I am a student volunteering some time for the country and conducting a happiness survey to understand the happiness quotient of our country.' They were told that while they shouldn't tell people how to vote, they should 'kindle the feeling that a stable, experienced government is required in today's situation and that it is good practice to rotate power to prevent corruption and increase responsibility.' Question 7 could, according to the instructions, be introduced by saying, 'You are probably aware of the significant number of corruption issues that have arisen over the last few years and the significant increase in the price of basic goods . . . ' With the backing of Art of Living, the Modi ecosystem had just absorbed a powerful new ally.

Modi was well aware of the enormous 'added value' that support from outside the conventional political arena could bring to his campaign. 'A key feature of the election,' he told me, 'was indeed the many independent institutions that backed us all across the nation. There were a lot of people and groups who would not want to come into politics or elections, but all wanted to participate in a mass movement either individually or through various organisations and make a difference.' Along with Baba Ramdev and Art of Living, he singled out the veteran singer Lata Mangeshkar, who has lent her voice to over a thousand Hindi films in a career spanning seven decades, and who now said she 'prayed to God' that Modi would become prime minister. It wasn't just the rich and famous, he said, but 'such was the enthusiasm all across the nation that folk artists were composing local songs and many artists were painting their vision of India, all related to the elections and the Modi effect.'

One Congress party leader unwisely demanded that Lata Mangeshkar should be stripped of her 'Bharat Ratna', India's highest civilian honour, for having the temerity to support Modi. But it often seemed that people within Congress's own ranks were acting as recruiting sergeants for the BJP leader. At different times all three members of the parties' uncomfortable triumvirate of leaders found themselves helping to promote his interests when their intentions had been exactly the reverse. The outgoing prime minister, Manmohan Singh, made few memorable interventions in the campaign. He did, however, inadvertently provide the BJP with perhaps its most successful slogan. Known as the silent prime minister, he almost never held news conferences. But to mark the start of the new year in 2014, he called only the third in his decade in the job. He probably wished afterwards that he'd stuck to his preference for keeping his own counsel. He told the assembled journalists that he wouldn't serve a third term as PM, whatever the result of the elections, instantly consigning himself to 'lame duck' status in the their eyes. He said he believed history would be kinder to him than the contemporary media and he might well have been right, although that was of little use to his party in the middle of a battle that had to be fought in the here and now. There was a bit of fighting talk when he said it would be disastrous for the country to have Narendra Modi as prime minister and spoke of Rahul Gandhi's 'outstanding credentials'. But what he wanted most was to defend his government's efforts to safeguard the Indian economy, the issue closest to his heart.

Under his watch, India had seen several years with some of the highest growth figures in the nation's history. During his

Young Modi in the uniform of the National Cadet Corps.

During the 'Emergency' period Modi went in disguise to avoid arrest.

At his school in Vadnagar, Modi's schoolteacher, Prahlad Patel, remembers an 'average student'.

Modi made his name as a proficient organiser. With chief minister Prem Kumar Dhumal and prime minister Atal Bihari Vajpayee.

Fifty-nine people were killed in the Godhra train burning in 2002 which led to the Gujarat riots and over 1,000 deaths.

Modi improved Gujarat's image with projects like solar power to provide twenty-four-hour electricity.

Modi's Gujarat re-election campaign in 2012 was vital to his chances of becoming prime minister.

Welcoming visitors to 'Vibrant Gujarat 2013', including British High Commissioner, Sir James Bevan (bottom right).

After being elected prime minister Modi received a traditional blessing from his mother, Hiraba.

His first speech to the nation at Delhi's Red Fort on the 68th anniversary of Independence set out his plans to transform India.

The anti-corruption campaigners Baba Ramdev and Anna Hazare helped prepare the ground for Modi's election.

In September 2013 Modi was made BJP candidate for prime minister. With Sushma Swaraj, Rajnath Singh and Arun Jaitley.

Modi's mentor L.K. Advani at the festival of Holi. He resisted Modi's candidature.

Modi loves head-dresses, but he never wore a Muslim skull cap.

Bombs exploded in and around the site of Modi's rally in Patna killing six people.

The crowd was one of the largest of the campaign and most stayed despite the attacks.

Modi took to the stage and appealed for calm in defiance of the bombers.

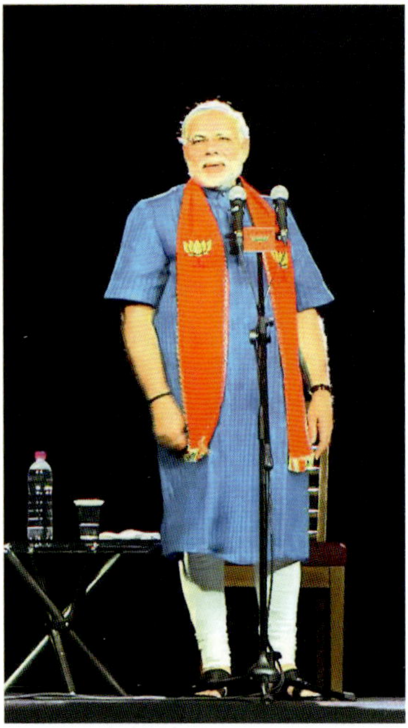

Modi's 3D holograms were transmitted to around fifteen million people.

Chats over tea highlighted Modi's childhood as a *chai wala*. They discussed issues such as women's safety.

Modi's selfie after he voted broke the election rules.

Modi logs on soon after waking up. 'I was seen as very tech savvy from the early days'.

Online campaigns backed Modi's zero tolerance agenda.

Narendra Modi was promoted on t-shirts like Superman.

Security for women was a big issue prompting his supporters to market a NaMo pepper spray.

Modi dolls went on sale based on Obama's.

Modi travelled 300,000 km. The media struggled to keep up.

Rahul Kanwal from *Headlines Today*. Modi was 'great copy'.

second term the economy was growing at around 9% a year until the impact of the global financial crisis hit. And even in his last two years, despite dropping below 5%, it continued to outstrip most western nations. Singh predicted that growth would soon revive once more and that 'yes, we are facing bad days now but the good days will be coming soon.'

That phrase alone gave Modi his cue. Six days later he appeared to strike a conciliatory note, saying, 'I agree with the prime minister. Good days are ahead for India.' But the sting was in the tail. The better days would arrive only when he took over. 'We should wait for four to six months, but good days are coming.' The BJP had its slogan to match Tony Blair's, 'Things can only get better' or Bill Clinton's, 'Don't stop thinking about tomorrow.' The refrain '*Acche Din Aane Waley Hain*', or 'Good days are coming', would be heard all across India over the next few months. It became the title of the BJP campaign song, written by the Bollywood lyricist Prasoon Joshi, and led to the unusual sight of Modi at least swaying to, if not exactly dancing to, the music in the online video.

Modi is nothing if not a serious-minded politician, although he frequently smiles in private conversation, most often when he's pleased with his own *bon mots*. He resorted to a touch of sarcastic, even bitter, humour only when seeking to undermine his younger opponent. When Rahul Gandhi said on a number of occasions that the Gujarat model of development was a 'toffee model', because of all the land he claimed had been given away to big business for the price of a toffee, and predicted that it was a 'balloon' that would burst come election day, Modi again saw his chance. Without naming him, as usual, he said, 'There is a player who doesn't move away from childishness. Such an important election about the country's future but for ten days the word that gripped him was "balloon". For ten days he kept repeating it. However, children don't stick to a toy for too long and now he has caught on to the word "toffee".' If the voters felt Gandhi was too inexperienced and unready for power, they now had an image of an immature schoolboy to go with it.

Modi was getting the better of the tit-for-tat exchanges, but he started to worry that they were in danger of over-shadowing his serious agenda. The one charge levelled against him by Gandhi that he felt could do some damage was that he was a showman, quick to trade barbs and deliver clever ripostes but slow to offer considered solutions to the nation's problems. His answer was a thoughtful speech on the 'Idea of India', delivered in the third week of January. Modi put a lot of work into the speech, helped by his more cerebral advisers. He criticised the long-standing approach of the Congress Party, with its many subsidies and handouts to the poor and disadvantaged, usually distributed through the states. It was, he said, a 'big brother attitude' in which Delhi knew best. Promising to change the nation's direction, he went on: 'There is no younger or big brother. The attitude should be that both the brothers are together taking the country ahead with equal efforts and strength.' He promised to extend what he called the 'slow but steady development' taking place in the west of the country, including Gujarat, to the centre and the east, asking, 'Why is there such a situation, such an imbalance?' And he identified seven key priority issues that he would address as prime minister: the family, agriculture, women, the environment, youth, democracy and knowledge. He set out some detailed proposals for all of them and declared that a vote for each was a vote for India.

The speech added weight and substance to Modi's offer to the electorate and some clear ideological dividing lines between the statist Congress approach and the BJP's faith in all Indians as individuals. It was the nearest he came to a classic left/right analysis that we are familiar with in the west. But it wasn't completely devoid of the trademark Modi one-liners. None of his speeches ever is. Referring to the absence of a Congress Party candidate for PM, he had some tongue in cheek praise for Sonia Gandhi. 'Which mother will sacrifice her son on the political path? At last a mother's heart decided to save her son!' And, as ever, he had a word to say about the latest brickbat to have been thrown his way. He told his audience that 'these days the tea vendors are being treated very well. Every tea vendor in the country is walking with pride.'

Time and again Modi has proved adept at quickly turning attacks on him to his advantage. He did so when the words were brutal and direct, as when Sonia Gandhi had called him a 'merchant of death' (see Chapter Three). And he did it again and again whenever his opponents tried to get under his skin. He seemed to thrive on the abuse that was directed his way. As he said himself, 'People keep throwing stones at me but I convert these stones into a ladder'. The stones didn't have to be large or to be thrown with great force. Modi had slipped in that line about the tea vendors because just two days earlier a hapless Congress leader had unwisely accused him of being something he gladly conceded was true, a former *chai wala*.

CHAPTER NINE
TEA BREAK

As the All India Congress Committee (AICC), the party's central decision-making body, met at Delhi's Talkatora Stadium in January 2014, they had precious little to smile about. They cheered and applauded every speaker, nonetheless, as if they were a movement on the brink of another five years in power. Rahul Gandhi, the party vice president, was the star turn; in a speech reminding the assembled crowds of what Manmohan Singh's government had achieved in the previous ten years, he cracked a joke designed once again to portray Narendra Modi as a showman. 'Opposition parties can say anything,' he said. 'Their marketing is very good. They have used everything, name, shine and song. They are the ones who will sell combs to the bald.' It wouldn't go down in history as one of the great political jokes, but it had a serious point. 'We live in a world,' he complained, 'where packaging and selling politics seems to replace the essence of real issues and real people.' Some follicly challenged men took offence, complaining their feelings had been hurt and that 'baldness is a natural process', but Modi, who still had a respectable head of hair for a man in his mid-sixties, seemed to take Gandhi's words as a compliment. 'I used to sell tea,' he told a TV audience later in the campaign. 'I never sold combs, but if the information that I can do it has reached them, it is a sort of achievement for me.' Yet the meeting would not be remembered for the fiction that Modi sold anything to bald people, but for the fact that he once sold tea on trains, something of which he was certainly not ashamed.

Modi had been making reference to his poor upbringing and his experience selling tea since his first speech as the prime ministerial candidate. It was paying dividends with potential voters who were themselves from lower castes and whose support the BJP had often struggled to get in previous elections. And there was no doubting the political value of setting a candidate who had worked hard for everything he had achieved against a man from a privileged background who was frequently reported to be jetting out of India to enjoy the pleasures of western nightspots and holiday destinations. In addition Modi had twelve years as a chief minister under his belt, while Gandhi had never held any position of executive authority, so when Congress leaders tried to argue that Modi didn't have what it takes to be prime minister while Gandhi did, it was always going to be a hard sell. In any case, whatever their social status, voters rarely respond well to attacks that appear patronising or just plain rude. Historically the Congress might have been the party of the poor, but its leaders generally were anything but. All the more reason for them to choose their words with care.

Mani Shankar Aiyar attended some of India's best schools before going to university first in Delhi and then Cambridge. He's a qualified chartered accountant with a taste for somewhat dapper-looking clothes and a reputation for dry, caustic wit. What he lacks, it seems, is an eye for the political bear trap. When he strode out from the AICC meeting on 17 January he jumped in with both feet. 'I promise you,' he said to the waiting TV crew from CNN-IBN, 'in this twenty-first century, Narendra Modi will never become the prime minister of this country. He won't. He won't. If he wants to come and sell tea here we can make some room for him.' The channel knew it had a story and some Congress Party allies could see it too. Omar Abdullah, the British-born chief minister of the state of Jammu and Kashmir, tweeted, 'Modi has a lot of negatives but his humble origins are a positive some of us can't claim. We aren't helping our campaign by mocking him.' Having jumped in, Mr Aiyar then forgot the one about being in a hole and not digging. Although his words had been broadcast nationwide, he tried to claim he'd been misquoted. And then he said it again. Back in front of the cameras, he said he hadn't insulted the BJP leader. 'It is Modi who keeps bringing to the fore his background of being a tea stall owner while making a pitch to the people of India for the elections. Therefore, I just said that Modi will never be the prime minister of India, but if he wants, we can set up a tea stall for him here.'

Once it was obvious that the remark had badly backfired, Congress tried to find proof that Modi had been exaggerating his own *chai wala* story for electoral benefit. Sonia Gandhi's political secretary, Ahmed Patel, accused him of misleading the voters. 'Tea seller associations have told us that he was not a tea vendor but he was a canteen contractor.' Once again the party simply highlighted an issue that by now was working heavily in Modi's favour.

If Manmohan Singh had given the BJP their slogan and the title of their campaign song, Mani Shankar Aiyar is often credited with giving Modi his cue to exploit his *chai wala* past to great advantage. The facts are slightly different. It was a less well-known politician, Naresh Agarwal, of the Samajwadi Party (SP) based in the state of Uttar Pradesh, who first tried to use Modi's history of tea selling against him the previous November. 'Someone rising from a tea shop can never have a national perspective,' he said. Agarwal later retracted the comment but it had already helped plant an idea in Modi's mind. Mani Shankar Aiyar merely gave Modi the chance to do something much more ambitious with it, and to do so with an even bigger surge of publicity.

Modi had decided it was time to create a storm over a teacup. To date the campaign had been marked by its mammoth rallies, but now he wanted to try something a little more intimate. Personal contact can be one of the most effective ways for politicians to win people over, but even in an average-sized country like the UK it is impossible for a candidate to meet enough voters one-to-one to make much of a difference to the overall result. The population of India is two thousand times greater than Britain's, so Modi wasn't going to get very far by winning votes one person at a time. The answer was to keep the conversation small but to make sure as many people as possible felt that they were part of it.

The concept became known as '*Chai pe Charcha*', which roughly translates as 'a discussion over a cup of tea'. And this being Modi, it could be no ordinary chat over a cuppa. The idea had been conceived initially not as a way of contacting voters directly but to help motivate some of the campaign's online volunteers. The Campaign for Accountable Governance had set up 300 separate Facebook pages in constituencies covering more than half the country, with names like 'With NaMo for Delhi'. The plan was that one or more people in each seat would keep the pages up to date with local news and discussions, but the results were a little patchy. In some places the volunteers were wildly enthusiastic and even seemed to think it was Modi himself who was replying to their messages, which of course he wasn't. Elsewhere there was very little activity and the pages were rarely being changed. In December

2013, Prashant Kishor of the CAG discussed the problem with Modi, who agreed to do a tweet or two himself to kick-start the initiative. Modi hates to see anything fail and Kishor recalls that 'By the time I moved from his office to the CAG office, I got a call from him saying why can't we organise something over a tea stall?' It wasn't exactly a flash of inspiration. 'NaMo Tea Parties' had already been tried out in the electorally critical state of Uttar Pradesh. BJP and RSS leaders had been meeting academics, students, lawyers and other professionals over tea to discuss Modi's campaign priorities, and the events had proved popular. Modi and Kishor were already planning to step them up a gear by the time the own goal by the Congress Party made them realise the idea could go national and go big.

The CAG team were asked to find a way of involving as many members of the public as possible. Why not broadcast conversations with BJP leaders, including Modi himself, to hundreds of locations simultaneously, giving people the chance to ask questions, whether they were there in person or not? It started off with a target of 300 sites but was quickly increased to 1,000, with tea being served at each and every one. They were to be linked by an array of technologies, including video conferencing, outside broadcast vans and satellite receivers. The chats would be streamed live on YouTube and mobile phone apps. There was a lot that could go wrong and the team were understandably nervous, especially if Modi was to be at the centre of this technological web.

'We took extra precautions and had contingency plans at each step to ensure that there are no slippages in the entire event,' according to one of the organisers. 'But in such a large setup, things don't always go as we want. We had identified three volunteers for each location – one primary and two secondary – to manage the event at the ground level. In case one doesn't turn up, the other two could be contacted. We prepared a detailed set of guidelines to select the locations. They should be able to host 200–300 people at the bare minimum, be in one of the busy locations of the city, have a tea stall with a tea seller who was happy to have the event there.' Nothing was left to chance. 'The volunteer would have to send us pictures of the location and also details of the tea seller who we would later call to verify the details. The volunteers would then be sent publicity including banners and posters to be used for mobilising people at the venue. Each location was mapped in order to have the TV screens, satellite machines and all the other instruments required to carry out the event.'

Delivery day was scheduled for 12 February, but it wasn't an easy birth. In one key location the young student volunteer refused to go out at the last minute, saying he had an exam the next day. He couldn't be persuaded and after a while stopped answering his phone. The persistent caller eventually found himself speaking to an angry father wanting to know why his son was being disturbed. When the situation was explained, the man agreed to take over the event himself. That was the least of the communication problems. The satellite links between the central location where Modi was due to appear and the waiting crowds were malfunctioning. An hour before the much-publicised launch, Kishor called Modi to tell him, 'Things are not coming together.' Modi told him to keep going, but just to be on the safe side tweeted to his followers, 'I am using new technology. I need your blessings.' He must have received them because things started to fall into place, and Kishor was thankful for Modi's 'keep calm and carry on' attitude when the event passed off successfully.

For the second *Chai pe Charcha* on the subject of 'Women's Empowerment', the team tried to learn from its mistakes while also making it yet more ambitious in scope. The number of locations was increased to 1,500, including thirty in other countries around the world. With the help of the 'Friends of BJP' group, Modi's supporters in Britain and in the United States (where 'tea party' has a whole different meaning) would be able to participate via satellite. If that sounded risky, the problems proved to be closer to home. The Election Commission had now declared the nine separate dates on which the voters in different states would be going to the polls. The election had to be staggered so that security and other personnel weren't too thinly stretched and could move from region to region with each phase of polling. The announcement meant that henceforward all campaign activity came under the Commission's very strict rules, codified in a 'Model Code of Conduct'. Permission had to be granted by every district office and from the police for any event, and this was not always straightforward when it came to the *Chai pe Charcha*. In a couple of locations, when the paperwork was deemed unsatisfactory, the organisers were taken into custody and the equipment was seized. A volunteer at one site recalled that 'Finally, after three full days sitting in the police station, the inspector said, "I can give you one of the screens, but leave the other one here, we will use it in the station." And it was not just the policemen who were looking for an opportunity to get free screens, even a few of the tea vendors and local party leaders had the belief that the screens were meant to be given to them once the events were over.' He added, with a gift for understatement, 'Elections are not that straightforward in India.' In Uttar Pradesh, the chief electoral officer threatened to impose a total ban on the grounds that a cup of tea could be a bribe and 'Any kind of allurement or enticement of voters during the poll process is not permissible as per law.' He had to be overruled from Delhi, where the commission declared that a cup of tea worth two rupees, or two British pence, could not be an enticement, although the cost of providing it would have to be declared as an election expense.

The third in the series had Modi sipping tea with farmers in the state of Maharashtra. Agricultural workers make up about half of all those employed in India, and he wanted to show he understood their problems, in particular the worrying incidence of suicides among farmers as a result of financial problems. This time it all went much more smoothly, but it was to be the last of its kind. The chats had generated massive free publicity but the turnout hadn't always been as great as the organisers had hoped. The return on all that investment in technology and the nervous energy required to make it work didn't justify carrying on. The tea had gone cold.

Modi decided to concentrate on his traditional rallies and on the same kind of 3D hologram events that had proved so successful two years earlier in Gujarat (see Chapter Four). He certainly wasn't turning his back on new technology. One BJP leader was quoted as saying, 'Modi is focusing on organising as many rallies through 3D appearances as possible. *Chai pe Charcha* was proving more time-consuming and was technically more complicated than 3D technology.' That was debatable, to say the very least. Closer to the truth was that the 3D rallies were better box office. Rajdeep Sardesai, who covered the election for the CNN-IBN network, reflected the view of many journalists when he wrote that he didn't find the content of the tea stall chats very newsworthy. 'The questions had been carefully vetted. Most of the time Modi would give lengthy answers, and no cross-questions were posed. As a journalistic exercise or an exercise in democratic questioning of a politician, it didn't really work.' Though he added that as a public relations exercise it was a classic poverty-to-power script and 'a cracking success'.

The hologram rallies that had proved such a game-changer in Gujarat had been revived at about the same time that Modi was sitting down for his first big discussion over tea. Here too the team had found themselves pushing at the limits of what was technically possible. They wanted to beam Modi to 100 different locations, almost double his best in 2012. Each show required five key people on the ground, one each to supervise building the stage, establish the satellite signal, operate the projector, look after the generator and handle the transportation. For the larger venues, the entire stage was built in the city of Pune and then driven by container lorry to the location.

The first rally was due to be broadcast on 6 April and the party had run extensive awareness campaigns, both door to door and using loudspeakers mounted on rickshaws. Huge banners and posters of 'NaMo in 3D' were put up around the locality, and as many as 50,000 pamphlets had been printed and distributed. When it was obvious that in too many places things were running dangerously behind schedule, the rally was postponed by a day to give everybody an extra twenty-four hours to prepare. Volunteers fanned out to warn people of the change and the posters and banners were hastily updated. By the morning of the 7th it became clear that only thirty-five of the venues were ready. It was a tense day for all concerned. One volunteer recalled that 'At five p.m. in the location where I was standing, they were still struggling with the projector and the sound systems. I got a call at five thirty p.m. from the central office in Delhi telling me that the rallies had been cancelled. Cancelled at all one hundred locations.' A press conference was hastily convened to announce that 'The poll rallies using 3D technology have been postponed due to a technical reason.' TV and radio carried the news but it was too late for the newspapers, leaving many of those planning to attend unsure of what was going on.

The launch date was changed again, this time to 11 April. Volunteers were under strict instructions to send smartphone pictures back to the war room to prove that everything was in place. There were still problems, down to something as simple as the bolts jamming on the containers. The watching villagers garlanded one volunteer with flowers when the door finally swung free. 'I just opened one of the stuck bolts and these people went crazy. I was amazed to see how eager they were to see Modi in 3D.' Although probably not as eager as Modi was for it all to go according to plan at last. For the effect to work, the hologram could be turned on only after it was completely dark. Other local dignitaries were invited to speak to keep the audience engaged, although never the local candidate, as his or her appearance would have meant the whole event having to be declared on the constituency election expenses, busting the legal spending limits in one go. When the projectors whirred into action, all people could see was a chair, a microphone and a flower pot, but the effect was still electric, with some locals apparently convinced they were real and had been beamed down by some Star Trek-style transporter. Then Modi appeared and sat down and the show could begin. 'We used this technology for the first time during the Gujarat assembly poll in 2012,' he said with evident relief. 'It caught the eyes of the entire world. We reached fifty-three places at one time and made it to the *Guinness Book of World Records*. I have broken my record today.' He went on to say he wanted to make India into a digital nation and said the campaign so far had been an education for him as well as 'for the people.' Occasionally he would reach for his water or turn as if to talk to somebody in the room with him. In rehearsals he had appeared too static and the team were worried the illusion wouldn't be believable if he didn't move about a bit. They even installed a fan so that his hair would move a little in the breeze.

From then on the jinx had been broken and the 3D rallies continued to the end of the campaign, usually late in the evening after he had been out flying around the country addressing huge crowds in person. He rarely seemed to tire, and the production team found him easy to work with. His taste for colourful shirts was a bonus as they stood out well in the holograms. 'He is a very colourful man with a great sense of style,' Senthil Kumar, one of the cinematographers who had returned to India for the elections, told rediff.com. 'I have not seen another politician dress so well. He would have a choice of four or five sets of clothes for each shoot, and would ask me, "Hey hippie, which one should I wear?" I would choose a colour that would suit the 3D hologram and he would wear that.'

Modi had asked the team to arrange for what's called a reverse feed from various parts of the country, so that he could see the throngs of people on screens in front of him while giving the speech. He would then start by addressing the crowds in specific locations so they got the impression he was talking to them directly. The rallies proved so popular that local campaign teams started to inundate the war room with requests to be included. The number and frequency of the rallies was increased, putting yet more strain on the logistics. In rural areas lorries would get stuck on muddy roads, loose electrical wires would prevent the tall trucks from passing and trees would obstruct the route. But there was an almost overwhelming demand from the public to be met – so much so that one afternoon an organiser rang the central controllers in fear. One of the trucks carrying power equipment was still a hundred kilometres away and he told them, 'These village people are saying they will not let me go if a 3D rally doesn't happen here today'. The situation was resolved at the last minute and Modi made a point of name-checking the village so his volunteer could sleep easy that night.

The appeal of the holograms is not hard to fathom. They were pure spectacle, bringing a touch of glamour to places that were often far from a cinema and where perhaps only a few – if any – of the villagers had access to a television. But the BJP's official spokesman during the campaign, Prakash Javadekar, suggested that it wasn't just the element of extravaganza that caught the people's imagination. Modi was close to becoming deified. 'In Hindu mythology,' he told me, 'like in other religions, God is omnipresent. If you are a believer, you believe God is everywhere. So, Modi is addressing them from a different place but he is there. Thousands were listening and people could photograph themselves with him. The photograph would also have Modi in the picture. So it was a big hit, especially in the rural areas.' Were the people looking for another God? I asked him. He hesitated briefly. 'Another hero.'

Turning Modi into a three-dimensional hero figure was a phenomenally expensive exercise and questions were already being asked about where all the money had come from (see Chapter Seventeen), but Chandrashekhar Sharma, who had the unenviable job of supervising the logistics from Delhi, said, 'The 3D technology has been a huge asset for the Modi campaign.' By the time the trucks finally returned to base for the last time, he had addressed close to 1,400 3D rallies. More than 2,500 staff and volunteers had been involved in keeping the shows on the road but – according to the team's own estimates – the holograms had reached some 15 million potential voters. Even those who hadn't attended in person had almost certainly heard about them. Prashant Kishor and his colleagues at the CAG had been closely involved in helping ensure both the tea stalls and the 3D rallies eventually came off. 'In my head,' he told me, 'it was always like make him omnipresent. Just think about it. All of rural India is talking about this guy appearing in thin air. This image that only he can do it was the essential theme behind all these activities.' The last time the hologram Modi appeared he told the crowds that if he didn't win the election, 'I can always go back to selling tea.' For once, I suspect, they didn't believe him.

CHAPTER TEN
IMODI

Narendra Modi is an early riser. He is awake before dawn and soon ready for the yoga and meditation routines that help prepare him mentally, physically and spiritually for the day ahead. Before he settles into position to follow an exercise regime that has its roots in centuries of Indian tradition, however, he has a more contemporary reflex that will not wait. He connects to the internet.

'Yes I do have the habit of doing this,' he told me. 'I am up daily by five a.m. and do not need any time to settle down before I am online checking my messages. It's a mechanical process now for me to reach out for my iPad within the first four to five minutes after I wake. Likewise every day before I go to bed I take a look at my emails and check any relevant news that I may not have heard about and want to read. Honestly, I never take breaks and never really switch off.' His internet habit started, he said, as long ago as the late 1990s, when he was effectively in political exile from his native Gujarat. He discovered it was the best way to keep in touch with what was happening back home and he has been obsessed with keeping up with the latest online applications ever since. So much so that it has often been Modi who introduced his younger staff to the latest technology. 'I was seen as very tech savvy from the early days and was the first to use a digital camera in the 1999 elections.' As chief minister from 2001 onwards he consistently tried to stay ahead of the game. 'Another example of my forward thinking relevant to the technology world is my prediction around WhatsApp. When WhatsApp had just started, and long before it had become popular I was telling my people to start using this as a means for communication as it would be a major messaging platform in the days to come.' Had Modi failed to become prime minister, he might not have gone back to selling tea, but there would have been a career waiting for him in digital marketing.

Modi signed up to Facebook and Twitter in 2009, and from a slow start his number of 'friends' and followers grew steadily. One of the skills he looked for in the young men he recruited at that time was their ability to use social media to its best effect. One recalled, 'It was our very first meeting and he asked how he could double his Facebook likes.' His enthusiasm for online communication caught the attention of the BJP's national head of IT in Delhi. Arvind Gupta had been trying to persuade the party leadership that it had to start moving with the times. Having worked in both Silicon Valley in California and India's own IT capital, Bangalore, he joined the party staff full time in early 2010 and said that the BJP was barely in the game when it came to online campaigning. 'I said, you can't just start doing these things three months before the election. We needed a structured approach, collecting data, using that data effectively, engagement with people over the long term so you are not just engaging with your volunteers and your voters just ad hoc before the elections. If you do that your brand loyalty, if I can call it that, becomes much higher.' To Gupta it seemed that Modi was alone among the party's top names in understanding the potential. 'Yes, he was the only one. He understood the power of the medium.'

With Narendra Modi as the candidate there was never any doubt that the 2014 general election would be not only the most internet-savvy election in India's history – that was inevitable with all the technological advances since the last one in 2009 – but also the most advanced anywhere in the world. The BJP was not alone in recognising that the world had moved on, of course. With far more limited resources but some very enthusiastic volunteers, the newly formed AAP had an online presence that helped the party punch above its weight. Congress, too, had its IT experts and social media enthusiasts. What it lacked was a leader who was ready to embrace all the opportunities digital communications now had to offer a political campaign.

Rahul Gandhi was twenty years Modi's junior. He had spent a lot of time outside India, going to college first in Florida and then in Cambridge, and afterwards working as a management consultant in London. Yet he thought he knew how Indian politics worked better than the man who had spent his whole life travelling around the country. One communications expert, who was later recruited to Team Modi, said he and his colleagues first approached Gandhi and offered to work for him. 'We had some common friends so we had an interaction with Rahul,' he told me. 'We were young chaps, very excited to meet him. Here was the next-generation leader who we thought could use social media to communicate. I said to him, let's do it. Let's reach out to the people and you can change the country. But he said no, that the real India does not live in the online world. I was, like, what? He said you are all urban guys, you think it's all about urban India but this is a poor country. He gave us this socialist speech. So I walked away disillusioned. I didn't go to him for political philosophy, I went as a youngster so I was very disappointed. I met Modi a year after that and at once I thought, this guy speaks my language.'

While it is true that in parts of rural India there is still no electricity, never mind a usable internet connection, it was estimated that over 240 million people were online by the middle of 2014, with a year-on-year increase of around 28%. Of those, 185 million were connecting via their mobile phones. So while Rahul Gandhi was right to say not all Indians were ready to get the message via social media, many were, and those who did would often pass on what they had learned to friends, relatives and neighbours by word of mouth.

The internet being what it is, there was a fair amount of online mischief-making too. And, once again, Rahul Gandhi came off worst. The parallel spoof campaign featured characters called *Pappu* (which means 'stupid') representing Rahul Gandhi, *Feku* ('boastful') was Modi, and *Nayak* ('leader or hero') was the satirical name for the head of the AAP, Arvind Kejriwal, who had turned his back on leadership in Delhi. The website, www.pappupedia.com, had the same format as a Wikipedia page. It featured a caricature of Sonia Gandhi with a quote saying 'We indulge in scams because we need money for Pappu's brain transplant. You can help us mend our ways by donating.' On the other side there was www.pheku.in, started by critics of Modi, which promised to expose facts about him that had been 'buried under the mountains of lies and deceits'.

The BJP divided the country's 543 constituencies approximately into thirds. 'There were three elections happening at the same time,' according to one of the team. 'There was a pre-modern election in about two hundred seats which didn't require a social media campaign at all. Then there was the modern election, which would include semi-urban towns. And finally we identified one hundred and fifty-five constituencies that could be said to be involved in a digital election.' And use of the internet was not just about disseminating party propaganda or recruiting volunteers. It was a two-way process, with the IT cell in Delhi and the many freelance operators out in the ecosystem using the web to pick up intelligence about what was going on and what people were saying, documenting it all in a specially created 'National Digital Operations Cell' or N-Doc, and then passing it on to the Modi ground operation.

The purpose of the digital campaign was not merely to increase his number of 'likes' or Twitter followers, although he would eventually accumulate over 14 million Facebook fans, second only to Obama as a political leader. Almost one in six of all Facebook users in India were following Modi by the end of the campaign. But the real objective was to turn 'likes' into votes.

For those involved in it, the digital campaign was both exciting and challenging. The excitement kept hundreds if not thousands of enthusiastic young volunteers busy for months. 'The challenge', in Modi's own words, 'was there was no campaign before on this scale using social media and technology that had been managed anywhere in the world and hence we had no comparative basis from which to learn.' Every conceivable online platform was exploited, including BuzzFeed, Pinterest, Tumblr and StumbleUpon, which I have to confess I had never stumbled upon, but clearly more avid internet users than me had. Banner ads went up in a multitude of languages, and users were encouraged to interact as much as possible. They could use their mouse and cursor to 'rub off' whatever bugged them most, like corruption or underdevelopment, and discover who had the solution to their problems underneath. There is no need for me to reveal who that turned out to be. And as the 'selfie' craze gathered momentum, anybody who chose to could submit a selfie of their own and see it form part of a huge mosaic of similar photos that formed an image of you-know-who. #SelfieWithModi was the top trending hashtag on social media within two minutes of its launch, not just in India, but worldwide. On Holi, the festival of colours in March every year, thousands of people spray each other with brightly coloured paint or have water fights with colourful balloons. Modi sprayed his followers with multi-hued messages on Twitter asking them to 'spread the colours of peace, prosperity and happiness all over.'

In return he invited them to shower him with ideas. Before each of his big speeches, an open forum would be created on the India 272+ website (see Chapter Six). He first tried the idea of crowd-sourcing material in July 2013 when he was due to address students at Fergusson College in Pune. He used his Facebook page to ask for suggestions and received over 2,500 replies. Such was the response that Modi said he wanted to make crowd-sourcing a regular feature of his campaign. Shashi Shekhar, CEO of Niti Digital, which hosted the site, took me through how the process worked. 'A week or so ahead of every speech we would create an open forum and publicise it through our blog. Then forty-eight hours before the speech we would take a dump of all the comments, analyse it, come up with a summary and that would then be shared with Mr Modi's office. He would get to read it on the plane on the way to wherever he was going, and some of the ideas would then actually appear in his speeches. Modi was particularly keen to pick up local issues and concerns that he and his staff might otherwise miss. 'I had to talk about how central government could impact life locally which meant that an understanding of the regional flavour was critical through our research and real-time feeds,' he told me.

Analysing so many comments was no easy task, and the technology was not able to spot the nuggets in the mass transfer of information or 'dump'. 'A manual scan was needed to sort out the serious comments from the non-serious,' said Shekhar. 'We tried some automation towards the end but it was not very efficient because it's very hard to tell what is a serious comment and what isn't.' The majority of the comments and suggestions were positive, but not all. When the call went out asking what Modi should say in his first 3D hologram projection, Shekhar was surprised by what came back. 'Before that he had been doing these rallies and had been attacking Congress hard, but there was a very strong feedback in the open forum that you have attacked Congress enough. Now talk about your vision. We conveyed that to his office and in his first 3D speech you can see that he actually toned down his attacks on the Congress and talked more about his own ideas.'

Technological limitations also made it difficult for all the data that was collected on individuals to be used as effectively as they would have liked. For once, having so many different sites working to promote Modi was a disadvantage, according to one insider. 'If a supporter landed on any of our websites we had no way of recognising them. So we were not distinguishing between hard-core supporters and not so committed supporters or a neutral person. That information was available on social media if you read everything but we just didn't have the engines to do it for us, so we couldn't get the websites to use that intelligence and interact with these guys.' It was, he concluded, at best a semi-digital election. Nevertheless, Rahul Gandhi's reluctance fully to embrace social media meant he was not just missing one trick, he was missing a magician's case full of them. And of all the ways in which digital campaigning influenced the outcome, the most significant was arguably the impact it had on a comparatively tiny number of users. Journalists.

When Modi is alone with his iPad in the early morning or late at night, he regularly checks to see what the news pages are saying. For a long time Google Alerts was a favourite tool, set to scour the net for references to 'Narendra Modi', that is until the number of pages it threw up became unmanageable. But like most senior politicians in my experience, he has an ambivalent relationship with the journalists' profession. He is desperate to know what they are saying about him and puts an enormous effort into trying to ensure they write about him in the way he wants, usually with great success (see Chapter Eleven). And yet he is more than ready to blame them for most of his ills. 'Media distortion' ranks second only to 'Congress lies' in his response to any criticism. From his early days as chief minister in Gujarat, Modi has been convinced that the media, and especially the English-speaking media, is out to undermine him at any and every opportunity. One man who knows him well said, 'There's a history to this. If you look at Mr Modi, especially after the 2002 riots, he's been at the receiving end of the majority of the media. So he saw a big need to communicate directly with the people because the media was not going to be positive to him, it was going to be hostile to him. Its default position towards him would be hostile.' So for Modi, social media was not just a passion, it was a necessity.

At BJP headquarters, Arvind Gupta said it wasn't merely a question of hostility to Modi, but the desire of the media to set the agenda by deciding what they would and would not report. In previous elections the party leadership had felt powerless. 'Our responses were totally dependent on the mainstream media who could choose to show our messages or not. Social media changed the whole scenario.' By the clever use of the right tweet at the right time, the party found it could take control of the agenda and all but force TV, radio and the print media to follow along behind. In this respect at least, Shashi Shekhar of Niti Digital believes that Modi was able to dominate the election in ways that no western leader has yet been able to achieve, for all their trying. 'Unlike in the west, where the television and the news cycle sets the agenda to a large extent, in India at this election it was Mr Modi who was setting the agenda. He was not reacting all the time. He was defining the debate and then the media would react.'

By the 2014 election, Aatish Shrivastava had been covering the BJP for seven years as a reporter, and then as deputy political editor for the twenty-four hours news network NewsX. He has had to accept that many of the stories he is now asked to follow up have been put into the public domain through social media. A late convert to Twitter himself, he realised that he and his whole profession had to change when his news desk would start to ring him up about stories that he knew nothing about. 'I said where? Check on the social media, they said. I realised that this is something which is now giving me stiff competition. Twitter is part of the job and I have to save my job as well.' By starting a debate online during the day and getting thousands of their supporters to join in, the BJP found they could very often influence what subjects the networks would debate in their studio discussions the same evening. 'Editors take a cue from that,' said Shrivastava. 'They say, this is trending, OK, so let us also have a debate on that.'

Modi was happy to participate in online debates using Google Hangouts or Facebook Talks, but only when his people had arranged them and he had the discussion to himself. Social media may be an 'open' forum allowing anybody to take part but, even here, Modi wanted to stay in control. In March he pulled out of a 'Facebook Talks Live' debate at the last minute because he didn't like the format. He would have had to take part alongside politicians without the same support across the country, like Arvind Kejriwal of the AAP, and he didn't want to boost their credentials by doing so. To make matters worse, the broadcast partner for the event was NDTV, his least favourite television network. The Newslaundry website, which had come up with the idea, said the BJP had known about the format for weeks. In a statement they said that: 'Just two days before his interaction, Mr Modi laid down some conditions which we cannot fulfil. Mr Modi then decided to cancel. He is best placed to state the reasons.'

Rajdeep Sardesai first met Narendra Modi in 1990 when he was a young reporter on the *Times of India* in Mumbai. After switching to broadcasting he covered the aftermath of the Godhra attack for NDTV and indeed got caught up in the ensuing violence himself. In his book on the 2014 election, he recounts numerous occasions when Modi would remonstrate about how the media was treating him. Having switched to CNN-IBN, Sardesai was the leading frontman for the network during the campaign and was able to see first hand how the use of social media had turned the tables. 'By building a large and devout Twitter following,' he wrote, 'Modi was able to challenge the monopoly of the traditional media on opinion making. Modi was always convinced that a large section of the English-language media would never let him forget the 2002 riots. Now, thousands of handles on Twitter systematically attacked any narrative that challenged Modi in particular and the BJP in general. Journalists increasingly tend to follow Twitter like a wire service and watching social media has become part of a reporter's duties. Thus, by sheer force of numbers, Team Modi wielded social media's power over mainstream media's news priorities.'

By so dominating the Twittersphere, the Modi campaign could not just get a story into the headlines, it could help douse the fires when a potentially negative one was starting to gather force. A good example came when, in order to complete his nomination papers, Modi had no choice but to reveal that he was married as a teenager and still had a wife (see Chapter Two). The story started to go awry for the Modi camp when questions were raised about his attitude to women more generally. 'Can women of this country trust a man who deprives his wife of her right?' asked the Congress general secretary, Digvijaya Singh. Shashi Shekhar remembered the day clearly. 'If there had been no social media this would have been a huge mainstream media controversy. The kind of story the mainstream media would paint was "here was a woman who was abandoned, so how can you talk about women's rights if you didn't show proper responsibility" and so on. But the moment the news broke out you had people on social media reacting with counter-stories and facts and the issue fizzled out. It was marriage when he was a teenager, it was never consummated; all these things came out. It wasn't a decision that he made, it was a decision that was forced on him. That full counter-narrative had to be brought out and that's what social media did.'

It might have been only a semi-digital election, but the impact of what was said and done online was felt well beyond those constituencies with the highest number of internet users. Even a passionate social media advocate like Shekhar agreed that 'overall the impact was on the conversation and the narrative, not so much in the actual votes, because I don't think digital has penetrated yet to such an extent that it was affecting the outcomes at the polling booth level. Maybe at the next election.' Modi felt comfortable and in control in the social media world. He learned from it but it didn't answer back. Or, if it did, he didn't have to respond immediately under the full glare of the television lights. Yet Modi was leaving nothing to chance and ceding no battleground to the enemy. Like it or not, he would have to engage directly with those inconvenient journalists.

CHAPTER ELEVEN
'SUPERSTAR'

At the height of the election battle, Narendra Modi found himself standing alongside one of the professional consultants who had offered his services for the duration of the campaign. 'So what are your English-speaking media saying about me now?' he asked. Modi was dominating the headlines and setting the agenda, but still he felt sections of the media were out to undermine him at any opportunity. It's a familiar trait in politicians. I found while working for Tony Blair, when he was at his most popular and most of the media were eating out of his hands, a constant feeling inside Downing Street that they were out to get him. Other prime ministers I saw at close hand, including Gordon Brown and John Major, both of whom admittedly received a far worse press, were driven literally to distraction by what was said and written about them. Modi, by contrast, was relatively sanguine. He had grown used to criticism and didn't let it distract him for long.

Looking in from the outside, most observers came to the conclusion that Team Modi had very little to complain about in the way the campaign was being covered. Sandeep Bhushan, a fellow at the Jamia Millia Islamia university centre for culture, media and governance, observed that, 'In the run-up to the general election, it appeared as if every TV channel was pushing Modi. The coverage was unprecedented. He was omnipresent. It was similar to an ad barrage.

People were yearning for better, corruption-free governance and Modi was projected as a huge, happening symbol of change. It was certainly a watershed moment for the Indian news media.' For his part, the BJP's official spokesman, Prakash Javadekar, had no complaints. Had Modi been reported fairly, I asked him? 'Absolutely,' he replied, although he felt some of the papers were being positive almost in spite of themselves. 'Newspapers who were opposed to what Modi was saying, still they could not shun him. Because he was speaking something new. New quotable quotes. He used to give at least twenty quotable quotes a day. As a journalist how can you stall that? So I have no complaint about the coverage given by the media.' Rahul Kanwal, who covered the election for *Headlines Today*, agreed that Modi constantly gave journalists what they wanted most: stories. 'He is brilliant copy. He's the best copy India has ever had.'

Almost everything he did made news: the tea stalls, the holograms, the mammoth open-air rallies. For Kanwal, as a television journalist, Modi was a dream. 'When he is speaking, he is the director, the producer, the editor, the copywriter, the actor, the superstar, all in the same person. Because when he is speaking you see, when he wants the crowd to respond to what he is saying, he turns the mic towards them. So he is very theatrical, very Bollywood in that sense. He has a better sense of occasion, of timing, of television, of cameras, of production than virtually anybody else. He is smarter when it comes to production than most TV producers.' And if that includes speaking over the heads of the journalists, through social media or at public rallies, 'It's not something that you like, but what option do you have? He functions in the way that he does. You can't change it. You can clamour as much as you want, you can crib as much as you want, he's not going to change.' Aatish Srivastava, who covered the BJP for the NewsX channel, concurred. 'You can't ignore it when there are seven or eight hundred thousand people coming out of their houses to listen to Narendra Modi. You can't keep your eyes shut on that. Even suppose I am a heavy critic of Narendra Modi, that I don't like him, but how much can I afford to dislike him? I have to go and report on him and what will I report? I have to report something positive, each and every statement of Narendra Modi has hundreds of thousands of people clapping it. You can't keep your eyes and ears shut on it. So suddenly the media, which was dead against him, realised that he is going to be the prime minister of the country.' And some journalists were prepared to admit that there were other constraints on what they could write. 'We are all corporate-run media houses now. There is no one who is doing it as a social service,' said one.

It is a view that strikes a chord with Professor Zoya Hasan from Jawaharlal Nehru University. 'I think media and money played a very important role, an exceptionally important role in this election. It is certainly about ownership because ours is a corporate-controlled media. Some of the biggest newspapers and television channels are owned by the corporate sector. And Modi has been assiduously courting the corporate sector.' His message wasn't just attractive to wealthy businesspeople, in her view, but to many journalists themselves. 'Most of the journalists are very middle class or upper caste. So, as far as the media is concerned, I think it follows a middle-class agenda, and the middle class in India has turned to the right, or at least the centre-right.'

In my experience, some of the most left-wing journalists come from middle- or upper-middle-class backgrounds but, in any event, Modi's media strategy was not based on appealing to the self-interest of journalists as individuals. He had decided to dominate the news headlines from day one and, barring a few unhelpful controversies, that is exactly what he did. And he did it by making news. As for the charge of avoiding cross-examination by journalists and going over the heads of the media, Prakash Javadekar was unapologetic. 'He was not speaking over their heads. Maybe some journalists wanted to ask questions just to divert the issue, but he was talking from his heart to the people. That was news in itself. And in every speech there were new ideas, new slogans, new articulations, so for the journalists it was a feast.'

Javadekar ran a relatively conventional press office operation with the help of his head of media, Shrikant Sharma. Everybody was at their desks by 6.30 in the morning to read the newspapers and monitor the main national radio and television broadcasts between 7.00 a.m. and 11.00 a.m. At nine o'clock there would be a teleconference with the main political leaders, like Arun Jaitley and Rajnath Singh. They would discuss the main issues that were running in the media and decide how the party should respond. At 11.00 somebody, usually one of the politicians, would make a statement in front of the cameras on behalf of the party and perhaps take one or two questions. The main news conference would be at 3.00 p.m., when journalists could ask whatever they liked. The team would then meet again to assess how their stories were running in the media and to answer any last-minute questions from the BJP spokespeople who would represent the party on the evening discussion shows. These programmes took up a lot of time and effort and it was part of Javadekar's job to make sure all the spokespeople around the country knew what to say – 'the line to take'. He would hold a teleconference call, using audio bridge technology, every afternoon. 'There are nearly two hundred state-level spokesmen and panellists who go on the various TV shows. In every Indian language now, in each state, there are at least ten news channels, out of which at least five do live debates in the evening. So, it's a big thing.'

It was also, in reality, a sideshow. The main event, day after day, was Modi, and it was Modi whom all the channel executives wanted to see on their screens. The Holy Grail was an exclusive interview with the man himself, and they were very few and far between.

Modi was wary of the big TV interviews because he believed, quite rightly, that he would almost certainly be asked about the riots and there was a risk that whatever he said in reply could overshadow the positive message he wanted to put across. For that reason it was decided not to do any studio interviews at all at the start of the campaign. Prakash Javadekar explained the logic. 'If you start with interviews right from the first day then unnecessary controversies will be raised and the headlines become different.' Better to wait a couple of months, by which time the themes that Modi wants to talk about have been widely discussed and the agenda has been set. 'After things were established in the minds of people, then we chose to give interviews.'

Every journalist preparing for a major political interview hopes that it will make a splash. Occasionally the politician will come into the studio with a big piece of news that they have decided to break in an interview with you, in which case your work has been done for you, but that is a very rare occurrence. I interviewed every British prime minister from James Callaghan to Gordon Brown, over a period covering more than thirty years, and many other leading politicians too. They had usually decided what they wanted to say in advance and stuck to it rigidly. I tried to tempt them into making news, but if that failed I would goad them or even provoke them, in the hope of producing a dramatic and newsworthy reaction. A flash of anger is always good. A walkout guarantees that your interview will get noticed.

It happened to me only once when, as a young reporter in Northern Ireland, I interviewed the fiery preacher-cum-politician, the Reverend Ian Paisley. It was being pre-recorded and when he didn't like my line of questioning, he ripped off his microphone and stormed out in a fury, slamming the door behind him. Somebody must have told him that wasn't such a smart thing to do and a few minutes later he came back in and suggested I should put the question to him again. By this time, of course, he had an answer ready. That evening I decided to transmit the whole thing, walkout and all, and as soon as it was broadcast he was straight on the phone threatening never to speak to me again and to boycott the programme I worked for. He didn't carry out either threat, and was completely charming the next time I saw him, which taught me an early lesson about standing up to political bullies. But when it became my turn to advise politicians on how to conduct interviews, my two pieces of wisdom were: never say 'no comment' and never walk out.

To this day, one of the most talked-about interviews on Indian television took place in October 2007. It was the occasion when Narendra Modi walked out of an interview with Karan Thapar for the CNN-IBN show, *Devil's Advocate*. Thapar suggested to Modi that he had an 'image problem' as a result of the riots. He pressed the point firmly but politely:

> Thapar: Why can't you say that you regret the killings that happened? Why can't you say maybe the government should have done more to protect Muslims?

Modi: What I had to say I have said at that time, and you can find out my statements.

Thapar: Just say it again.

Modi: Not necessary. I have to talk about in 2007. Everything you want to talk about.

Thapar: But by not saying it again, by not letting people hear the message repeatedly, you are allowing an image contrary to the interest of Gujarat to continue. It's in your hands to change it.

Modi: (Takes the microphone off.) I'll have to rest. I need some water.

At that Modi walked away, saying, 'I can't do this interview.' On behalf of the BJP, Javedakar told the press the programme had given assurances that the questions would be about current issues and not the riots. Thapar, who had a reputation as a particularly combative interviewer, said no conditions had been set in advance. Although Modi promised their friendship would be unaffected, it was an encounter he never forgot. If he was going to make headlines in 2014, and he most assuredly was, then they were going to be the headlines he wanted.

Thorough preparation is not something reserved for the interviewer ahead of a big televised encounter. The interviewee, too, must be well briefed, confident and prepared for the likely direction of the questioning. And, as with most things in life, experience helps.

Modi knew that, but it seemed that Rahul Gandhi did not. He met the *Times Now* editor in chief, Arnab Goswami, on 27 January, for the programme *Frankly Speaking*. It was the first interview of its kind he had ever done, and it went so badly that it might even have been better if he had walked out. The first question was about why he wasn't putting himself forward as the Congress Party's candidate for prime minister. He dodged it and got bogged down in constitutional detail and history. But it was when he was asked about the anti-Sikh rioting that followed the assassination of his grandmother, Indira Gandhi, by her Sikh bodyguards in 1984 that he showed his vulnerability. There had been over eight thousand deaths, a casualty rate that was far higher than in Gujarat in 2002. The Congress Party was widely accused of complicity in the revenge attacks, but Rahul felt unable to either accept any responsibility on behalf of his party or to apologise. Rahul spoke movingly about the murder of both his grandmother and his father, Rajiv, but the interview soon degenerated into a lengthy effort by him to avoid answering almost all the questions that were put to him. One Congress Party media manager said afterwards that they had hoped it would boost Rahul's image to see him being quizzed by a tough interviewer. The idea was that it 'would establish Rahul as a politician who was open to public scrutiny, unlike Modi who walked out of interviews. I guess we just didn't know how badly Rahul would end up looking.'

Modi, meanwhile, was sticking to his political strategy of using attacks on the record of Congress in government and the inexperience of its young pretender to generate a demand for strong leadership that only he could fill. It had been decided that most of the news he and the other BJP spokespeople would try to make should be based on a 'charge sheet' against the government. Modi was quite happy to let the media report on his rallies and the content of his speeches. For now, he preferred to avoid giving interviews and if he did they were usually while he was out and about, never in the studio, and generally concentrated on local issues.

Then, in February, he took a calculated risk. 'I decided that I would not be available to the media,' he told me. 'I did this intentionally to create a vacuum and get attention because of the vacuum.' Modi used the time to busy himself with practicalities, like overseeing the selection of candidates. 'Thus the month of February was no interviews and mostly silence. My supporters were anxious and my detractors were happy, little realising that this was my strategic intent as we readied for the last few days before polling began.' And with polling staggered across the nine different phases, when he emerged from his self-imposed media purdah he did it with one eye firmly on the election calendar. 'The TV interviews were carefully planned before any election in a state and I was specifically doing the interviews focused on where the elections were going to be held. What this did was to allow me to customise my message all the time and not to spill all the beans at once and keep the curiosity of people alive in terms of what would I say next. I went full-fledged to the national media only towards the end, first to the Hindi channels and then to the English.'

Modi finally appeared on screen in a national television studio on Saturday 12 April, by which time the first two rounds of voting had already happened. He chose to grant the exclusive to the popular Hindi-language show *Aap ki Adalat* ('Your Court'). It was presented by the editor in chief of India TV, Rajat Sharma, a friend of Modi's for over forty years. The studio was set up as usual in a courtroom format, with the interviewee 'in the dock' in the centre and the audience surrounding him at a distance. The programme received the highest TV ratings in India's history. Official monitoring figures showed that 74% of news viewers in the country tuned in to watch. Despite a hectic day on the campaign trail, Modi was in sparkling form, buoyed up by the enthusiastic reaction of the studio audience, who started chanting his name and applauding as soon as he appeared. It went on for over an hour, and while it wasn't exactly a grilling, and Modi was clearly in control of what he wanted to say, nobody could claim that the difficult issues hadn't been raised. He was asked about the Gujarat riots, the ban on him entering the United States, his attitude towards Muslims, the charge that his image was all spin and didn't always fit the facts, and much else besides.

The day after it was broadcast, the success of the interview was marred by the resignation of India TV's editorial director, Qamar Waheed Naqvi. It was rumoured that he had gone because he thought the show had been 'fixed'. He later confirmed that, in his view, 'The entire programme was part of the Modi propaganda machine. No hard questions were asked and the audience was full of Modi *bhakts* [devotees] who were only there to cheer for him.' India TV put out a statement saying they were surprised at the reasons being circulated on social media for Naqvi's resignation. 'Such reasons are baseless, and we condemn the effort being made to use it for political gains,' it said. The interview was shown again many times during the remainder of the campaign, with consistently high viewing figures suggesting that the row had done little damage.

For the next month Modi did interview after interview. Television journalists would be invited to Gandhinagar, where Modi would return after many long hours of travelling and speaking at up to three rallies a day. His stamina was extraordinary and his staff often noted that the reporters seemed more tired than he was. Most, but not all, of the networks were granted interviews, although the English-speaking channels were, as he had intended, left until last. The editor-in-chief of *Times Now,* Arnab Goswami, got his interview only on May 8, by which time eight of the nine phases of voting had already been completed. The one channel that was excluded altogether was NDTV, where Rajdeep Sardesai worked before moving to CNN-IBN in 2005. He wrote that 'Modi, it seems, still hadn't forgiven or forgotten the reporting done by the NDTV channels (yours truly included) during the Gujarat riots and its aftermath.' Modi's dislike of NDTV was common knowledge in journalistic circles and he was well known for never forgetting when a media organisation or individual journalist had, in his view, let him down. When I asked one of his advisers if Modi really disliked NDTV so much, the reply was simply, 'The feeling was mutual.' Over at *Headlines Today*, part of the *India Today* group, Rahul Kanwal told me, 'There are people he believes are on his side. He likes those people. His system gives access to them. Then there is a whole bunch of journalists who he had a falling out with during the 2002 riots. Them he doesn't like, them he can't stand.'

To favoured journalists, Modi was surprisingly accessible on the telephone during the campaign although, given his thirst for political intelligence and feedback, it was more often to seek information than to impart it. He would ring local journalists before a big rally to get a sense of the mood in the area and then sometimes afterwards to see how his speech had gone down. Aatish Srivastava at NewsX said Modi was 'very inquisitive to know what the media is thinking about him, about his campaign, about the words which he uses, the amount of aggression he shows on screen.' But when it came to reporters asking him questions, 'He does not really want to open up with journalists. He does have good friends in the media, where people do visit him but he does not open up.'

Again, according to Rahul Kanwal, it depended who you were. 'He has got very strong likes and dislikes. If he trusts you he would be very frank and very open. If he doesn't trust you, he would not come on the phone at all. It's like the Great Wall of China, you can keep banging your head against it.'

Headlines Today was clearly one of those that he was usually happy to talk to. 'When he is campaigning, he constantly wants feedback. So, for example, I would speak to him virtually every week or ten days during the campaign. Once he gets over with work at night, say at 10.30 or 11.00, then people can call him and chat with him. You call up the switchboard number and you tell them who it is and they patch you through and then he speaks to you for a very long time. Now he is prime minister, of course, he speaks for far shorter periods, but earlier he would speak for one and a half hours, or two hours.' Did that, I asked him, lead to an unhealthily cosy relationship and to the risk of self-censorship by journalists who wanted to stay in his good books? 'I think each person does what he wants himself. There can be no rule on that. The way we try and do it is that we don't let access or lack of it impact our journalism.'

Most political journalists have to balance their need for good sources, who will trust them enough to impart information, with the risk of getting too close and so compromising their integrity. There is another form of journalism, however, where the transaction is more straightforward, although just as hard to prove. It is known as 'paid news' and results in stories appearing in the media that appear to be independent but which have, in fact, been paid for. It is not illegal, but the Election Commission thinks it should be outlawed. The former chief election commissioner, S.Y. Quraishi, has written that, 'In recent years, corruption within the Indian media has gone far beyond the corruption of individual journalists and specific media organisations. From "planting" information and views in lieu of favours received in cash or kind, to more institutionalised and organised forms of corruption, wherein newspapers and television channels receive funds for publishing or broadcasting information.'

It was nothing new, and had been going on for years with stories promoting the interests of corporations, film producers, actors, and anybody else with something to sell. But, said Mr Quraishi, 'the phenomenon of "paid news" acquired a new and more pernicious dimension by entering the sphere of political "news" or "reporting" on candidates contesting elections over the last few years.' Without the power to intervene, the EC and the Press Council of India had been able to collect only circumstantial evidence. All the main parties were suspected of being involved, although because of the overwhelming amount of coverage sympathetic to the BJP, and its perceived closeness to some big corporate interests, Modi's party was scrutinised more closely than most. Given the scale and variety of the media across the country and the sheer volume of stories that were generated during the campaign by journalists going about their jobs to the best of their abilities, it seems highly unlikely that paid news had any significant impact on the results. And overall, Mr Quraishi concluded that 'the Indian media has been discharging its responsibility with spectacular effect.'

The American writer H. L. Mencken famously said that, 'journalist is to politician as dog is to lamppost.' In India there is a saying that a horse and grass can never be friends, which amounts to much the same thing. Modi might have stopped feeding some journalists who wrote or said things he didn't like, but he usually mellowed after a while and gave them another chance. At the end of the day, he needed them as much as they needed him. The doyen of social media also wanted to be taken seriously as a politician of real substance with an ambitious policy agenda, and there is, after all, only so much you can say in a 140-character tweet. Politics isn't all about sound bites and at times, thankfully, some serious analysis is called for. And away from the studio lights there was a different kind of election going on – less glamorous, perhaps, but no less important if Modi was to make the transition from delivering good copy to delivering on his promises.

CHAPTER TWELVE
VOTE LOTUS

While it was the TV debates, the chatter on social media, the 3D rallies and the satellite-linked tea stalls that were capturing the imagination of the journalists, in the various committee rooms a great deal of much more mundane but essential work was going on to ensure that the BJP captured the votes of the electorate when it mattered. It was all very well for the campaign to break new ground in the use of modern technology and innovative ideas, but the party couldn't afford to neglect the basics of fighting elections. If it did there was a risk that the chances of victory could yet disappear as fast as the face of Mr Modi when the plug was pulled on the hologram machine. Feet on the ground would be far more important in delivering victory than a thousand images in thin air or a million tweets in the Twittersphere.

For all his love of social media and new technology, Modi remained a man with his own feet very firmly on the ground. His years as an organiser 'behind the curtains' taught him never to underestimate the importance of meticulous planning and a rigorous attention to detail. Once he was the prime ministerial candidate himself he had to leave much of this work to others, but the campaign structure he had put in place before his elevation continued to function – with varying degrees of success. The different committees met and set about fashioning the blocks on which the long-hoped-for victory could be built. Some took longer about their business than others, and not all met the deadlines that had been set for them. Agreeing the text of the party manifesto, in particular, proved to be a delicate and time-consuming task.

I have yet to meet anybody anywhere outside the small community of political cave-dwellers who has actually read a manifesto from cover to cover, but the documents do matter. If necessary the promises thrown out with a rhetorical flourish in campaign speeches and interviews can be quietly forgotten or reinterpreted to meet the needs of the more sober business of government. The manifesto, on the other hand, is there in black and white; or more often these days in colour, in a vain attempt to get anybody to take an interest in it. If a party stands a decent chance of winning, there will be dozens of stakeholders all trying to ensure that their pet idea gets the imprimatur of inclusion in this important but unloved declaration of intent. In the case of the BJP, they included the various party leaders hoping to become ministers, the different party cells and regional bodies, outside supporters including from the corporate sector, and of course the RSS, which still regarded itself as the keeper of the party's conscience. At the same time it was important to avoid any hostages to fortune. The other parties would have troglodytes of their own ready to dig for hidden gems that could be unearthed and turned into weapons.

Under the chairmanship of Dr Murli Manohar Joshi, the BJP manifesto committee finally unveiled its work on 7 April, after numerous delays. They were cutting it fine, to say the least. It was the same day that voting began in the first phase of the election. In two states, Assam and Tripura, it was already polling day, so those casting their votes there had no chance to make a decision based on what it said, even if they'd wanted to. The timing created a headache for the broadcasters, who were uncertain whether it was even legal for them to cover the launch while polling was in progress. Despite suspicions that the BJP might even have chosen the date deliberately, the editors decided to go ahead on the grounds that it was a newsworthy event that should be covered in the national interest.

Whether or not the BJP was pulling a fast one by choosing that particular day, they claimed that the delay had been caused by logistical problems. By the time the manifesto was at last ready to go to the printers, many of the top brass who needed to sign it off were spread across the country campaigning. Some of the committee members, including Dr Joshi, were themselves candidates, and were busy ensuring their own nomination papers were filed in time. When the public finally got to see it, Congress called it a 'cut and paste' manifesto and claimed the BJP had put off publication so it could steal their best ideas. The most significant factor behind the hold-up, however, was a feeling among many of those who were given the final draft to read that it just wasn't good enough. It was considered to be too much of a laundry list of promises that needed to be made more 'lean and mean'. One told the *Economic Times*: 'In the age of 140-character Twitter messages, who has the time to read such a lengthy document?'

It wasn't just the number of words that was a problem, but the policy content too. The RSS was said to be demanding that it appeal more forcefully to Hindu nationalists. And it was widely reported that one man who had held up publication was the self-proclaimed master of organisation himself, Narendra Modi. It wasn't a case of being disorganised – that would have been be very un-Modi-like – but a concern that the manifesto didn't put enough emphasis on economic and development issues and had failed to include some of the big ideas he wanted to push, like establishing dozens of new 'cities of the future'. At the end of the day, after the document was revised, the pledge was included and it promised, 'We will initiate building 100 new cities, enabled with the latest technology and infrastructure – adhering to concepts like sustainability, walk to work etc.'

Modi's twin priorities of good governance and economic development were finally at the heart of the manifesto, and there was much else that reflected those personal ambitions for India that he would later articulate so effectively in his first 'state of the union' speech as prime minister (see Chapter One). The party was now committed to 'Create an open-defecation free India by awareness campaign and enabling people to build toilets in their home as well as in schools and public places.' There would be 'a national campaign for saving the girl child and educating her.' Manufacturing industry would be encouraged to put quality first and 'focus on zero defect products.'

It soon became apparent to me that the status of an Indian manifesto is not exactly the same as one in Britain, for example. In Whitehall a manifesto is as close as you can get to a list of firm commitments to be delivered in the time-frame of the parliament to come. The convention is that if something is in your manifesto and you win the election, then you have a mandate to deliver it and you are expected to do so. The BJP manifesto was rather more a mixture of hard and fast promises and a wish list for the more distant future. Some of the commitments were decidedly vague, although anybody who has travelled on Indian trains would welcome the promise of 'railways modernisation' including 'state of the art technology'. Others were highly ambitious, to the point of being dismissed as pie in the sky, something no manifesto writer in Britain would be allowed to get away with. With admirable ambition the manifesto says that 'The time of knee jerk reactions and incremental change has gone. What we need is a quantum leap and a total change.' So perhaps the BJP government will manage to 'modernise and equip all stations with requisite infrastructure and public utilities', but we shall have to see. Likewise with the pledge to 'facilitate piped water to all households'. None of these promises is costed. Perhaps most ambitious of all is the 'low cost housing programme' which will be expected 'to ensure that by the time the nation completes 75 years of independence, every family will have a *pucca* house of its own.' That celebration falls in the year 2022, while the latest census figures in 2011 showed that almost 1.8 million people were without a home across the country.

The influence of the ideological priorities of the RSS was most evident on page 41 in the section on 'Cultural Heritage'. The first item listed stated that 'The BJP reiterates its stand to explore all possibilities within the framework of the constitution to facilitate the construction of the Ram Temple in Ayodhya.' This was, of course, the city from which the victims of the Godhra train massacre in Gujarat had been travelling (see Chapter Three). Murli Manohar Joshi, who chaired the manifesto committee, had been among the nationalist leaders who had encouraged the demolition of a mosque on the site back in 1992. But the manifesto promise to rebuild the Ram temple was not as incendiary as it may have sounded. The BJP had made the same pledge many times before, and its inclusion could be seen an article of faith as much as anything. Significantly, while the word 'Ayodhya' appeared just once in the manifesto, 'technology' was repeated fifty-eight times. Nevertheless, it did show that Modi's agenda continued to include issues dear to the heart of the more fervent nationalists. The desire to defend Hindu culture and traditions was reflected in additional promises to clean up the holy River Ganges, protect cows and their calves and to promote Indian languages. The offer to Indian Muslims, by contrast, was principally economic: 'It is unfortunate that even after several decades of independence, a large section of the minority, and especially Muslim community continues to be stymied in poverty. Modern India must be a nation of equal opportunity. BJP is committed to ensure that all communities are equal partners in India's progress, as we believe India cannot progress if any segment of Indians is left behind.'

There was some concern in western capitals at the pledge to 'Study in detail India's nuclear doctrine, and revise and update it, to make it relevant to challenges of current times', and to follow a nuclear programme 'unencumbered by foreign pressure and influence, for civilian and military purposes.' This could be read as an intention to revise India's 'no first use' policy with regard to its nuclear weapons, especially when combined with the statement that 'In our neighbourhood we will pursue friendly relations. However, where required we will not hesitate from taking strong stand and steps.' BJP sources said it was really about indicating that India would rebuild its strength and regain its self-respect on the international stage.

The leaner and meaner manifesto had finally been cut down from sixty pages to forty-two, but the process of agreeing what should go in and what shouldn't had been so protracted and painful that plans for a 'vision document', designed to paint a picture of the party's longer-term hopes for India, had to be shelved altogether. It was reported to be running to an ungainly 200 pages or more. Party sources were quoted as saying that the voters, especially the young, had neither the time nor the inclination to wade through a text that was high on political philosophy and low on practical measures. And what was the point, anyway? According to one insider, 'Now Modi is the manifesto, Modi is the vision. Nothing else is required.'

If only it were that simple. He might have been the party's greatest asset but, despite the efforts of the hologram team to transmit him to the darkest corners of the country, there was still just one Narendra Modi. Under Indian election law he was permitted to stand in two constituencies, and so in both Vadodara in Gujarat and Varanasi in Uttar Pradesh (UP), people could vote for him personally, but that still left 541 seats where his name would not be found anywhere on the ballot paper. Choosing the men and women to contest those seats was another time-consuming exercise, and one that was again left almost until the last minute. This time, however, the delay was entirely deliberate. Just as Modi had decided to avoid debating his ideas on TV until he had established the agenda on his own terms, so he made up his mind not to have too many candidates in the field who might distract from the message he was seeking to convey.

Some well-established MPs who met with his approval knew that they would be defending the same seats again. Others he wanted to move to different constituencies and some he wanted to drop altogether. If the BJP was to get anywhere close to a majority, then lots of newcomers were going to find themselves elected to parliament. Why risk rows and controversies over who was standing where until you had to? And, the later it was left, the greater the pressure on all concerned to keep quiet and get on with the task of winning. According to the journalist Aatish Srivastava, some party leaders confirmed the strategy privately. 'They said why should we announce the candidates when we will fight only on Narendra Modi? Let there be a delay, it is going to be fought only on Modi. So suppose they announced my name from Varanasi 100 days before the elections, then my short-comings will become the debating point in that particular constituency. They don't want that situation, so they want until the last moment so people will only talk about Modi and, as for the candidate, be it good or bad, they will not have that much time to debate his character.'

Modi was delighted with how it had worked out. 'The way we picked our candidates was also a surprise,' he told me. 'Their past election track record was not a criteria, just as political background was not. This approach came from my experience and is something that Modi has always done.' He said he had used exactly the same approach when he was chief minister in Gujarat. The downside, of course, was that the party found itself with a very large number of inexperienced candidates with little or no voter recognition in the seats they were expected to fight. 'At that time many in the party saw this as a big risk as there was no history of vote-winning ability of several of the representatives. As expected there were some dissident activities, but the fact that we won the elections by a huge margin is a sign of the strength of the organisation and the ability to get people to fall into line and be aligned if the core organisation is built on strong foundations.' The late announcement also had the effect of making the campaign even more presidential than it would otherwise have been, something that suited Modi's strategy perfectly.

Much of the responsibility for building those strong foundations fell to party vice president Mukhtar Abbas Naqvi, who was put in charge of election management and logistics. Without the option to clone the party leader, and with so many new candidates, he had to ensure that voters knew which button to press if they wanted Modi to be PM. 'Nobody was voting for the local leader or MP,' he told me, 'everybody was voting for Modi. We were concerned that on voting day when people would go to cast their vote and not find Modi's picture on the electronic voting machines, they won't know who to vote for.' Some candidates running against the BJP had even been caught using Modi's name or photo to cause deliberate confusion. The solution was to promote the party symbol, the lotus flower, which would be printed on the ballot paper alongside the name of every BJP candidate. Modi agreed to wear a pin badge with the lotus flower on it whenever he appeared in public. The lotus featured prominently on all the party's posters, TV adverts and literature, sometimes with the message, 'Don't forget two things: Narendra Modi and the Lotus Flower'. Naqvi knew that even that would not be enough. People led busy lives, and while it might have felt as though everybody was talking about the election, they could not be expected to get the message so easily. His task was to see to it that as many voters were contacted face to face as humanly possible.

The BJP had some catching up to do if it was to challenge the well-established political machine built up by Congress over many decades. In the event that machine, which had grown rusty and unreliable with age, was pushed aside like an old wreck as the Modi juggernaut passed through. Naqvi's boss, party president Rajnath Singh, had appointed one key individual in each state to oversee the management of the campaign. By far the most significant of these was Amit Shah, who was sent to the electorally vital state of UP. Alongside the so-called 'party in charge', like Shah, every state had an organisation secretary and a 'war room in charge'. Between them they would have to determine who were the best candidates to stand in each constituency, look after the finances and organise the campaign on the ground. At the same time they had to ensure it all stayed within the rules laid down by the Election Commission, or be answerable if it did not.

The state-wide apparatus was still very remote from the individual voter. Almost 200 million people live in UP alone, for example. If it were an independent country, it would be the sixth largest in the world. So each state was divided into districts with their own presidents, coordinators and committees. And so it went on down, with officers in charge of constituencies, subdivisions within constituencies, and finally to the level of the polling both. The 'booth in charge' was at the lowest level of the structure but had one of the most important jobs. Most constituencies had between 1,200 and 2,000 polling booths, and he or she (it was usually he) had the ultimate responsibility of delivering the voters on election day.

Many of those appointed to supervise key electoral battlegrounds were outsiders, and deliberately so. This enabled them to take a fresh look at whether the party apparatus needed an overhaul without having a stake in the status quo. Others were given new roles that they were unfamiliar with. There was a lot of learning on the job, but that too brought a sense of urgency to the business of getting the right structures and people in place. Shrikant Bhartiya was asked to take over the war room in Mumbai, capital of the state of Maharashtra, second only to UP in terms of size and electoral importance. He wasn't even sure what a war room was, so he looked it up online. First up came Winston Churchill, but that was a different kind of war. 'After that I saw Obama had used a similar concept during the last two US elections. I studied those models and tried to implement some of the aspects here in Maharashtra. For example, the BJP is a core network organisation and we have 89,000 booth in-charges. Earlier we used to have only one-way communication with them. If we look at the Obama campaign, they collected a lot of feedback from the field and adjusted the campaign accordingly. So we tried to do that here. Secondly, we learned about using technology to effectively communicate with the network in the quickest manner – emails, WhatsApp, social media; all of them helped big time.'

Equally there were some good old-fashioned methods that had never lost their effectiveness. Bhartiya and thousands like him would have to ensure there were enough loudspeaker vans to go out touring the constituencies; posters, flags and leaflets had to be printed, public meetings organised and voters canvassed. In some important respects the Modi phenomenon wasn't just about pushing the boundaries when it came to innovative techniques, but also reviving and revitalising traditional ones. Political rallies and public meetings had been falling out of favour in Indian elections, just as they had in many countries. According to one BJP leader, 'More and more we found that people would rather stay at home and listen to the speeches on TV. Modi reversed all that.' And, inspired once again by the Obama campaign, party workers in Delhi, Mumbai and the big urban areas were sent out to knock on doors and ask people face to face for their support, something that had never been tried before on such a large scale.

Rural districts required a different kind of on-the-ground operation; the more remote the constituency, the greater the challenges. Mukhtar Abbas Naqvi sits in the upper house, the Rajya Sabha, so he didn't have an election of his own to contest. But, like many in his position in the high command, he was given a lower house Lok Sabah seat to supervise. Unlike most of his colleagues, he's also a Muslim, so the seat he was assigned was Leh and Kargil, up in the mountains in the north-western state of Jammu and Kashmir, where the Muslim vote is critical. The BJP had always fared very badly here, but Modi told him it could be won. It was also one of the most formidable challenges in terms of logistics. In the winter months many of its towns and villages are completely cut off by snow. Helicopters were used to get officials in and out when possible, but Naqvi was forced to cancel a personal appearance because of the weather. 'So I recorded a video message instead,' he told me. 'We sent it by horse and cart and it took two days to arrive.'

Unable to find a Muslim candidate who was acceptable to the different sections of the community, Naqvi selected a Buddhist, 67-year-old Thupstan Chhewang. Geographically Mr Chhewang might have had the highest constituency in India to fight, but on the day the results came in he had the lowest majority, just thirty-six votes. An astonishing 73% of voters had braved the weather and turned out. So if you want to know about the importance of going after every vote, just ask Mukhtar Abbas Naqvi.

When he wasn't worrying about the weather in the Himalayas, Naqvi also had overall responsibility for the logistics of Modi's frantic schedule of rallies and visits as well as those of a dozen other party leaders. He would gather his team together at 5.30 most mornings, conscious that Modi was awake by 5.00 a.m. and could ring at any time. Working closely with the officials and advisers at the chief minister's office in Gujarat, the Delhi-based election management committee would plan the itineraries down to the smallest detail. Modi's years as an RSS worker had taken him all over India, and with his own intimate knowledge of the country he would frequently make suggestions himself. He often tried to switch between campaigning in the north or west one day and the south or east the next.

There was inevitably a concentration on what were regarded as winnable seats, but Modi had already demonstrated that he had a more ambitious view of where was winnable than the rest of them. By the end he was doing as many as six rallies a day. He would spend up to seven hours a day travelling, so getting the transportation right was key. Modi had two helicopters at his disposal, so they could leap-frog each other and get to the next destination by the time the candidate's plane landed at the nearest airport. He would work while in the air, reading the notes he had been given for the next place on his itinerary. Simple food would be available for him to eat and occasionally he would take a nap. Very few staff joined him as he travelled because, under the election rules, the cost of any extra people had to be added to the expenditure of each candidate, which was capped. The most important were his long-serving personal assistants Om Prakash Singh Chandel, Dinesh Thakur and Tanmay Mehta.

Sticking to the rules was one thing, dealing with hurdles that they were certain had been deliberately put in their way was another. Permissions to fly and to land often had to be granted at a national or state level by officials whose political bosses were no friends of the BJP. 'We had lots of problems,' Naqvi recalled. 'Sometimes from local officials, sometimes from Delhi, maybe because of instructions from the government. But, despite everything, we were adamant that we would never cancel any rally of Modi. It only happened once due to the death of the candidate.' It seems Modi never lost his temper in circumstances that in Britain or the US would have seen the leader turning the air blue or taking it out on the seats. 'When we would speak with him his words were always encouraging. He would never complain. One day I remember permission for his helicopter to land had not been given and refuelling arrangements for his aircraft were not there because the government and some local officials and some central air traffic control system had not cooperated. At that time he was sitting at Delhi airport for two hours and in some other place for about an hour. He called us up to ask what was going on. We knew that they were deliberately trying to disturb our election programme and the rally, but despite this he reached it two or three hours late. There was no cancellation.'

The thousands of BJP party workers across the country, working alongside the dedicated volunteers from the RSS, were the unsung heroes of the 2014 election. Theirs was not glamorous work and it rarely excited the interest of the media, but without them the result would have been very different. They carried the party symbol with them wherever they went, hoping that people would get the message that if they wanted to vote Modi they had to vote lotus. Shrikant Bhartiya's experience in Maharashtra was typical. He recognised that a vast swathe of voters weren't deeply engaged politically. 'The common man is the bottom line of Indian democracy. And a common man's EQ [emotional quotient] is stronger than his IQ [intelligence quotient]. People are emotional. People vote for a person, a person who can lead the nation. The same has happened in the past, be it for Indira Gandhi, Rajiv Gandhi, Jai Prakash Narayan or Atal Bihar Vajpayee. So there are three types of votes that we get – votes in support of the party, votes in support of the philosophy and then a significant number of votes in support of the leader – in this case Modi.'

The man himself, who liked to say to his party, 'Like all of you, I am just an ordinary worker', overstepped the mark in his own efforts to promote the image of the lotus flower. On the last day of April, nine states including Gujarat were going to the polls. Modi cast his own vote in Ahmedabad and then emerged from the booth and took a selfie on his phone with the metal lotus badge held in his fingers, one of which was inked to show he'd voted. The picture went viral almost immediately. Modi told the cheering crowds that in his estimation, 'After analysing the election process and the voter's mind until now, I can say that this time nothing can save the mother-son government.'

The BJP already had form for stretching the rules on polling days, but now Modi had stretched them to breaking point. Political speeches and campaigning are not allowed while voting is going on. The Election Commission said that 'from the substance, tone and tenor of the address,' and the 'manner in which the symbol, lotus, of the BJP was being displayed by him . . . thereby displaying to the public election matter by means of television in areas going to polls today', it was evident that it 'was in the nature of political speech intended and calculated to influence and affect the result of elections in the constituencies going to polls today, not only in Ahmedabad but also in all other constituencies in Gujarat and elsewhere in the country.' The deputy commissioner of police, Himanshu Shukla said he was starting an investigation, 'against chief minister Narendra Modi as directed by the EC under Section 126 (1) (a) and 126 (1) (b) of the Representation of the People Act, 1951, and Section 188 of the Indian Penal Code.' He said a complaint had also been received against some media channels for covering the event. No charges were ever brought and the case was closed in August after Modi had become prime minister.

When I asked Modi about the incident he was all innocence. 'The selfie was a natural reaction and was just for social media.

It was part of what I was always doing and the youth of the nation were in my mind when I did it. There was no other objective – but obviously the media wanted to write about it and spin it.' He conceded that like all Indian politicians he looked for 'auspicious' days to help ensure 'our message got the attention it deserved to keep the election momentum going.'

Modi was content to be the main vehicle for carrying the message, and indeed in many ways he was the message. Even that was not enough for Team Modi. To raise his profile still further and to ensure that so far as possible his face was known in every town and village across the country, including those where his helicopter would never land, Modi was turned into more than just a politician with something important to say. Once again they were ready to push the limits of what had been done before to promote a political leader in India – or anywhere else for that matter – and to create a new, must-have fashion accessory, Brand Modi.

CHAPTER THIRTEEN
BRAND MODI

A man in his mid-sixties with glasses, grey hair and a beard is not everybody's idea of a fashion icon. But it is one of the many apparent contradictions that make Modi so unusual that this self-proclaimed 'man of the people' is as fashion-conscious as any leader on the world stage. Even the *New York Times* fashion blog has been moved to note that 'Mr Modi stands out. Literally and strategically.' I remember the lengthy discussions inside 10 Downing Street when Tony Blair realised for the first time that he needed glasses. He fancied himself in a pair of Calvin Klein's, but we in the communications team insisted he should get an NHS pair so he wouldn't be accused of being too flash. Narendra Modi had no such inhibitions. It has been widely reported that his glasses are from Bvlgari, his watch is a Movado and the pen that often pokes from his top pocket is by Mont Blanc. The shirts themselves, a short-sleeved version of the traditional round-necked kurta, have become an internationally sought-after brand. He has them hand-made, and is often seen to change them several times a day, even switching colours so they go well with the background when he speaks.

His own account of the birth of the Modi Kurta has itself become legendary. He claims it was merely a way of making life easier before he was famous and was just a nomad travelling the country with a small bag. 'I had to wash my own clothes. So I thought my shirt occupied too much effort in washing and space too. I cut the sleeves myself. So my shirt became half sleeved. I have been wearing such clothes for over twenty-five years. Yes, I like to dress up well and stay clean. God has gifted me the sense of mixing and matching colours. So I manage everything on my own. Since I'm God gifted I fit well in everything. I have no fashion designer but I'm happy to hear that I dress well.'

Modi's fashionable tastes are said to be one reason that some traditionalists in the RSS, with its austere customs, became suspicious of him. In a sense his clothes and accessories are a very visible expression of what does indeed set him apart from the strict nationalist tradition. For him they symbolise his commitment to modernisation, ambition and good-quality products, although I'm sure there is a touch of vanity behind his choice of clothes too. Men across India didn't exactly rush out to buy short-sleeved shirts once Modi and his kurtas were on the TV every night, but the garment industry realised there was a marketing opportunity to exploit and both high-end and cheaper versions of the kurtas soon started appearing in shops and markets.

Every craze in the world, it seems, generates its own t-shirts and the Modi phenomenon was certainly no exception. Some of the first to appear were designed even before he became the candidate, by young supporters who had created an online campaign called 'Modi-fying India'. Tajinder Pal Singh Bagga had represented the party's youth wing on the BJP national executive for four years when he decided more should be done to make politics, and Modi in particular, more attractive to younger voters. 'If you see the scenario two years back,' he told me, 'when you spoke with the youth they would say I am not interested, everybody is a thief. But they saw a ray of hope in Modi.' Having watched Bruce Springsteen perform for Barack Obama, he and some friends staged a small rock concert. Concerts need t-shirts and these, too, were a deliberate attempt to copy the Obama campaign, although with a very Indian twist. 'We launched t-shirts because there were many people blaming Modi for the 2002 riots,' said Bagga. 'The first t-shirt was with the quote from Modi, "India First is my definition of secularism". And the second t-shirt had Modi's face with the tagline, "Face of Development".'

They were hardly the sort of slogans you can imagine fashion-conscious young Indians wanting to see emblazoned on their chests, but this was just the beginning. Once his campaign was properly up and running a huge market opened up for Modi-related products. An online shop, thenamostore.com, was quickly established and there were t-shirts galore available at the click of a button. Most of the designs prominently displayed his face, while others featured political slogans like 'sip the change', alongside a kettle pouring out a cup of tea. One simply replaced the 'S' in the iconic Superman symbol with an 'N'.

Modi was well aware of the use being made of his image and wholeheartedly approved. Another volunteer recalled going to show him some of the products. 'We showed him various things like cups and Superman tees with his face on it. He loved it and he said, "Go ahead and do it".' As the merchandising really took off, modimania.com joined the online sales drive and new products were made available. There were better-designed clothes for both men and women, stationery, watches, key-rings, mouse mats and toys. With a keen eye for the news agenda, some products were launched on particular dates, like NaMo chocolates for Diwali and the NaMo pepper spray that came out on International Women's Day.

When a specific controversy arose, new t-shirt designs could be quickly produced to take advantage of the situation. So when Modi decided to fight back against the *chai wala* jibes, Tajinder Pal Singh Bagga and his friends at Modi-fying India printed hundreds of thousands of t-shirts with a picture of Modi and the lotus symbol on the front and a rather lengthy slogan in Hindi on the back that read, 'Why can't a tea-seller become PM? Why can't the one who changed Gujarat change India too? Modi – my PM.' The garments were then distributed to tea vendors all over India.

Inevitably, cheaply produced copies of some of the t-shirts and other merchandising started to appear on market stalls just about everywhere. This presented no problem for the campaign team. They had no patents to protect. Indeed, quite the reverse, the rip-off products were just another kind of free advertising and it was obvious for all to see that there was no equivalent demand for Rahul Gandhi apparel. At the same time, promoting Brand Modi had to be about more than clothes, key-rings and assorted accessories. To do the job properly, the party needed some help from the experts.

Piyush Pandey is the Don Draper of India's advertising world. Not quite so young and dashing perhaps, although he told me working on the Modi campaign had made him feel twenty years younger. The allusion to the hit American show *Mad Men* brought a smile to his lips under his huge bushy moustache. We were sitting in his stylish apartment, tastefully decorated and with jazz posters on the walls. He stretched out and picked up his second large whisky. 'No, life is very different to *Mad Men*. We actually have to work hard.' In a short but intensive campaign, Pandey and his team regularly put in up to twenty hours a day trying to keep up with the demands of the election schedule. 'I think this campaign was the most memorable of my life,' he said, 'because for six weeks every day God was on my side.' Not that he needed divine inspiration. He signed up for the role only in February 2014, by which time the market was more than receptive to what he was about to market. He didn't demur. 'How many times do we get a product so easy to sell?'

Pandey knew Modi of old. The company he worked for as executive chairman and creative director, Ogilvy & Mather, had handled the contract for Gujarat's tourism push for nearly four years. But the founder of O&M, David Ogilvy, had made it a rule not to do political advertising, and so Pandey had turned down the contract for the 2012 Gujarat elections and did so again when Modi asked him to handle the general election. Then, at the end of January, the phone rang again. 'He said, "You must reconsider, I think I need you". So I agreed to think it over.' The solution was to take on the job not on behalf of O&M but the subsidiary company Soho Square, which he also chaired.

The man in charge of the day-to-day running of Soho Square, Samrat Bedi, readily agreed, and a meeting was quickly arranged with Piyush Goyal, chair of the Election Information Campaign Committee. Goyal shared the findings of the public opinion survey he had commissioned (see Chapter Six), which had shown that Modi's personal popularity was running around 20% higher than that of the BJP. He wasn't just out-performing his party, but was far ahead of any of his colleagues in the leadership. That meant, in advertising speak, according to Bedi, 'Mr Modi had far more equity than any other leader in the party, which led them to take a decision that Mr Modi would be the face of the campaign and that a presidential form of campaign would be run. It was unanimously decided that, instead of having multiple leaders, there would be just one brand, one face and one leader, Mr Modi. Just like it is done in US. That was the starting point for us.'

In line with the political strategy already in place, it was decided to go for a two-peg advertising campaign, one negative and one positive. Although with so little time left before polling, they would run more or less concurrently. 'The first peg was attack,' said Bedi, 'which was to use anti-incumbency as a tool to attack the opposition. This part of the campaign was primarily based on issues faced by different sections of the society, and the theme was '*Janta maaf nahin karegi*' or 'people will not forgive'. The issues we took up were women's empowerment and safety, unemployment and corruption. Then the second peg was around hope based on the theme '*achche din aane wale hain*' (good times are coming). This was designed to show people the bright future and it evolved into a message that only if people give the BJP an absolute majority will the good days come.'

In the west political advertising usually has to pass the 'focus group' test. Possible slogans and images are shown in private to carefully selected groups of voters to see how they react. If they don't like them, the ads are unlikely ever to appear. Modi, in keeping with his general mistrust of professional opinion surveying, prefers to do things his own way. He recalled for me a slogan he had come up with himself for an earlier state election, '*Jeetega Gujarat*' (Gujarat will win). 'I had a thought that perhaps people in the state may see this as somewhat arrogant, with us saying that if the BJP won it meant Gujarat won.' So Modi had a banner put up in a part of Mumbai, in the neighbouring state of Maharashtra, where many Gujaratis lived. Party workers were posted on the street to ask passers-by what they made of it. 'People loved the directness of it so this was a good validation for us to proceed,' Modi told me.

He did the same with the phrase *'Bus, aave to BJP'* (Enough, now it needs to be the BJP), which was painted on a few walls. 'The simplicity of the slogan captured the voice of the people and struck a chord,' he said. The ad went ahead and Modi's faith in the feedback of what he likes to call 'the common man' was reinforced.

To be effective, the advertising had to keep up with the changing dynamics of the political campaign. And that meant daily meetings and endless telephone calls, many of which would go on late into the night. Almost without fail the Soho House team would meet Goyal and his colleagues at one in the afternoon, before which they would go through all the newspapers, watch the news bulletins and try to anticipate what the politicians would require. Ads would be prepared for radio, television, newspapers, magazines and billboards both nationally and in the different states, which meant producing material in as many as ten different languages. And the designers and copy-writers had to be mindful not just of their client's expectations but the limitations imposed by law. Paid political TV advertising is all-pervasive in the US, but banned completely in Britain. In India, as with so much else, the powerful Election Commission keeps a very close eye on what happens. Every proposed ad has to be sent to the EC for approval, and anything that amounts to a personal attack or to the use of religion or communal politics is quickly rejected. The agency produced 230 adverts in the course of the campaign and a number of others failed to make it on air.

'The Election Commission was getting sick of us,' recalled Piyush Pandey. 'They said, "Do you think you are the only party? Every morning you come up with fifty scripts." Some got rejected when we went a little overboard with our attacks against Congress. And there were some borderline cases. But we always prepared fifty more that could be used just in case. Sometimes we were on the edge, sometime we went over the edge and if they rejected them we accepted it with good grace.'

I thought back to an earlier conversation with Narendra Modi in which he expressed some scepticism about the value of professional advertising. 'They know how to market products but not ideas,' he had told me. In previous campaigns he had become frustrated. 'We saw that ninety per cent of the inputs came from our side and, rather than helping us, they were actually slowing us down. This made me realise that while we can hire the advertisement companies to support us, in a hugely diverse country like India, we ourselves are best positioned to know what matters to the people.' For the 2014 campaign things would have to be different, but an effective way of working was quickly established. 'We wouldn't know what was happening in places like Jamshedpur or Ranchi,' admitted Samrat Bedi, 'so the party would tell us what needs to be communicated. The briefs would come from the party – what are the problems which need to be highlighted in UP or in Bihar. So the "what" of the messaging came from the party, while "how" it needs to be done was our job.' Piyush Pandey would sometimes attend the planning meetings, although most of his work was done over the phone with Goyal. He was full of praise for how quickly decisions were made. 'They were speedy, energetic and decisive. Possibly it wouldn't have been like this if we had more time. So, in hindsight, thank God they called us late. It didn't give too much time for everybody to comment on what we were doing. We did it. We agreed. We moved on.'

Modi left most of the work to his Election Information Campaign Committee, although Piyush Goyal would regularly update him on what was going on. Pandey would meet

Modi when he wanted to film him for one of the TV spots or take a photo for a newspaper ad or a poster. He found him, as ever, highly focused and interested in the detail. He remembered one occasion when 'It was a little late, when we went to shoot him for the print campaign and the design of the ad was still to be finalised. We had not agreed some design elements with the local team.

'So Modi and I, we designed it together. How much green should there be and where should it come? He said we should have a touch of green. "Make the lotus half in green and half out". He was actually a part of the creative team. He was my art director.'

Pandey put his drink down and went in search of some of the storyboards he had worked on a few months earlier. He wanted to show me his favourite campaign, which didn't feature Modi at all and came close to the edge of the EC's rules on personal attacks. By chance the ICC World Twenty20 cricket championships took place in the middle of the elections. Pandey, who is a passionate cricket fan, saw an opening. He decided that in the middle of an exciting game a 'soapy TV commercial' wouldn't work, and besides, the broadcasters would allow them only twenty-second slots while the matches were being aired. So he designed a series of animated cartoons to be run in the short ad breaks, aimed particularly at younger viewers. His favourite showed the pitch just before the match with the umpire calling the two captains forward for the toss of a coin that would decide who went in to bat first. But there is only one captain. The caption read simply, 'A team without a captain doesn't win, this time vote Modi.' 'The youth went beserk,' he said. And he knew it had worked when the nineteen-year-old daughter of a friend told him the BJP was 'a cool party to vote for.'

If Piyush Pandey is the Don Draper of India, then Prasoon Joshi, who wrote the campaign anthem, is the Andrew Lloyd Webber. With dozens of Bollywood scores to his credit, his songs are instantly recognisable by most Indians. He's also a poet, Indi-pop lyricist and, more recently, chairman and CEO of another large advertising agency, McCann India.

Through McCann and its subsidiary TAG, Joshi made a team of twelve people available twenty-four hours a day to support the Modi campaign whenever required. Although O&M was the lead agency, TAG handled some of the regional campaigns, including in Punjab. We met over tea at one of Delhi's fashionable five-star hotels, where he told me that the theatrical impresario in him could see the value of connecting Modi with younger voters through the song and its video, but the hard-headed ad man believed that the BJP campaign connected with younger voters because it was willing to take their concerns seriously. 'People misunderstand the youth, not just in India, but also worldwide,' he told me. 'That's the reason a lot of youth campaigns fail. In my opinion, youth is not frothy and shallow. They have a sense of depth and a sense of honesty about things. The real difference between a young person and an older person is that the young person doesn't think about what can't be done, because nobody has told him about the limitations. A child thinks he can fly, that anything is possible.' Was he suggesting, I asked, that Modi was child-like in his belief that anything could be done with enough will to succeed? 'Exactly. That is what youth is all about. In India a lot of people say: "Use the word chilled, use the word yo, use the lingo of youth and you become cool"; no it's nothing to do with that. Youth is about not considering the limitations but what can be done. When you're building a brand you have to understand that. Young is a state of mind.

It's a thought process. So Modi is a very young 64-year-old or whatever.'

It struck me that Prasoon Joshi's analysis is every bit as valid in Britain, where political leaders have made fools of themselves by appearing in pop videos or wearing baseball caps to try to look trendy. Politics is not a brand like a soap powder or a mobile phone that can be jazzed up by fancy advertising. 'When you're building a brand you have to focus on the USP of the product,' he said, 'and to succeed in political advertising you have to go to the core, to the DNA. You can't rewrite it overnight, you have to be in synch with it. And that is why the philosophical voice of the BJP is so important.' When I challenged him with the thought that to many people the philosophy of the party was based on a rather old-fashioned Hindu nationalist ideology, he said that Modi's great achievement was to put what he called 'all that fuzzy stuff' behind him and concentrate on his development agenda. 'I hear you out that he has these cultural issues, he has this ideology, but overall what do I buy into, what does he do, he delivers. I have heard x, y, z but I have seen a, b and c. The distillation of Brand Modi is very modern, not at all fuddy-duddy, and very focused on what the youth of the country wants. The USP was forward looking.'

Tajinder Pal Singh Bagga, still in his twenties, agreed. When he dreamed up the first NaMo t-shirts they were decidedly untrendy. 'If we had wanted a good-looking person we would have gone to Bollywood.' He and his friends used social media to try to find out what people of their generation wanted from politics. 'The main issues that came up were corruption – everybody was frustrated with the corruption in India – then eighty per cent of girls said women's safety is the main issue, especially in Delhi. And the third one was education.' Bagga believes no other candidate could have connected with younger voters in the same way and that his age was never a factor. 'We were choosing a person who was good for the country, who has proved himself, and who people believe can change the nation.'

Those who saw Modi regularly were impressed by his willingness to listen to suggestions, no matter who they came from, even the youngest person in the room. It was the quality of the advice that counted. And while he may often seem young at heart, he has an older man's experience when it comes to organisation and team management. He's clearly not averse to a bit of creative tension within the various parts of his ecosystem in order to help bring out the best in people. And it was obvious that the advertising agencies recruited to help with the campaign were keeping a wary eye on each other. The sheer pace of the election helped prevent this rivalry causing too many problems and, as it moved into top gear from the end of April, the demands on the copywriters, the film-makers and the picture editors would become even more acute.

CHAPTER FOURTEEN
MOTHER GANGES

Four hundred years ago, so legend has it, a Brahmin poet by the name of Jagannatha broke the taboos of his caste and fell in love with a Muslim girl. As a devout Hindu he tried to persuade his elders that love was sacred and transcended all man-made divisions, but they refused to accept his pleadings. In despair he went to the holy River Ganges to seek the blessing of the Goddess Ganga. Sitting atop a flight of steps, he wrote fifty-two verses, and with each one the waters rose until eventually he was carried away. The beautiful lyrics spoke of his anguish as he wrote:

> I come to you as a child to his mother.
> I come as an orphan to you, moist with love.
> I come without refuge to you, giver of sacred rest.

It is a story rich with resonance for the India of today.

Narendra Modi went to the sacred city of Varanasi, on the banks of the Ganges, not in despair but full of hope. There were many good reasons for him to select Varanasi as the constituency to represent in parliament. It is in Uttar Pradesh, far and away the most electorally significant state in the country, and as the holiest of the seven sacred cities revered by Hindus, it sent the clearest possible message to his ultra-nationalist supporters, without causing serious offence to the more liberal voters and those of different religions – or none – who he needed to attract. As he arrived in the city on 24 April to file his nomination papers with the district magistrate he said, 'I don't think anyone has sent me here, or I have come here. I feel Mother Ganga has called me to Varanasi.'

The city attracts pilgrims, artists, scholars and tourists alike to its crowded and dirty streets. Funeral pyres are often lit on the banks of the Ganges and it is here that many Hindus bring the ashes of their loved ones to have them scattered into the sacred if filthy waters. Even Jawaharlal Nehru, India's first and avowedly secular, agnostic prime minister, asked to have a handful of his ashes cast into the river. On that day in April 2014, however, it was the man most likely to be India's fifteenth prime minister who was drawing the crowds. And what crowds they were. It was the largest turnout so far in the largest election on earth. The journey from the helipad that would normally have taken around thirty minutes lasted over four hours as the open-topped truck edged through the throng.

After submitting his papers, Modi spoke, and his words were unusually modest. He said he was overwhelmed by the love the people were showing him and that he wanted to serve the land and to see the waters cleaned. He singled out the city's weavers, almost all of them poor Muslims, who he said he hoped to support with modern technology, branding, design and marketing. Again for Modi it was an unusually short speech, just a few minutes long. The news channels broadcast it live, as they would with almost everything Modi said or did. And, not for the first time, it caused an unholy row. The reason Modi had kept it short and largely apolitical was that he knew he had chosen a day when voters in other parts of the country were already going to the polls. One BJP leader admitted to Rajdeep Sardesai of CNN-IBN, 'We knew that if we created a mega television event, the cameras would focus on Modi and we could capture eyeballs even while the voting was on.' Congress complained that the Election Commission rules had again been violated, prompting the BJP's spokesman, Prakash Javadekar, to respond that 'The Election Commission has not banned the filing of nominations on dates of voting . . . so what's wrong with the procession?' Congress shot back that by garlanding the statues of iconic Hindu leaders, Modi had flouted the ban on courting votes on the basis of religion. 'There's nothing religious about it, that's nationalism,' retorted Mr Javadekar. The speech might have been brief but, back in Delhi, Piyush Goyal, overseeing the BJP's own marketing, identified seven different messages that could be turned into short TV adverts.

That Modi would win Varanasi was never in doubt, although the leader of the upstart Aam Aadmi party (AAP), Arvind Kejriwal, had optimistically thrown his hat into the ring. The BJP had held the seat at the last election in 2009, although not with a very large majority, and this time around it had been flooded with enthusiastic volunteers from both the party and the RSS. According to the BJP campaign manager, Sunil Deodhar, 'Modi was going to win, so victory was not a target for us. Our target was the size of the lead. By what margin he wins. If Modi wins by 50,000 then it would be shameful for us. It would be almost like defeat.' To some of the young activists who had come to Varanasi to be part of the action, talk of a certain victory sounded like dangerous complacency. Pankaj Jangid was brought up in a Congress-supporting family. He had never been involved in politics but he was drawn to the anti-corruption movement in which Kejriwal had played such a prominent part (see Chapter Five). Yet it was for Modi and Modi alone – he corrected me when I suggested it was for Modi and the BJP – that he took a month's unpaid leave from his job in Delhi and travelled to Varanasi to campaign. He helped conduct surveys to see what issues most concerned the people. 'It was mainly cleanliness and unemployment. It is very dirty there and that's a major cause of concern for people.' At first he sensed that the AAP were doing better than expected. Their first survey in the district of Rohania showed 50% support for the BJP and 35–36% for the AAP, which Jangid thought was too close for comfort. 'People would sit on the *ghats* [flights of steps leading down to the river] in several small groups and discuss the political scenario. Initially mostly everybody was neutral but later, after the AAP did some negative campaigning that was against Modi, talking about the Godhra riots and all, we could see a shift in stance by some Muslim shopkeepers, etc.' Further surveys were more encouraging, but Jangid admits that they tampered with the results to make them appear worse than they really were before sending them to the party HQ. 'We tweaked the surveys because we thought that the BJP was not doing enough work in those areas.'

Sunil Deodhar, although always confident of victory, conceded that the party did have problems at first. The previous MP hadn't been universally popular and the BJP attracted some bad publicity, something he put down to dirty tricks by their opponents. 'Eggs were thrown at Mr Arvind Kejriwal when he visited the Kashi Vishwanath temple. Allegations were made that it was the BJP which did it and that harms the religious beliefs of people.' For the first time, Deodhar encountered young Muslims actively campaigning against the party and trying to persuade their Hindu friends not to vote for him either. 'They were saying he will divide this country and all the usual allegations because of the Gujarat riots.' The party calculated that the Godhra issue would have very little impact on Hindu voters but, as campaign manager, Deodhar made no effort to go after the votes of Muslims. 'Not at all,' he told me. Stressing that it was his personal opinion and not that of the party, he said, 'Varanasi is an orthodox city and the Hindus are staunch Hindus. In the last few days of every election it takes a communal turn. Hindus become Hindus and Muslims become Muslims and I knew this time it was going to happen. If a Hindu BJP leader goes among Muslims and tries to woo their votes then there will be a negative effect on Hindu votes. It is not that I have any hatred for them. I have much love for them, but winning an election is something different. If something is going to decrease my margin, why should I take that risk?'

What the campaign team did do was to make a special drive to attract female voters. 'In Uttar Pradesh very low voting of women used to take place,' said Deodhar. 'If you go to a village and organise a meeting only men will come. Women they will not allow. This time we decided to target women. Modi always speaks passionately about girls' education and the empowerment of women. If you go early morning to any village you will find all men, but if you go after 10.00 a.m., all the men would have gone to work in the fields or to the market or town and until the evening only ladies and youngsters are to be seen in the homes. So we would call women to our meetings to motivate them and tell them they should vote. That was the best time for campaigning.'

The TV journalist Rahul Kanwal had seen the impact Modi had on many women as he filmed his on-the-road reports, and noted that Modi himself was more than aware of it. 'He is convinced that he is the epitome of manhood to this whole universe of middle-aged Indian women who come from a very simple background. Not so much the western, liberated, urban, educated women who have travelled abroad, but to the typical middle-class, small-town, rural or urban woman, he's a rock star. He's got cult popularity. Because he doesn't smoke, he doesn't drink, he's very straight, very focused, very committed, hard-working, non-corrupt, and industrious. They love all that about him.'

In that respect, Varanasi was just like any other seat in the country. Modi was the party's strongest card with women voters, just as he was for men. 'The people were ahead of the party. The party was left behind. They just wanted Modi,' said one team member.

His face was everywhere, on posters and leaflets, but he didn't appear in his own constituency in person until nomination day. The judgement was taken that his time was better employed in more marginal areas. When he finally came to file his papers, everything changed. The crowds were vast, and while Congress accused the BJP of paying people to attend and bussing them in from outside the area, a common practice in Indian elections, in fact, said Deodhar, the reverse was true. 'People from adjacent districts were calling us saying they wanted to attend and we refused. We said please don't come because there will be insufficient place for you and I was worried about a stampede.'

It was the beginning of the end for the Kejriwal campaign too. There had been brawls between the younger BJP and AAP volunteers, according to Pankaj Jangid. 'They would come and say things like, if Modi comes to power then the poor will suffer, so then someone or the other would get annoyed and get in an altercation with them. We would intervene and say that this behaviour will also mean negative publicity for Modi and stop them.' After the nomination rally, however, the fight had gone out of the opposition. 'Even the AAP could sense the huge Modi wave that had developed, and eventually even they gave up. Some of the AAP workers were staying in a guesthouse opposite ours and they just left ten days before the polling.'

If the Election Commission could do nothing to stop Modi filing his nomination papers with a gargantuan entourage on a day when voters were going to the polls, two weeks later they would show that they were far from being a paper tiger. In the evening of 5 May, the BJP called up the local electoral officer and asked for permission for a rally in the Beniyabagh area of the city, which has a large Muslim population, on the following day. The go-ahead was given verbally and the party was asked to submit a written application first thing in the morning. During the following day, however, the officer, who was also a district magistrate, changed his mind. The venue was double booked, he claimed, and the intelligence bureau had warned of a security threat. The scene was set for a showdown. For the BJP, Arun Jaitley said that 'unbelievable' excuses had been put forward to deny a rally that was the candidate's right. 'This is not a banana republic,' he said. A party official who preferred not to be named warned that, 'We will have to compensate . . . in some form or the other.'

In conversation with me, Narendra Modi put the blame for the ban, as he did for most things, on the Congress Party. 'The Congress was trying to stop me through any means possible, and what they did at Varanasi proved this point. Can you even imagine that a prime-ministerial candidate is prevented from being able to give a speech in the same constituency where he was a candidate? However even with all this going on, I chose to stay silent and stay in line like a democratic leader should always do.' Well, up to a point. On the morning of 8 May, Modi tweeted an apology to Mother Ganges, who was not previously known to have a Twitter account, for being unable to perform a Hindu ritual that day. 'My profound apologies to Ganga Maa for not being able to perform Aarti today. Wish these people know that a Mother's love is above politics.' The schedule might have been changed but the venue had not. Modi flew into the helipad at the Banaras Hindu University at 5.30 p.m. There would be no 'rally', but he would instead simply drive to his campaign headquarters. Party leaders had been in Varanasi all day to protest about the decision of the Election Commission. 'Timid men can dwarf high offices,' said one. The chief election officer, V. S. Sampath, responded by requesting 'leaders to use proper discourse while referring to a constitutional body like the EC.' Arun Jaitley was still an angry man. 'India is not under British rule,' he said. 'It is a free country. To drive on the roads of Varanasi we don't need any damn permission from this returning officer. Just like you can drive, Mr Modi can also drive on the roads.'

Inevitably, after all the publicity for the row, the crowds were as huge as ever. Party estimates put the figure in excess of 100,000 people. *The Hindu* reported that 'As his convoy arrived, led by a rally of motorcycles with party supporters, the slogan-shouting reached a crescendo. Paramilitary forces struggled to control the crowd from breaching the security cordon.' It took Modi over five hours to drive six kilometres. Tensions had been raised to such a pitch that many in the throng were still furious, and some scuffles broke out, only to be captured by the TV cameras. True to his word, Modi didn't make a speech, but for another whole day he was the running story on all the news channels.

Advertising guru Piyush Pandey had seen the events unfold on TV, so when the phone rang he was not surprised to find the other Piyush – Goyal – on the line. He wanted an urgent ad prepared for broadcast within twenty-four hours. Goyal was still fired up with a sense of injustice. He approved a doubling of the advertising budget for the day and ordered a short film that would reflect the passions of the occasion. 'The message was to be around, "we will not stop, whatever happens",' he told me. Pandey duly obliged, working long into the night to complete the hardest-hitting spot of the whole campaign. At 4.31 a.m. he attached the video to a WhatsApp message and pressed send. Three months later, as I sat around the dinner table with Goyal and his wife, he pulled out his phone. He had kept the message and passed me the device so I could watch it. Even without understanding the Hindi commentary, I could tell immediately that it was powerful stuff. The young men in the crowds looked threatening and the musical overlay was like something from the trailer to a horror movie. He told me that the key section of the voice-over, delivered in a portentous tone, translated as, 'We are unstoppable, this fire will not stop. Greetings to the citizens, this is a storm of change.' I couldn't help but feel that it was more reminiscent of scenes from a Hitler Youth rally than a democratic protest.

After a few hours' sleep, Goyal awoke and realised the ad was a big mistake. 'I realised the first idea was not a good one. We could not end on an aggressive note,' he said. 'Now was the time to go more softly, to bring in inclusiveness and talk about the love and affection shown by the people. So I called up Piyush and asked him to make the ad again. After three or four iterations, the script was finalised at 1.00 p.m.' This version, which he also showed me, had some of the same footage, but the intimidating music had gone and the tone sounded much more positive. 'I got a WhatsApp message at 5.45 p.m.

saying that the ad had been approved by the Election Commission and at 6.30 p.m. it broke on TV.' He had missed the deadline he had set for himself, but only by thirty minutes.

By tradition nobody is ever denied the blessing of Mother Ganges and she had certainly been good to Narendra Modi. He would go on to win the Varanasi seat with a huge majority of 371,784 over Arvind Kejriwal who was in second place. Modi had not gone to the sacred city to win one parliamentary seat, however, but to help secure victory in enough other constituencies to enable the BJP to govern alone. And to do that, the state of Uttar Pradesh, with Varanasi in its south-easterly corner, was critical. It is a truism of Indian politics that the road to power in Delhi leads through Uttar Pradesh. It has by far the largest number of seats of any state, eighty, with the runner-up, Maharashtra, having just forty-eight by comparison. Without winning in UP, and winning big, Modi was not on his way to the prime minister's residence at 7 Race Course Road. Nothing, but nothing, could be left to chance.

CHAPTER FIFTEEN
THE ONLY WAY IS UP

The general election of 2014 turned Amit Shah from just another politician, albeit a controversial one, into a legend. When the campaign started, Shah, a former home minister in Gujarat, was out on bail facing serious criminal charges relating to the deaths of prisoners who had been shot dead by the police. After the elections he was made president of the BJP, and was widely regarded as the second most important politician in the country. The charges against him were dropped and he was free to do what he does best: advance the political interests of Narendra Modi.

Amit Shah is perhaps the only person that Modi trusts completely. It is no exaggeration to say that, without him, Modi would not hold the power he does today. Shah gave him his majority in parliament. Or rather, the voters of Uttar Pradesh gave him his majority, and it was Shah who made sure that they did.

At first sight, the prospects for the BJP in the state did not look good. At the previous election in 2009, the party had won only ten of the eighty seats in UP with just 17.5% of the vote. In 2014, under Shah's direction, the party took all but seven of the seats, a breath-taking turnaround that greatly exceeded the expectations of everybody, including Shah himself. Professor Zoya Hasan has followed the politics of UP closely for many years. She told me that the whole election hinged on that one state and the significance of the result there could not be overestimated. 'The fact that the BJP got seventy-three out of eighty seats really turned the election. It was being projected in the middle of this enormously long campaign that they would get up to a maximum of forty seats. Now they got thirty-five more than that and it gave them the majority in parliament.' The journalist Aatish Srivastava was brought up in Varanasi and watched the campaign in his home state closely. 'When I came back from UP at the end of the elections, I went on air saying that I really doubt if they will cross forty seats in Uttar Pradesh, but they won seventy-three. That was unbelievable.'

UP is not merely huge in terms of geography and population, but also hugely complex with regard to its demographics, caste and political affiliations. The undercurrents of shifting loyalties were all but impossible for anybody to track with precision, so it was not surprising that both scholars and journalists with an intimate knowledge of the state failed to spot the scale of what was going on.

Exactly how Amit Shah turned the situation around will be the subject of academic scrutiny and political debate for years to come. I would have liked to ask him myself, but he is a man who is notoriously tight-lipped and often wary of journalists and writers. I sat outside his office on three separate occasions, only to be told he was in a meeting or running a high temperature and too ill to see me at the time we had agreed. On subsequent occasions he was always away, busy trying to repeat his success in the by-elections and regional polls that followed hard on the heels of the general election victory. I submitted my questions by email, as I was asked to do, but ten weeks later I had yet to receive a reply. I have no idea how frank he would have been if we had ever met. He is a master at sticking to the party line, as he should be in the job that he holds.

What I was able to do was to consult some of those who worked on the inside of the campaign, and they were remarkably frank so long as what they told me was 'off the record'. By reputation, Shah, like his master, never forgets and rarely forgives. The party line, as might be expected, is that voters in UP were drawn to Modi's positive, development-driven agenda, just like those elsewhere in the country, and rewarded the party accordingly. That is part of the story, certainly, but, according to campaign insiders, as well those doing their best to analyse what went on, only a part.

So important was UP to Modi's calculations that he appointed Shah to oversee the state as early as June 2013. Uttar Pradesh was not one of those places where the battle was a straight fight with the Congress Party. Congress had traditionally had a strong base there, and it was the home state of the Nehru-Gandhi dynasty, but had been in decline for many years. Regional parties that drew their support largely from specific castes were now dominant. In the 2012 state legislative elections, when the BJP slipped yet further to a 15% vote share and just forty-seven of the 403 assembly seats, the largest party had been the Samajwadi Party (SP), which secured 224 seats. Second was the Bahujan Samaj Party (BSP), which had previously governed the state under its combative and colourful leader, Mayawati, one of those high-profile figures who is known only by her first name. Both parties had their roots among the poorest communities. The BSP drew its support largely from the Dalits, once known as the untouchables, and had many Muslim voters. The SP was particularly strong with the 'other backward classes' (OBCs).

UP is not one of India's economic powerhouses. Eight out of the fourteen Indian prime ministers before Modi had come from the state, but it had made comparatively little material progress in that time. Dr A. K. Verma, who lectures in politics at Christ Church College in Kanpur, wrote that, in UP, 'Politics is greatly influenced by the primordial affiliations of caste and religion. In a state where the fruits of development have not reached people even after more than half a century since Independence, they are forced to look to their own caste leaders for petty favours of daily life.' If Indian politics was to be recast, as Modi hoped, there would be no greater challenge to doing so than in Uttar Pradesh.

When Amit Shah landed at the airport at Lucknow, UP's capital, on 12 June 2013, he immediately went to the party's offices and called together the BJP's local leaders. Although he didn't say so in as many words, worrying about the demographics was his problem, sorting out the party on the ground was theirs. 'You have to concentrate on the booths,' he was reported as telling them. 'That is where it will all start and that is where everything will fall into place.' Booth-level workers were thin on the ground and the call went out to recruit more and bring in outside volunteers, not just in the big cities like Lucknow and Varanasi, but across the state. There were to be no 'no-go' areas. According to Poornima Joshi, political editor of the *Hindu Business Line*, even the party's state president, Laxmikant Vajpayee, agreed to adopt a booth by way of setting an example.

One insider described for me the party's organisational structure as being 'in complete disarray'. Shah reconstituted all the committees at booth level 'with precise caste representation', to make sure local voters would be hearing from somebody who understood their concerns. The RSS was called upon to provide its own grassroots support and, not insignificantly, to keep an eye on the party appointees and make sure they were doing what was expected of them. First priority was given to those seats that the BJP had lost by a margin of 50,000 votes or fewer, which Shah considered eminently winnable. But that could only be the beginning. He now had to go for those places where his party had, until now, been little more than also-rans.

The most significant breakthrough came with the announcement that Narendra Modi was to be the BJP prime minister-designate. And when it became known that he would also be contesting from a UP constituency, Varanasi, the tectonic plates really started to shift. One consequence of UP's relative poverty was that a disproportionate number of its people travelled outside the state to find work. Many of these economic migrants went to Gujarat and came home with stories of better roads, 24-hour electricity and the chance to earn a decent living. When Modi spoke of his development agenda and claimed that his record in Gujarat proved that he could deliver, the first-hand testimony of people who had been there and seen it for themselves made it more than just election rhetoric. In this way the talk of economic development appealed not just to younger voters, who hoped for a better life than their parents, or to the business community, but also to some of the poorest in society.

It was not just what Modi said but how and where he said it that seemed to have special resonance in UP. At a rally in Gorakhpur on 23 January, Modi asked the crowd, 'How many hours do you get electricity?' They responded with a cacophony of shouts along the lines of, 'We don't get power.' Modi reminded them that in Gujarat there was 24-hour electricity, and taunted the leader of the SP state government, Akhilesh Yadav, saying he would never be able to turn UP into Gujarat. 'You need a 56-inch chest to do that.' Because of its significance, the state got more than its fair share of mega-rallies, which, as they did everywhere, saw people travelling huge distances just for the chance to hear him speak. UP was also a prime target for the hologram machines. Shah identified around 35,000 so-called 'dark villages' in the state, places where there was often no television to be found and where it was possible people were all but oblivious to the fact that an election was going on. The lucky ones got to see Modi in 3D, and in places with no electricity supply of their own the impact of that was beyond electric. In others, specially prepared videos would be shown with the help of generators brought in for the purpose. Shah gave the project a distinctly messianic name: *Modi Aane Wala Hai* ('Modi's arrival is imminent'). He asked the CAG team to plan for some 400 GPS-enabled video vans equipped with 54-inch LCD screens to take Modi's speeches into the dark zones.

The GPS was not just to help the vans find their way, but also to enable the war room in the state capital, Lucknow, to monitor their progress. One campaign insider explained why to the dnaindia.com website. 'Normally, party workers turn up at the party office in the morning before leaving for campaigning. But few of them actually end up doing any ground work as they are used to resting at a place of their comfort,' said a party leader, on condition of anonymity. 'In the evening, these workers paint a rosy picture of all the hard work they put in while campaigning the entire day. With GPS monitoring, their movement will be under constant watch. Any attempt to mislead the party leadership after the installation of these GPS device will be futile.'

As the vans fanned out across the state, children and adults alike were showered with campaign goodies like flags, t-shirts and cardboard Modi masks. It was no accident that much of it was in the party colour, saffron, which carries great religious significance for Hindus. One volunteer recalled that 'There was a huge craze for caps because the colour of the caps was saffron. So if a cap fell down, people would pick it up, bow their heads and rub it against their forehead and then keep it. It was the first time I saw such a thing. There was also a huge demand for the saffron scarf, which was always in short supply and we often had to order more supplies.'

Modi had something else that, although he likes to play down its electoral significance, was crucial to Amit Shah's strategy: his caste. By dint of his birth, Modi is an OBC, and 'other backward classes' make up over 40% of the population of UP. The Dalits comprise another 21%. The upper castes, where BJP support was traditionally strongest, are around 19%. Muslims, who fall outside the Hindu caste system, account for 18.5%. Whether he liked it or not, politics based on communal identity was ingrained in the way elections had always been fought in UP, perhaps more so than in any other state in the country. When I asked Modi about it he asked rhetorically, 'Why would one want to target caste politics?'

The answer is in the arithmetic. He insisted that he was directing his campaign instead at the young, first-time voters, and women in particular, which left 'no room for caste politics', but in UP at least the facts on the ground tell a more nuanced story. One person who watched the campaign from the inside said, 'Ultimately a calibrated effort towards the amalgamation of Mr Modi's OBC status and his development-centric campaign was able to break the complex matrix of UP's castes and sub-castes.' Academic observers reached the same conclusion. According to Dr A. K. Verma, the BJP were deliberately cracking the caste code, and 'by bringing Modi and highlighting his backward caste, the BJP . . . sought to revisit and redefine the OBC discourse', which had previously been dominated by the caste-based parties like the SP. Professor Zoya Hasan agreed. 'Have they have been able to cast away caste? No, not really. Or to do away with identity politics? No. In UP I think it was development and identity politics. It was development and Hindutva. So development may have been the text but Hindutva was definitely the sub-text.' Modi never talked about Hindu nationalist ideology in so many words, but in UP, right from the decision to stand in the sacred city of Varanasi, the message was conveyed in other ways.

It is one thing to put up a candidate from a particular caste and hope that others from the same background will be more inclined to vote for him. All parties do that, and the selection of who should fight which seats clearly took caste into account. It is another thing to stir up antagonism between castes or religions in the hope of reaping the electoral benefit. According to Professor Hasan, the BJP were guilty of just that. 'To say that the BJP campaign was only about development would be turning a blind eye to the division of labour which has always been a part and parcel of the BJP. That is to say that you always have top leaders who talk about development and so on, but you also have any number of other people, including the RSS and the whole assortment of organisations that are attached and affiliated to them, who do work on the ground which is divisive, communal and polarising, something they are continuing to do to this day.'

Inter-communal violence has besmirched Uttar Pradesh for decades. Attempts to apportion blame for the attacks, murders and rioting are often made all but impossible by conflicting reports of what actually happened and who started it, but it is fair to say that responsibility is shared by Hindus and Muslims and that nobody's hands are clean. The outbreak that followed the murder of a Muslim boy and two Hindu youths from the Jat population close to the city of Muzaffarnagar on 27 August 2013 was one of the worst for many years. In the subsequent rioting, which continued into September, more than sixty people were killed, and tens of thousands were displaced from their homes. Rajesh Verma, a journalist working for the IBN7 TV channel, died after being shot in the chest. For the first time since the rioting that followed the destruction of the Babri Masjid mosque at Ayodhya in 1992, the army had to be called into UP to try to quell the violence. It was inevitable, so close to the election, that the events around Muzaffarnagar would take on a political dimension. This was western UP, where the BJP had never been strong. The governing Samajwadi Party was at the forefront of the accusations but members of the BJP were also implicated. 'Murky politics are already at work,' wrote the London-based *The Economist* magazine. 'A triple murder sparked the latest violence . . . but low-level politicians stirred up fury at public meetings. Others failed, deliberately or not, to stop anger spreading. Some victims say politicians paid village headmen to start killing. On 18 September a court in Muzaffarnagar ordered the arrest of 16 politicians and community leaders for inciting violence. Critics of the opposition Bharatiya Janata Party (BJP), such as local Muslims, warn that a campaign has begun to fire up Hindu supporters.'

It was described for me by one well-informed insider from the Modi campaign as 'the watershed incident, which changed the political landscape of Uttar Pradesh.' He claimed that, 'The hostility between Jats and Muslims yielded rich electoral dividends for the BJP because the party immediately projected the local riot as a bigger battle between Hindus and Muslims. The caste identity of Jats was consequently merged into the larger Hindu identity, and the violence against the Jats was projected as an attack on all Hindus. And the BJP positioned itself as the only party willing to fight the discrimination suffered by Hindus.' According to this analysis, the previous political loyalties were fragmented to the detriment of the regional caste-oriented parties and to the immense benefit of the BJP.

Aatish Srivastava watched the political developments first hand. 'We went to Muzaffarnagar. BJP workers were there, BJP leaders were there, and there were some fringe elements who incited passions, who wanted some kind of defensive reaction to creep in because the BJP never had a good track record in western UP, with only stray seats here and there,' he told me. There was no evidence that the party had been behind the violence, he said, but 'when it got sparked off, there were local leaders of the BJP there who were continuously looking out for such an opportunity. The opportunity came to them and they used it.' The BJP even went so far as to announce that three politicians who had been named in connection with fanning the violence would be among their candidates at the election.

Shah himself was accused of exploiting the issue as polling got closer. He visited Muzaffarnagar in early April and was reported as referring to the killing of Hindus and saying the election was 'about revenge and protecting honour.' According to the *Times of India*, Shah was heard saying, 'This not just another election. This is the time to avenge the insult meted out to our community.' For the BJP, Mukhtar Abbas Naqvi responded that Shah had merely been criticising the UP state government for maligning the victims of the rioting. 'It is not the question whether a person is Hindu or Muslim. It is about rubbing salt instead of medicine on the backs of those who suffered in those riots,' he said. 'Then they said that the people living in camps are not the victims of the riots and that they are the supporters of political parties. This is nothing but an insult to the people. Therefore this insult has to be paid back.' A few days later, however, the Election Commission officially banned both Amit Shah and a senior SP leader, Azam Khan, from addressing any more public meetings, accusing them of making 'highly inflammatory speeches'. The BJP called it a 'monstrosity of judgement'. But Shah was in trouble again in early May when he referred to Azamgarh in eastern UP, which has a large Muslim population, as a 'base of terrorists'. The SP said it was further evidence of the BJP's communal and anti-Muslim politics, while the BJP said he had been referring to the lack of development in the area.

While all this was going on, Narendra Modi was careful to ensure that no accusations of divisive politics could be levelled at him directly, although he was repeatedly criticised for not condemning the comments of Shah and others. And he did make a point of reminding voters of his lower caste background as the campaign drew to a close. When Rahul Gandhi's sister, Priyanka, accused him of 'low-level politics', he said, 'You can insult Modi as much as you like, you can hang him. But do not insult the lower caste'. He was content to be seen as the defender of the lower castes, but not as an apologist for the politics of caste or religious identity, which he firmly attributed to the Congress Party. He spoke of wanting Muslims in places like UP and neighbouring Bihar state to be as rich as they were in Gujarat. 'They should have the Koran in one hand and a computer in the other,' he said. When asked why he had once refused to wear a Muslim skull cap, when he was famous for wearing regional and tribal headgear when campaigning round the country, he again turned it on Congress, telling India TV 'I have never seen Gandhi, Patel or Nehru wearing such a skull cap. Indian politics has deteriorated. They can do anything for appeasement. I believe in respecting the traditions of all religions. But at the same time, I have to respect my own tradition as well, although I respect all traditions. I can't hoodwink people by wearing such skull caps. But I believe in taking action against those who show disrespect to other's caps.'

In the last few days of campaigning in UP, Modi met Colonel Nizamuddin, a Muslim war veteran who was said to be 114 years old. Modi touched his feet as a mark of respect and received his blessing. Sunil Deodhar, Modi's campaign manager, had personally called Amit Shah to ask if the colonel could be invited. Deodhar said, 'The strategy was to show that Mr Modi is a nationalist and respects people who have given sacrifices even if they are Muslims.'

Modi would not be the first political leader in the world to look the other way while others in his party were getting involved in dubious political manoeuvres. And the fact that the BJP indulged in caste-based politics in Uttar Pradesh does not mean that Modi was insincere when he said he wanted political debate in India to be about what people thought, not who their parents were. It merely shows that he, or Amit Shah on his behalf, recognised that the country was not yet at that stage. As prime minister, Modi has continued to call for an end to political violence. At his Red Fort speech on Independence Day he spoke eloquently of the 'poison of casteism and communalism'. 'How long will these evils continue?' he asked. 'Whom does it benefit? We have had enough of fights. Many have been killed. Friends, look behind you and you will find that nobody has benefited from it. Except in casting a slur on Mother India, we have done nothing.'

Modi's enemies in the 2014 election were not the Muslims, they were the leaders of the Congress Party. This was as true in Uttar Pradesh as anywhere else in the country, and he was more than ready to wade into the Gandhi family's final stronghold in UP to prove the point.

CHAPTER SIXTEEN
RALLY DRIVER

From two and a half months from early March until the very last person had cast his or her vote, the Modi machine was in overdrive. It was, in the words of one BJP leader, designed to be 'a 360-degree campaign'. Whichever way you turned and wherever you looked, you would see Modi. In the morning newspaper, on the billboards beside the road while driving or walking to work, in every nook and crevice of the internet and all over the television screens in the evening. Close your eyes and he was there on the radio or in the chatter on the streets or in the markets. Pick up your mobile and don't be surprised to find an SMS or a WhatsApp message from him waiting to be read.

With the finishing line in sight and the competition already left somewhere far behind in the dust, the man in the driving seat never once took his foot off the accelerator. Modi was now doing four or five big rallies a day before flying home to do another of his 3D extravaganzas or a TV interview or both. The requests from state and constituency level party bosses flooded in to the office of Sanjay Bhavsar, whose job it was to manage the schedule. Every aspiring candidate across the country was hoping for a visit. 'It was believed that if Mr Modi did a rally in any seat, the BJP will positively win it,' said Dr Subhas Sarkar, who was running in West Bengal.

Dr Sarkar's wish was granted on 4 May. His constituency of Bankura was down as the first stop. The police and paramilitary commandos from the National Security Guard (NSG) had already checked out the venue. The barricades were in place to control the crowd, the stage was ready, the PA system and microphones had all been tested and then tested again. The massive gantries had been erected to guarantee the best pictures would be captured by the BJP's own cameramen, to be passed on to the TV networks. Two dozen local dignitaries had already been told they would be seated alongside the man they were all waiting to see. The loudspeaker vans had been out, and party workers and volunteers despatched far and wide armed with posters, leaflets and banners to alert people to the impending event. Others were busy on social media, creating a buzz and asking for suggestions to go into the speech. As many as 200 vehicles were ready to transport people to the venue if they couldn't get there under their own steam.

Modi was out of bed, as usual, by 5.00 a.m. The rally was due to start at 7.40 a.m. Bankura is a small district without an airport of its own, so first Modi flew by chartered plane to Bokaro Steel City in neighbouring Jharkhand, accompanied by just his personal secretary and a doctor. From there he took a helicopter to the Bankura Stadium, where a bullet-proof car was waiting for him. Thousands of people lined the route, hoping to catch a glimpse of him on the short drive to the stage.

Modi got out of the car and put his arm around Dr Sarkar's shoulder. 'Let's go,' he said. They could hear the chants of 'Modi, Modi' from the crowd that had been estimated at 150,000 people from Bankura and the neighbouring constituency of Bishnupur. Back at the office in Gandhinagar, the team were ready to start tweeting. 'Shri Narendra Modi addresses rallies in West Bengal @narendramodi' was the first. Then a more personalised, 'I came to Bengal a few days ago and I understood the direction of the wind. BJP is going to win here. Shri Modi in WB @narendramodi'. Sitting close to the stage, ten volunteers had the social media sites divided between them, ready to go to work as soon as Modi began speaking.

As always Modi started with some local references, and when, as now, he was in territory controlled by another party, a dig or two at the local leadership. Mamta Banerjee had split from the Congress Party eighteen years earlier to form her own party, and had been West Bengal's chief minister since winning a landslide election in 2011. Mamta, known popularly as 'Didi' (elder sister), had called Modi a paper tiger. That was too easy for a performer like Modi. 'I am surprised, Didi, why are you afraid of a paper tiger?' he asked mockingly. 'What will happen if a real tiger comes before you?' It was good knockabout stuff and the crowd loved it. Then it was time for the serious business. He accused Didi's government of being soft on illegal immigration from across the border in Bangladesh. 'They must go back. They are robbing the youths of India of their livelihood,' he thundered.

From Bankura, Modi flew by helicopter straight to Asansol, also in West Bengal. Here the BJP was fielding a high-profile singer, Babul Supriyo, as its candidate. The rally had been planned only five days before when Modi and his team realised that the state, where they had picked up just one seat in 2009, could have some rich pickings this time around. Nirmal Karmakar, the rally coordinator, said that, despite the short notice, 'This was the biggest rally which ever took place in Asansol.' Karmakar put the crowd at over 250,000, and Modi suggested that political pundits who wanted to do 'political weather forecasting' should take note. He tweeted, 'Amazing rally in Asansol. Urged people to elect Babul Supriyo, a youngster devoted to serving people of Bengal.' By contrast

Modi accused Didi's administration of vote-rigging and of letting down the Muslim voters she claimed to want to help. Muslims in Gujarat, he said, were better off, and many more could therefore afford to make the annual Haj pilgrimage to Mecca. In response, her party, the TMC, filed a complaint against him to the Election Commission, accusing him of seeking votes in the name of religion and trying to spread communal disharmony.

After speaking for thirty-five minutes and leaving controversy in his wake, Modi was back in his helicopter and heading for the airport and a plane to Uttar Pradesh. His next stop, Bhadohi, was again in a remote spot, so a second helicopter was waiting for him as soon as he landed at Varanasi. The rally almost didn't happen. The police had been worried that the field was too close to a main road and to overhead power cables, while the landowner had come under political pressure not to allow it. The local coordinator, Santosh Pandey, had managed to overcome all the obstacles, however, and with the help of hundreds of volunteers and as many as three thousand buses and cars, a massive crowd had been assembled. It was impossible to get independent estimates of just how big it was but, according to Pandey, 'About 350,000 people turned up, which was at least three times as many as the local BJP functionaries had expected.' Before the helicopter arrived he was warned to make sure the sound quality from the public address system was as good as possible. The schedule was starting to take a toll on Modi's voice and he had a sore throat.

Modi got to the field at 14.20 to fire the next salvo in what Amit Shah had dubbed 'The Battle of Purvanchal'. Purvanchal is a geographical rather than a political area, although there are those who would like it to become a state in its own right. It was one of the most hotly contested parts of UP, with

Modi's cavalcade jammed the streets of Varanasi in Uttar Pradesh after he was refused permission for a rally.

The Modi mask and the BJP's Lotus emblem were trademarks of the campaign.

Modi gave few interviews. Journalists had to make do with look-alikes.

Voters in Amethi. The BJP accused Rahul Gandhi of neglecting his constituents.

Modi motivated younger supporters across the country.

Modi needed two helicopters to ferry him to all his rallies.

The newly-formed AAP had passionate supporters but failed to break through at the election.

With Hugh Jackman at the Global Citizen Festival, Central Park.

Headlining at Madison Square Garden, New York.

Welcoming President Obama on Republic Day. Modi's suit had his own name sewn 1,000 times into the pinstripes.

A selfie with Tony Abbott, Melbourne Cricket Ground.

With Chinese President Xi Jinping at Mahatma Gandhi's ashram in Gujarat.

Sonia and Rahul Gandhi, leaders of the Congress Party. They held their seats but the party suffered huge losses.

Dr Manmohan Singh, prime minister 2004–14. The first Sikh to hold the job.

Amit Shah, Modi's closest colleague who helped him win a majority in parliament.

Arvind Kejriwal, leader of the AAP. Activist turned politician.

'Strength,' said Mahatma Gandhi, 'comes from an indomitable will'

Narendra Modi prides himself on his appearance and always makes time for the camera.

With the author at the prime minister's residence, 7 Race Course Road, Delhi.

Congress, the AAP and the main regional parties, the SP and BSP, all in the running. The rally, and the one that would follow that same afternoon, were crucial elements in Shah's strategy for the state. Rahul Gandhi was now back in the cross-hairs. Modi accused him of visiting poor families only so he could have his photograph taken with them. 'Like people go to the Taj Mahal, get a photo clicked and then upload it on WhatsApp, so Rahul . . . each year visits the house of one poor family along with a team of photographers and cameramen so that he can get a good photograph with a child that can be telecast on television,' he claimed. Things were getting a bit personal. 'Only the poor will understand the pain of being poor,' he added for good measure. In one sound bite, Modi had reminded the crowd both of his own humble upbringing and the allegations of corruption against Congress. He revived a line he'd used before, that while he might have sold tea on the railways, at least he didn't sell the country.

The crowds at his final rally of the day in Allahabad had been waiting for hours by the time his helicopter finally appeared in the sky above them at 15.30. He couldn't hear them above the noise of the rotor blades, but from the window he could see them waving and pointing in his direction. A sea of saffron flags and scarves was still visible even as the dust swirled around the helicopter as it landed. Clutching their machine guns to their chests, the NSG soldiers escorted him swiftly towards the stage. The rally coordinator, Ranjit Singh, was part of the welcoming committee. 'While receiving Mr Modi at the helipad I handed over a letter to him, mentioning the burning local issues and requesting him to address them in his rally speech.' Modi cast his eyes over the contents and mentally absorbed them. Minutes later he was at the microphone and slotted in Mr Singh's suggestions about help for local industry as he compared the BJP promise to deliver economic development with the failure of the other parties that had been in power in the state or at the centre. Back in Gandhinagar, Dr Hiren Joshi was watching it all on television and prepared a final Facebook posting to sum up the message to the voters of UP. On behalf of his boss, he wrote, 'Earlier today I addressed large rallies in Bhadohi & Allahabad (UP). I am sad to hear complaints of rigging & violence in parts of UP. EC should ensure such instances don't happen in coming phases. Instead of improving people's lives in UP, Cong leaders go to homes of poor for photo-ops. People will punish them for such insensitivity. SP & BSP ruled UP for years. Cong is in power in Delhi but none of these parties presented their work record to the people. Shameful.'

Modi arrived back at the airport at 18.20 and headed straight for the Gandhinagar campaign headquarters. He posed for photographs with party workers and CAG volunteers before going to the studio for the latest 3D rally. For forty minutes he was beamed to hundreds more locations, most of them in the states of UP and Bihar. This evening, however, the journalists were monitoring what he said with only half an ear. They had a much bigger story to write. The BJP had let it be known that he would be speaking the following day in Amethi, the constituency of Rahul Gandhi himself. Did this mean, they speculated, that Modi thought he could win even here, and so politically decapitate the heir to the Gandhi dynasty? Back in his residence, Modi was on the telephone to get the assessment of his own people on the ground. If it could be done, he was going to give it his very best shot. Political convention dictated that party leaders didn't attack each other on their home territories, but Modi had never allowed convention to get in his way.

The decision to go to Amethi was taken only after a visit to the seat on 2 May by Amit Shah. Until then the plan had been to bombard the area with hologram rallies. Five each had been scheduled for the 2nd, 3rd and 4th. What Shah heard when he met the local leaders persuaded him that there was the chance of pulling off the biggest upset of the election, but only if Modi were to go there in person. Every angle of the 360-degree campaign was activated at short notice. The advertising executive Piyush Pandey was in Goa where his mother-in-law was unwell. This time Piyush Goyal, the campaign information chief, had to resort to some verbal arm-twisting. 'We need you,' he told Pandey. 'We will always be in your debt and I will make it up to you.' A camera crew was sent to Amethi to get the pictures needed to illustrate the theme of the advert, that even with Rahul as the MP, the city had seen no development. The charge that the Gandhis took their supporters for granted and thought they could just bank their votes was reflected in the film's title, 'Amethi, a vote bank for Congress'. Pandey found the whole process exhilarating. 'Piyush Goyal sat with me in Ahmedabad till six in the morning with many other colleagues of ours,' he told me. 'There were still people shooting the footage in Amethi and at the same time we were writing the script in Ahmedabad and editing it.'

When Modi awoke at 5.00 a.m., Pandey and Goyal were still hard at work in the video suite. They all knew that while the campaign had seen some highly memorable days, this promised to be one of the biggest of them all. What none of them could anticipate was that their audacious assault on 'Prince' Rahul's fiefdom would come close to being overshadowed by an unnecessary row of the BJP's own making.

Modi left Ahmedabad airport on a private plane at 8.10 a.m. The whole day would be spent in Uttar Pradesh as, for much of the state, it was the last day of campaigning. He arrived at his first stop, Ambedkar Nagar, at 10.20 and went straight to the rally site. It was clear that he was already preparing himself for his full-frontal assault on the Gandhis later in the day. The warm-up was a teasing remark directed at Sonia. Mrs Gandhi had accused Modi of behaving as if he'd already won. 'Sonia says that Modi considers himself as PM. So what should I say?' He answered his own question by quoting a Hindi saying, '*Aap ke muh mein ghee-shakkar*' (May your words come true).

So far, so good. It was a twenty-minute flight by helicopter to the next venue, Faizabad, less than five kilometres from the disputed temple site at Ayodhya. The BJP hopeful for the seat, Lallu Singh, met him and accompanied him on stage, as so many candidates before him had done so. As soon as they appeared together in front of the crowd and the cameras, the journalists back in their newsrooms knew they had an unexpected story. The backdrop featured a huge picture of Lord Ram, one of the most sacred figures in the Hindu tradition. The use of religious images is explicitly forbidden in Indian elections, but with Lord Ram's head even larger than his own in the TV pictures, Modi said that the people of Faizabad should allow a lotus to bloom in 'the land of Shri Ram.' He avoided any reference to his manifesto pledge to restore the Hindu temple at Ayodhya, but invoked Lord Ram's name again when he said: 'This is the land of Lord Ram where people believed in "*pran jaye par vachan na jaye*" (one may lose one's life but one cannot break a promise). Can you pardon those who broke their promises?'

Modi's opponents immediately cried foul and the Election Commission launched an investigation. BJP sources let it be known that Modi had been 'furious' when he saw the image.

One party functionary, Harshvardhan Singh, said, 'the decision of having the Lord Ram backdrop was taken by the local district unit without the knowledge of the state or central party headquarters'. None of the images or the text of Modi's remarks appeared on his official website, but nor did he apologise; the picture of Modi alongside Lord Ram immediately became one of the most controversial and talked about of the whole campaign. Modi might have had good reason to be cross. The images his team had planned to dominate the news agenda were of him striding unapologetically into Rahul Gandhi's back yard.

The actress turned politician Smriti Irani had been told she had to go to Amethi and become its candidate just twenty-five days before the voters in the constituency were due to go to the polls. She had to start almost from scratch. There was no real BJP organisation on the ground and at the previous election the party had won fewer than 40,000 votes, while Rahul Gandhi had secured more than ten times as many, 464,195. 'It's the heart of the Gandhi family,' she told me, 'but I saw at first hand what people wanted and they wanted Modi.' On 5 May they got him. The Piyush Pandey video had been playing from the stage even before Modi's helicopter appeared and came in to land on the specially made helipad 500 metres from the stage. He emerged in an immaculate white kurta, holding a special 'manifesto for Amethi', promising development in place of neglect.

Smriti Irani spoke first. Her own starring role as an actress had been as Tulsi in the hit soap opera, *Kyunki Saas Bhi Kabhi Bahu Thi* (Because a mother-in-law was once a daughter-in-law too). She was still bristling after Rahul's sister, Priyanka, had responded with a dismissive 'Who?' when asked about Irani's candidature. But it was Modi who had the best answer to that one. 'I'll tell them who Smriti Irani is,' he said. 'She is my younger sister.' The comment brought tears to the eyes of the woman who had once said Modi should resign over the Gujarat riots (see Chapter Three). 'I did get emotional when he spoke,' she told me. 'I did get emotional. You question me about my remark of 2002 and the human being in him announced to the world that I am his younger sister in Amethi. That says a lot about the man and makes me feel smaller and smaller.'

While he was on the subject of family, he turned his attention to Sonia Gandhi. 'I know how difficult a time this is for a mother. This mother has suffered for ten years to get her son ready and to settle him. As a mother, your hard work is going down the drain and I can understand your troubles.' Once again he compared his own family with theirs. 'I am a four times chief minister,' he said, 'but when my mother, who is over ninety, went to vote, she went in an auto-rickshaw.' He denied that the BJP was trying to cause the Gandhi clan problems by campaigning so hard in the constituency. 'I have sent Tulsi to reduce Amethi's difficulties, not to increase Rahul's difficulties,' he said.

When the voters got their chance to give their verdict two days later, they opted to stick with the son rather than the sister. Smriti Irani didn't win the seat, although she came tantalisingly close. She increased the BJP vote from 37,000 to 300,748. Rahul Gandhi held on with 408,651. Sometimes there are prizes for coming second. Irani, already a member of the upper house, was given a place in Modi's first cabinet.

As Modi flew back to Gandhinagar, he could feel confident that the day's controversies would only help him electorally. His appearance in Amethi had sent a strong message about the BJP's almost unlimited ambitions, and the row over Lord

Ram had upset his opponents and the Election Commission more than it was likely to have troubled his core voters. If he had any regrets, it was that the decision to take on Rahul directly hadn't been taken sooner. 'We were a little late in starting,' he told me. 'If we had started about two weeks earlier in Amethi, I believe the results would have been different.' As it was, after forty-eight hours of campaigning at full throttle, he had given Team Modi the final boost it needed ahead of the finishing line that was now clearly in sight.

CHAPTER SEVENTEEN
GOTV

At 5.30 in the morning of 12 May, the temperature in the shade in Varanasi was already 32 degrees Celsius. By the middle of the afternoon it would climb to the mid-forties. The dawn heat didn't trouble the party workers too much. They had grown used to campaigning in these temperatures and, besides, most of them hadn't tried to get more than a couple of hours' sleep. This was the final day of polling in the world's biggest election, and the seat Modi hoped to represent in parliament was one of the last to open its doors to the public at 7.00 a.m.

Formal campaigning had ceased two days earlier under the Election Commission rules. Everybody's energy was now redirected to the job of 'GOTV' – get out the vote. After such a high-tech campaign, the business of getting the voters to the polling stations was a tried-and-tested formula. It was all about employing good organisers and getting plenty of feet on the ground, just as it always had been, except that on this occasion there were a whole lot more of them.

Every single voting booth had a BJP polling agent assigned to it. The rules stated that his or her name had to be notified to the commission in advance and they must be registered to vote in the same place themselves. No other party members were allowed within a 100-metre radius of the booth, except when casting their own ballots. Clamping down on bribery and corruption at the moment when the voter finally comes face to face with the electronic voting machine had long been one of the EC's top priorities. The polling agent would sit there all day, usually accompanied by those from the other parties, noting down how many people had voted and, so far as possible, who they were. This information was then passed on to the rest of the team who were busy scouring the constituency and ensuring that everybody who had said they would vote for the lotus candidate actually went down and did so. If a particular booth was registering a noticeably low turnout, then volunteers would be switched from neighbouring polling stations to help out.

The last hours of the campaign were the least digital in this most digital of elections. The internet professionals who had joined Team Modi had invested a lot of time and effort into turning the electoral registers into digital format, but these were available only in some states and, in any case, most of the workers at constituency level preferred to work with the old paper versions. SMS messages and social media could be used to remind people to vote, although at this late stage not to recommend who they should vote for. Minutes after the polling stations opened, Modi tweeted, 'My special request to the youth – go out & vote and take your family and friends along to the polling booth!'

Both the RSS and the CAG had done separate analyses of the seats. For the Sangh there were three categories: safe, swing and difficult. The CAG breakdown was into four groups: safe, favourable, battleground and difficult. Now that the message was simply 'get out and vote' rather than 'vote Modi' or 'vote BJP', all the elements of the ecosystem could cooperate more closely than ever before. Each BJP district president was given the materials and the budget to equip their teams. According to one, 'Booth level kits were prepared containing the voter lists, stationery, pens and voting slips in a carry bag. These kits were then despatched to the respective locations by rental car to get there two days before polling.' On the day, the teams were told to ensure that every voter they met knew the exact location of the polling booth where they were supposed to vote. If for any reason he or she couldn't get there easily, then transport was made available.

The BJP were convinced that the higher the turnout the better their candidates would do. They had two big advantages working in their favour, quite apart from their own dedicated workers and volunteers. Most important of all was that most people didn't need much persuading. There was clearly a genuine positive enthusiasm and determination among the electorate to exercise their democratic rights. Veteran observers of Indian democracy had seen nothing like it since the highly charged elections following Indira Gandhi's 'Emergency', when the voters wanted to punish her, and after her assassination when they wanted to honour her memory.

Narendra Modi says that democracy is 'part of India's DNA'; one of his party's older generation, the journalist and politician Arun Shourie, recounted for me a story to illustrate what he meant. 'A British anthropologist asked a woman who was not able to vote why she was crying. She said, "Do you know what I do? When the gunny bags come to the store, a few grains fall off. My job is to collect those grains and I am allowed to keep a part of what I have collected which I use to feed my children. So I know the value of every single grain."' That, he said, was one reason why so many millions of people were willing to wait in the searing heat for their turn to vote.

The second reason that turnout was always going to be high was the enormous effort made by the Election Commission to ensure that every citizen had the opportunity to vote. 'It may sound amusing at first,' wrote the EC's former chief commissioner, S. Y. Quaraishi, 'but all modes of transportation from the primitive to the ultra-modern – elephants, camels, boats, cycles, helicopters, trains and airplanes – are used to reach voters and to move men and materials through deserts, mountains, plains, forests, islands and coastal areas.' Up in the Himalayas, government employees were selected at random by computer for the task of hiking to some of the remotest villages. 'What miserable luck I have,' 25-year-old Gulzar Ahmad Dar told the *New York Times* at the start of a 35-kilometre trek into the Marka Valley, 'but somebody has to do it.' The presiding officer who accompanied him to register the votes of just 114 people added, 'My, this democracy thing is stupid, isn't it?'

Modi has a favourite story from his home state of Gujarat. 'A good example of how much we value democracy is evident from the fact that we are the country where we have a complete election booth only for one voter,' he told me. Mahant Bharatdas Darshandas is a temple priest in his sixties who lives alone in the Gir forest. The EC rules say that nobody should have to travel more than two kilometres to vote, so for this election, as in previous ones, a team of officials carried an entire polling booth and voting machine to his hamlet so he could do his duty as a citizen.

As polling came to an end, the party leaders issued their final messages. 'People are tired of false promises, corruption and the same old tape-recorded messages,' said Narendra Modi. And while the evidence from all the exit polls was that the Congress-led government was heading for a massive defeat, Rahul Gandhi said, 'I am confident that the voters will give a mandate to an inclusive, fair and unifying government.'

Early in the morning, the BJP posted its 'Modimeter',

showing that since 15 September he had travelled 300,000 kilometres and attended 5,857 events, including 1,350 3D rallies and 4,000 *chai pe charcha* tea stall chats.

By midday, some states were recording that over 40% of the eligible electorate had already voted. There were sporadic reports of scuffles and even some shots being fired, but overall the day was passing peacefully. The Election Commission was kept busy with complaints from various candidates that their opponents had been breaking the rules by, for example, wearing their party symbols inside the polling booths. The AAP berated the television networks for showing live pictures and sound of Modi while the Varanasi poll was still in progress. Just before the booths closed, Congress announced that it wouldn't be taking part in any of that evening's TV debates on the exit polls.

At 7.00 p.m. it was, at last, all over bar the shouting. What *Time* magazine called: 'The insanely huge and complex exercise known as the Indian election' was complete. Insane or not, it had done its job. Officially the polls had closed at 6.00 p.m., but with such a huge turnout, some leeway was allowed to make sure people who had queued for hours were not denied their vote. The doors were now shut and the process of moving all the electronic voting machines to the counting centres began. Figures would later show that 66.4% of the electorate had participated, the highest for sixty years. Modi's campaign to woo women voters appeared to have borne fruit. The number of women voting was up 10% on the previous election at 65.63%. For the first time people had been allowed to register their disapproval of all the candidates by indicating 'NOTA' – none of the above – although only just over 1% did so.

At 7.03 p.m. the TV channels started to flash up their own

exit polls. CNN-IBN put the BJP and its allies at 270–282 and the Congress-led alliance on 92–102. India TV had them at 290 and 107 respectively. Times Now was the least encouraging for Modi, giving him 249 seats, well short of a majority, against 148 for the outgoing government. Apart from the Chanakya survey, which did predict an overall majority, they all underestimated the scale of the BJP victory, but even on the most pessimistic figures there was no doubt Modi would be the next prime minister. At 7.40 p.m. he said it was time to resurrect the spirit of bipartisanship in Indian politics which had been temporarily lost in the election campaign. It was a statement that left commentators scratching their heads trying to recall when such a spirit had last been in evidence and wondering if Modi was really the man to bring it back.

It had been a bitterly fought election and, as the sun went down, giving up a little of its heat, the arguments about how it had been conducted were already simmering. At 8.03 p.m. the Election Commission raised questions about how honest all the parties, including the BJP and Congress, were likely to be when submitting their election expenses.

If there is a spirit of bipartisanship at election times, it is most evident in the conspiracy of silence over how much they spend and where they get their money from. Nobody knows for sure, but to add to all the other record-breaking statistics, it is quite possible that this was the most expensive election anywhere in the world, surpassing the seven billion dollars spent during the American presidential election of 2012. The reason we can't be sure is that the election laws, so strict in many ways, don't require financial disclosure by the parties. At constituency level, spending on every pencil and every litre of petrol has to be accounted for. At the national level, anything goes. One thing we can be sure of is that the BJP massively outspent their rivals. When I put this to Mr Quraishi, he was clear that it was none of his business. 'People asked how come the BJP spent so much money and the Election Commission took no action? I said everything they did was totally legal because there is no cap on spending by a political party. They used it to the hilt but good for them.'

The issue of campaign finance had come up sporadically over the past few months. Congress, which had traditionally been the wealthier party, looked at all the planes and helicopters Modi was using and the expense of transmitting himself in 3D around the country. 'Is it Modi's money?' asked Rahul Gandhi. He accused the BJP of taking 'hefty money' from two or three corporations and alleged that while Congress wanted to make the poor wealthier, Modi was looking after his friends in the business world. He singled out the billionaire Gautam Adani, who was known to be an old friend of Modi's and a fellow Gujarati. The AAP led by the former anti-corruption campaigner Arvind Kejriwal had frequently linked Modi with Adani as well as other wealthy industrialists like Mukesh Ambani and Ratan Tata, accusing Modi of being their 'property dealer'.

There was no doubt that Gautam Adani had done very well from his infrastructure and ports businesses during the years that Modi had been chief minister, but both men strongly denied allegations that Adani had been given special privileges and sold land by the state government at knock-down prices. Adani told the Reuters news agency that 'Crony capitalism should not be there. I definitely agree with that. But how you define crony capitalism is another matter. If you are, basically, working closely with the government that doesn't mean it's crony capitalism.' In a rare interview with CNN-IBN, he said, 'I have never received any special treatment from

Modi, nor do I expect any. In any of his discussions, Modi always talks about policy matters and never about individual companies.' And, just in case any of the viewers hadn't got the message, he added, 'I am not the BJP's ATM machine.'

India's richest businessmen have long been a major source of funds for both Congress and the BJP. The pressure group, Association of Democratic Reforms (ADR), has calculated that 87% of the total contribution to political parties from known sources has come from business interests. With such lax rules for disclosure, finding out where the parties get their money is no easy task, but individual company accounts offer some clues. The ADR, which campaigns for greater transparency, believes as much as 75% of the funding sources are never made public. Politics can be a costly business, and Modi's campaign was undoubtedly the most expensive in India's history. It is no surprise, therefore, that political leaders feel the need to turn to the corporate world for help. As long ago as 1925, Mahatma Gandhi described himself as 'a friend of the capitalists' and thanked the wealthy industrialist Sir Ratan Tata for his contributions to his campaign work. Tata's grandson, in his turn, has publicly supported Narendra Modi (see Chapter Three).

Gautam Adani makes no secret of his backing for Modi; indeed he appears to be proud of their connection. They have been photographed together at many major business-related events. During the campaign Modi was often spotted flying in corporate planes belonging to his group of companies, although Adani said the BJP paid 'fully' to hire them. When I asked Modi about his relationship with big corporate donors, he told me, 'Even in the Gujarat days I have collected money going house to house to fund my elections. I have raised money from the people. There was a lot of writing that we were using private aircraft from the corporates. Please keep in mind that if necessary I will also hire cycles to run the campaign. We needed aircraft to criss-cross the country to manage a campaign on this scale and handle the diversity in India. Our party paid for every bit of the expenses that were incurred in leasing anything that we used.'

The scale of the expenditure on the 2014 campaign increased the pressure for party spending limits to be introduced, or at the very least for them to be more transparent about their funding. While acknowledging that the commission he headed has no powers to intervene, Quraishi does believe there are serious issues at stake for Indian democracy. 'To spend that much,' he told me, 'they have to raise all kinds of money. It may be crime money, it may be drug money, it may be corporate money. And there is no free lunch. It has to be repaid.' And looking back over the recent election it was the corporations that troubled him most. 'One low point in the campaign is that the money power, the corporate money which was playing its role has its dangerous implications. Crony capitalism is a phrase that is used in TV debates all the time. What is crony capitalism? These guys fund the election and they run the country. Now obviously businessmen running the country as a business is not what democracy should be, so that of course raises a concern.' He is not optimistic about the chances of reform. 'All the main parties oppose our demand for transparency. They know the other parties are indulging in the same practice but they don't mind it because they are doing it themselves too.'

Where the commission can act, it does. And as a result of their efforts and those of the security forces, the actual business of casting a vote in India has become both safer and less open to bribery and corruption. S. Y. Quraishi reminded me that 'In the past there used to be polling day violence, hundreds of thousands of people used to get killed, but all of that is history.' Similarly, bribery, intimidation and dirty tricks were once all but synonymous with a general election. They have certainly not been eradicated altogether, but the incidence has been greatly reduced.

Mr Quraishi has listed forty ruses that the EC has identified and said, 'It's a cat and mouse game. The parties come up with all kinds of methods. It's like when they say that crime is always ahead of enforcement.' His list includes envelopes of cash delivered to people's doors with the morning newspaper or the milk, money paid to village headmen to ensure his villagers vote the right way, and bribery involving anything from free alcohol or seeds, to cows or mobile phones. His favourite story involved an election observer who noticed a huge feast going on. Nearly four hundred people were enjoying lavish food and plenty of liquor. He was told it was a wedding celebration but when he said he wanted to congratulate the happy couple, he discovered they didn't exist. It was one massive exercise in bribery.

So while the 2014 election was officially described as 'the most transparent and free' in the country's history, there were still problems. It says something that in the cleanest election to date, the authorities still seized three billion rupees in cash (over thirty million pounds), some 22 million litres of alcohol and 30,000 kilogrammes of illegal drugs by the end of the campaign. The vast majority of the bribes were handed out in the last two days before polling. Officially the BJP insisted its hands were clean as, of course, did all the parties. When I put this to activists who had seen what went on with their own eyes, they smiled. 'They all do it,' I was told. 'All of them.'

Corporate India was delighted to see the campaign come to

an end. Political uncertainty is never good for business, and most could now sit back and watch the rupee strengthen on the foreign exchanges and their share prices rise as the stock market responded enthusiastically to the prospect of a pro-enterprise, Modi-led administration. Not everybody was happy, however. Deepak Parekh, chairman of India's leading housing finance company HDFC, and Ashishkumar Chauhan, chairman of the Bombay Stock Exchange, had turned up to vote in Mumbai, only to find that their names were missing from the electoral register. Thousands of other residents in the state of Maharashtra had also discovered that they weren't entitled to vote. The BJP suspected political interference and claimed that the majority of those omitted were their supporters and that their names had been deliberately deleted. The Election Commission was embarrassed but said it was the responsibility of every individual to make sure his or her name was on the register.

The election hadn't been perfect by any means, but on past experience it could have been a whole lot worse. The complaints of irregularities were all examined and in a few places a re-run was ordered, but none of it was going to make any difference to the final result. The policies, past records and personal characters of the leading contenders for power had been picked over and scrutinised in detail. The electorate had made its choice and the outcome had been decisive. Democracy had done its job.

CHAPTER EIGHTEEN

INDIA RECAST

On the morning of 16 May 2014, hundreds of millions of people across India were glued to their radios, TV sets, mobile phones and computers. In the large Indian communities in Britain, North America, Australia and elsewhere, many were doing the same, even if it meant being awake in the middle of the night. After the longest and most exciting general election campaign any of them could remember, the results were finally being declared. Change was not just in the air and on the air. Out on the streets and in the fields, in the crowded market places as much as the smart office blocks of corporate India, people knew that who governed India and even how it was governed was being transfigured. Some were apprehensive. Many more dared to hope and believe that if they were lucky, and if the promises that had been made were kept, their own lives could be about to change for the better.

From eight in the morning the electronic voting machines from all those hundreds of thousands of polling stations started to give up their secrets. It was no secret to anybody that the Congress Party and its allies were on the way out. Whether the BJP had secured enough seats to form a stable new government on its own was yet to be revealed. India has over four hundred television news and current affairs channels – the statistics in this vast country never cease to boggle the mind – and they are highly excitable even on a quiet news day. This morning they were feverish.

As the commentators analysed the returns, and with the stock market soaring, the networks reported that the man everybody expected to become the next prime minister was nowhere to be seen. With presidents, prime ministers, corporate leaders and Bollywood stars all queuing up to congratulate him, Modi was said to be 'watching television for now.'

According to the man himself, this was just another example of the media claiming to know more than they did and getting it wrong. 'In the morning when the counting was going on,' he told me, 'I was totally alone and had no TV on. I was finishing off my own spiritual activities and enjoying my meditation time after the gruelling elections.' I suggested to him that many people outside India, and no doubt quite a few of his own citizens, would be amazed to hear that after having worked so hard for victory he didn't savour every moment as seat after seat fell to the BJP. 'Yes, I do have immense self-restraint and this was a good occasion to test it. I started taking calls only from 12 noon and the first call on the results was from the BJP president Rajnath Singh telling me that it was a foregone conclusion that we would sweep the polls.' Three days earlier Modi's number-crunchers had sent him a private note predicting that he would end up with somewhere around 260 seats, a figure which would have forced him to go into coalition. He hadn't believed it. 'I started feeling we would win well before anybody else,' he told me.

Modi may have a gift for reading the political tea leaves, but he is not always so good at accurately remembering the past. If he suffers from an occasional tendency to overlook inconvenient facts when it comes to crafting his public image, he certainly isn't the first prime minister to be guilty of that. It was actually at 10.26 a.m., not midday, that Rajnath Singh tweeted to his 977,000 followers, 'Congratulated Shri @ narendramodi over the phone on BJP's superb performance in the Lok Sabha elections. Trends indicate it is a landslide.' After such a tumultuous day, Modi might be forgiven for not remembering all the details.

And it was indeed at 12.07 that Narendra Modi tweeted to his 8.8 million followers, 'India has won. Good times are coming.'

The BJP headquarters in central Delhi was already festooned with flowers. Sweets were being handed out in a traditional gesture of giving thanks. Eight hundred kilometres away, in Varanasi, where Modi was about to become the MP, posters had gone up overnight welcoming a victory that had yet to be officially announced but which everybody knew was coming. Congress Party leaders had thrown in the towel before the first results came in. By the end of the day they would know they hadn't just lost, but had gone down to their worst defeat in history. They were left with just forty-four of the 543 seats in parliament. With less than 10% of the MPs they failed even to pass the threshold needed to claim the post of leader of the opposition. The BJP had 282 seats, giving it a comfortable majority. 272+ had become a reality with room to spare.

The TV channels flashed up Modi's tweet, but they were still waiting for the day's first glimpse of the man who had been dominating their screens for months. When he did appear it was to perform a very traditional ritual. Modi went straight to the home of his ninety-year old mother, Hiraba, to touch her feet and seek her blessing. It was more photo-opportunity than family occasion. Modi doesn't do family. Here was the most powerful man in India showing that he still knew how a dutiful son should behave. From there he went to thank his supporters and deliver a speech that was carried live across the country. Dressed in saffron orange, he promised that 'in letter and spirit I will take all Indians with me. This is our aim, and I will not leave any stone unturned.'

Modi had been elected in two places, Varanasi and Vadodara in Gujarat. He would promptly resign this second seat, necessitating a by-election, but he still wanted to thank the people of the state that had made him. 'After filing my nomination from Vadodara, I was able to spend only 50 minutes here, but you gave me 570,000 votes,' he said. The BJP had swept the board in the state, taking every one of the seats. Referring to his promise of 'with all and development for all', Modi said that it 'will be my government's motto and not an empty slogan. I hope I'll get cooperation from all political parties and leaders in running the nation.'

Throughout the day his tone was consistently conciliatory. 'Even if we've a clear majority to run the government, it's our responsibility to take everyone along in running India. To live free to determine our future is our dream. India's 1.25 billion people today should not be thinking about giving their lives for their country but living for it! If 1.25 billion people decide to live like this then my country will take 1.25 billion steps forward.'

Before leaving for Delhi, his pledge to the people of the whole country was to work as hard for them as he had done in Gujarat. 'You have faith in me and I have faith in you. The people of this country have given their verdict. This verdict says we have to make the dreams of 1.25 billion people come true. I must work hard. I am a labourer, a worker. The country has never seen such a labourer as me. Is there any doubt in your mind about my capacity for hard work? I guarantee you our mission is everyone's progress walking together, all together. There is a difference between running a state government and running a country. To run the country we are responsible for taking everyone with us together and I seek your blessings to succeed in this endeavour. We have a responsibility to take everyone with us.'

It was Modi's day and it would have sounded like sour grapes for anybody to point out that taking everybody along with him had been his responsibility as chief minister just as much as it was now as prime minister. Even so, not all his opponents managed to be gracious in defeat. The Congress Party spokesman, Rajeev Shukla, told reporters that 'Modi promised the moon and stars to the people. People bought that dream.'

Both Rahul Gandhi in Amethi and his mother Sonia in Rae Bareli had held on to their seats, the only Congress candidates in Uttar Pradesh to do so. Both stood ready to accept their share of responsibility for the national debacle. Appearing before reporters at 4.30 p.m. Rahul said, 'I would like to start by congratulating the new government. They have been given a mandate by the people of our country so I wish the new government all the best. For my part, the Congress Party has done pretty badly, and there is a lot for us to think about. As vice president of the party, I hold myself responsible for what has happened.' His mother, with a touch more defiance, said, 'We, with all humility, accept the mandate of the people and hope that the new government at the centre will uphold the unity and interests of the country. I congratulate the new government. Congress will continue to fight for its principles and will not make any compromise. As president, I take responsibility for the defeat.'

Modi's slogan, written for him by the outgoing prime minister Dr Manmohan Singh, '*Achche din aane wale hain*', 'Good times are coming', was the refrain of the day. Those days would be better for some than for others, it has to be said. As the old American political adage goes, 'to the victor the spoils.' The Congress Party was left licking its wounds. It quickly set up an internal inquiry into why it had done so badly, an inquiry that would eventually exonerate all the party leaders.

The upstart AAP faced the humiliation of winning just four seats in parliament. Arvind Kejriwal was down but not yet out. He would go on to stage a remarkable come back in the next Delhi legislative poll the following February. But for now the best he could muster was that the 2014 result 'was a good start for us for our first election.'

Some of Modi's own party elders, including L. K. Advani, his mentor turned tormentor, would soon discover that their fortunes had turned when they were removed from the BJP's ruling parliamentary committee and offered positions as 'mentors' instead. Advani would later be quoted as saying that the victory owed more to the mistakes of Congress than the achievements of Modi. 'The massive campaign carried out under the leadership of Narendra Modi also contributed to the victory. But the biggest contribution was from our opposition. Had they not committed so many grave errors and had people not witnessed so much corruption in the last ten years, then probably this kind of result would not have come.'

Modi had gone from 'pariah to prime minister', according to one of his colleagues, who added, 'This is nothing short of a miracle.' And this being 2014, to the victor came the tweets. Led by David Cameron, who had told him, 'It's great to be talking to someone who just got more votes than any other politician anywhere in the universe,' world leaders were busy following up their phone calls by finding 140 characters in which to say congratulations. The *New York Times* read a political snub into the order in which he chose to acknowledge them. First came the UK, then Canada, Russia, Japan,

South Africa, France and Germany. 'As the list of nations grew throughout the India day, the leader of the biggest western power, President Obama, began to look more and more like the kid who was picked last for teams during recess.' Modi hadn't forgotten that the United States had been the last, and most begrudging, of the western governments to invite him back into the diplomatic fold. Eventually, after thanking New Zealand and Fiji, Modi tweeted, '@BarackObama & I talked about further strengthening India–USA strategic partnership that will help both nations.'

The time had come at last to assess the true scale of the Modi wave, and for the most part the statistics were extremely impressive. Until today, no party other than Congress had managed to secure an overall majority on its own. For the first time in its history, the BJP had polled more of the popular vote than its rival. In six states it had taken every one of the seats up for grabs. But it hadn't swept the entire country. Its candidates had done much better in the north and west than in the south and east, but nevertheless the national map had been transformed. Nationwide, the younger voters that Modi had assiduously courted, those aged 18–22, had preferred the BJP to Congress by a margin of more than two to one. The BJP was ahead in every age group, although among those over fifty-five the party's lead was much smaller at 7%. Despite all his efforts to go after the female vote, however, women had been rather less impressed by Modi's party than men. While 33% of men had voted BJP, the figure for women was just 29%. And where it had been a straight fight between the two big parties, Muslim voters had preferred Congress candidates by almost four to one.

In Uttar Pradesh, the BJP won a staggering seventy-three of the eighty seats. In his book, *How Modi Won It,* the former

Congress party adviser Harish Khare noted that 'the BJP did not nominate a single Muslim candidate in UP, while one third of its candidates were OBCs. So successful was the Modi-Shah strategy of Hindu consolidation that for the first time since Independence, UP did not elect a single Muslim.'

Across the country as a whole, for the first time ever the BJP had outpolled its rivals among those at the bottom of the caste system, the Dalits, or 'untouchables', and among those identified as tribal voters. Until 2014 there was a lot of truth to the aphorism that, in India, 'you don't cast your vote, you vote your caste'. Modi had explicitly called on people to put this behind them when he urged voters to make their choice not on the basis of who they were but rather on what they thought about the issues confronting the country as a whole. Caste or 'identity' politics certainly didn't disappear altogether, however, and the BJP had engaged in its fair share of it where it felt it had to. But if the substantial breakdown of traditional loyalties that was revealed once the election results were analysed in detail proves durable, then Narendra Modi will have done something of far greater significance than winning an election. He really will have recast politics in India.

Even Modi's closest colleagues concede, however, that it is one thing to promise change and quite another to deliver it. Modi will not need to make good on all that he has said he will do in his first term to be judged a success. 'People are patient,' one of his loyal cabinet ministers told me. 'They will wait. But they won't wait for ever.' Indira Gandhi made it her ambition to 'abolish poverty' in 1971. It was a pledge she could never have met and towards which she had made little progress by the time she was cut down by assassins' bullets thirteen years later, but it has not stopped millions of people continuing to revere her memory.

The first few weeks or months in office are scarcely the time for political leaders to start worrying about how they will be remembered. But nor is it a time to be squandered. I worked inside Downing Street for Tony Blair during his first term when he had the authority and the parliamentary majority to do almost anything he wanted. By the time the next election came around he regretted not having acted with greater urgency. He, and arguably he alone, was haunted by the prospect of his opponents' fortunes reviving and his hold on power disappearing. In 2014 Modi already had his eyes on the next elections he had to win in some of the big state legislative assemblies. Victory in these could also help secure him a majority in the upper house of parliament, the Rajya Sabha, where most the members are elected by the state legislatures.

When I met the veteran BJP leader Arun Shourie, it was already two months since the results had been declared and he was a worried man. He had been passed over for the job of finance minister that he coveted, so perhaps he had reasons for being sour. But he is a Modi fan through and through and he told me, 'People have been saying, "Let's file a missing person's report, where is Modi? Can't seem to find him in the crowd".' He was disappointed that Modi had not hit the ground running. 'There is no time,' he told me, 'Five years is not enough. It's a short period. You need to act on what Buddha said: "Live every day like your hair is on fire".' Political honeymoons are getting shorter the world over. By the summer of 2014 Modi was still extraordinarily popular, but he was already the subject of intense public scrutiny, much of it trying to work out just what kind of prime minister he was turning out to be. Above all, how could he manage to satisfy all the people with so many strands of opinion, some of them contradictory, that had until now been ready to unite behind him?

CHAPTER NINETEEN

FROM PARIAH TO PM

One of Modi's most pressing tasks was to pick his team of ministers. His first cabinet was a slimmed-down affair, suggesting he had an eye to his campaign promise of 'less government, more governance.' His closest allies were rewarded with some of the best positions. Arun Jaitley became both finance and defence minister. Rajnath Singh got the home affairs department, with his old job of BJP party president going to Amit Shah. Smriti Irani went to the sensitive human resources department that included education policy and Piyush Goyal, while outside the cabinet, was put in charge of power and coal. There were places for some of his critics, too. Sushma Swaraj, who had been identified with the Advani camp, was made external affairs minister, although Modi watchers noted that he seemed determined to take most of the big decisions himself and that she wasn't always invited to accompany him when he travelled abroad.

Governments around the world were waiting to see what a Modi administration would mean for international relations and at the outset the omens were good. His first priority was India's nearest neighbours. Nawaz Sharif, prime minister of the old enemy Pakistan, was quickly invited to his swearing-in ceremony, alongside the president of Sri Lanka and all the other regional leaders. Soon afterwards visa regulations for some Bangladeshi citizens were relaxed; Modi became the first Indian leader in seventeen years to visit Nepal. While in Kathmandhu he reached back over two thousand years of history to remember perhaps the most revered of the Indian subcontinent, the Emperor Ashoka who, he said, 'having waged wars came in search of Buddha to tread the path of peace.'

On the campaign trail Modi had promised to restore India's standing in the world, but that could be achieved only if he succeeded in delivering on the key planks of his programme for the country at home, strengthening the economy and tackling corruption. Here the early signs were less encouraging. Just three weeks after the election, Modi had warned the country that it would need to take a 'bitter pill' in order to restore the nation's finances. And he appeared to be prepared for the political consequences when he said 'I know my popularity might go down due to these hard decisions, people might be annoyed with me, but they will appreciate it later.' That was the kind of talk the markets liked, and yet the budget in July was seen to contain too little harsh medicine not too much. There were few radical departures from the economic plans already announced by the previous government. One commentator, giving it 4.5 out of 10 in the *Economic Times*, said it was a Congress budget 'with saffron lipstick added'. Investor confidence had grown since the election but big business was disappointed that so many of the reforms it had hoped for were absent, and the stock market, which had soared with Modi's arrival in office, fell back in the wake of the budget.

There was better news on price inflation, which fell to a five-year low, thanks largely to cheaper food and fuel. The fall in global oil prices, rather than anything the government had done, was the major factor and the Indian central bank remained cautious about the future. The economy was certainly growing again, although many economists said the new government could not claim full credit for that either as the signs of a recovery had already been in evidence before the election. By the end of the year *The Economist* was reporting that growth was again slipping: 'Investment was especially weak. Credit growth has been feeble.'

The Jaitley budget was delivered within weeks of the election, and while it did suggest that insufficient attention had been given to what it should contain while the BJP was still in opposition, there would be time enough for more radical measures in the future. On corruption there could be no such grace period. Modi had reason to hope that his very presence in the PM's office at 7 Race Course Road would send a message to all ministers and officials that this prime minister, unlike the last, would not turn a blind eye to wrongdoing in government.

Modi promptly let it be known that not only was he changing the way the prime minister's office worked, but also that he expected the entire bureaucracy to change with him. Officials would be trusted with greater autonomy but in return they would have to be at their desks by 9.00 a.m. and work through until 5.30 p.m. with only half an hour for lunch. There would be no sloping off for a game of golf in the mornings, a diktat that was reported to have caused alarm at the elite Delhi Golf Club. A party spokesman, M. J. Akbar, said 'He wants to bring discipline into the government and he thinks solving India's problems requires 25-hour days. He's not anti-golf or anything, but just pro-work.'

Mohan Guruswamy, head of the Centre for Policy Alternatives in Delhi, said it was high time to end what he called the 'crony capitalist' relationships between civil servants and big business, where deals were often done over a game of golf. 'We have a bureaucracy which is undisciplined, corrupt and venal to the core. It's about time it was shaken up,' he told the *Daily Telegraph*. To the horror of some officials, Modi even went so far as to introduce biometric clocking-in devices and a new online portal, attendance.gov.in, through which anybody could check on the timekeeping of civil servants. Some of the abuses exposed by the new regimen were astounding. In January 2015, the government dismissed a junior civil servant in the public works department after discovering that he hadn't turned up for duty once since going on leave twenty-four years previously.

Officials in all the key departments were called in to make presentations to the prime minister. He asked them to identify eight to ten regulations in their ministries that could be done away with. They now knew they had the ear of the prime minister in a way that they had not been used to before, but they also knew he was keeping an eye on how they performed. The new modus operandi ruffled some feathers among Modi's new ministers too. They felt, with some justification, that he was going over their heads and trying to run their departments from the centre. One was quoted as telling a journalist privately, 'Even our secretaries and advisers are imposed on us. We don't have any decision-making powers.'

The information minister, Prakash Javadekar, dismissed such stories and said Modi trusted his ministerial colleagues. 'He gives us some freedom and has only one mantra for us that "you should have the courage to take decisions".' He dismissed as 'misinformation' a story about himself that had caused both amusement and alarm in the corridors of power. It was widely reported that Javadekar had been on his way to the airport to attend a conference in Kenya wearing a pair of jeans and t-shirt when the phone rang in his car. It was, so the story went, the prime minister's office, telling him to go home and change into something befitting his job. 'The prime minister's office is not so childish,' he said, calling the story an unsuccessful attempt to damage Modi's image.

What would damage Modi's image would be any backsliding on his anti-corruption agenda. But when it came to decisive action to clean up public life, it soon became clear that it was sometimes easier to make a campaign promise than to keep it. Modi had made much of his intention to bring back so-called 'black money', which had been hidden away in foreign banks to avoid paying tax. Some of his senior ministers had been quoted as saying it would start within his first 100 days. When that deadline passed, Jaitley was forced to admit that existing international agreements and confidentiality clauses had made the task more difficult than expected, although he promised the government would 'not rest until the last account is identified.'

Modi instigated a regular prime ministerial radio address in order to speak directly to the country. In his first broadcast, he urged all Indians to shed their despondency and use their skills for the betterment of all. The second addressed the corruption issue head on. 'As far as black money is concerned, I ask you to trust me. For me, it's an article of faith. India's poor money that has gone outside should come back,' he said.

Even while he was asking for their patience, the people of India had good reason to remain confident that the new occupant of the prime minister's residence was anything but personally corrupt. But while his own integrity was unchallenged, the same could not necessarily be said for the company he kept. The Supreme Court expressed dismay that thirteen of his forty-five ministers were facing pre-existing criminal charges, including rape, attempted murder and intimidation. The court warned that 'Corruption is the enemy of the nation. As a trustee of the constitution, the PM is expected not to appoint unwarranted persons as ministers.' When Modi expanded his cabinet in November, the number of ministers implicated grew to twenty out of sixty-six, almost a third. Arun Jaitley said any suggestion that there were criminals in the cabinet was 'completely baseless', adding that 'these are cases arising out of criminal accusations, not cases out of a crime.'

The Election Commission took a less benign view of the situation. It had proposed banning candidates facing serious criminal charges from standing for parliament at all, but the recommendation had got nowhere. No fewer than 34% of the total number of MPs elected in May had been charged with a serious offence, according to figures from the Association for Democratic Reforms. In December a draft bill to help tackle the problem was shelved, wrote the *Times of India*, 'for lack of consensus among the leading political parties.' The amendment to the Representation of the People Act would have disqualified any candidate from standing for election if there was a charge against them carrying a prison term of seven years or more.

At the end of the year a judge dismissed the charges against Amit Shah. Shah had always insisted that they were politically motivated and had thrown himself into the task of maintaining the momentum of the BJP's triumph as soon as the general election was over. At first it seemed possible he had lost his magic touch and that the BJP's political honeymoon would indeed be short-lived. Although Shah wasn't in charge of the day-to-day campaigning on this occasion, the party massively under-performed in a clutch of state by-elections called to fill vacancies including those left by members of the legislative assemblies who had become MPs. In Uttar Pradesh the BJP won just three of the eleven seats up for grabs and the accusations of religious polarisation resurfaced with a vengeance. Nationalists in the state raised the spectre of a 'love jihad', which they alleged involved the conversion of Hindu girls to Islam through seduction, marriage and bribery. The BJP didn't openly endorse the inflammatory phrase, but party activists along with their RSS sympathisers certainly tried to exploit the tension created by the allegations. The police were called in to investigate the claims, but found little or no evidence of any such conspiracy. The state's police chief, A. L. Banerjee, told the Reuters news agency that 'In most cases we found that a Hindu girl and Muslim boy were in love and had married against their parents' will. These are cases of love marriages and not love jihad.'

Amit Shah told the *Economic Times* that 'Love jihad is a media creation, not our terminology,' before adding, 'It's a grave social problem. Where injustice is done to a woman, then it is natural that BJP as a socio-political organisation will fight. But it is not true that we have started some big campaign on the issue.' Nevertheless, the 'love jihad' row dominated the political discourse both in UP and elsewhere, and was soon widened into a debate about whether religious conversions should be banned altogether. It all helped convince many liberal commentators that Modi was guilty either of endorsing such fundamentalist scaremongering or failing to silence those of his supporters who did. Numerous other comments by BJP figures were seen as evidence that below the shiny surface of Modi's modernisation and development agenda lay the same extremist Hindutva ideology that had always sought to denigrate those of other religious beliefs.

The man chosen to be the BJP's star campaigner in the UP

by-elections, Mahanth Yogi Adityanath, was an MP known for his outspoken Hindu nationalist opinions. He happily lived up to his reputation and was duly condemned by the Election Commission for allegedly promoting religious hatred. The failure of his tactics might suggest that what the voters wanted to hear from Modi's party was a lot more about development and a lot less about the religious divide.

While the BJP tried to analyse what had gone wrong in the by-elections, Amit Shah was determined that the party should put the setback behind them as quickly as possible. He played his part with just the kind of style he had demonstrated in getting Modi into power, delivering dramatic wins in the much larger and more significant state elections in Maharashtra and Haryana in mid-October. In Maharashtra the BJP's share of the vote rose from 16% in the previous elections to 42.4%, and in Haryana the figures were even more remarkable, up from 9% to 52.2%. At the same time Shah launched a membership drive in those parts of the country, mostly in the south and east, where the BJP had performed less well in the general election. The Congress Party might have been crippled in May, but Shah and Modi were determined that it should not be given the chance to recover. Their dream of a 'Congress-free India' was still very much alive. In this respect Modi was behaving as prime minister just as he had as chief minister in Gujarat. The campaigning didn't stop once an election was won.

While these victories showed the BJP could win convincingly when Modi and his development agenda were the central themes, the party was heavily defeated in the February 2015 Delhi Assembly elections. The AAP swept the board, taking sixty-seven seats to the BJP's three. Arvind Kejriwal's party was helped by a collapse in the Congress vote but it proved that the Modi bandwagon was not unstoppable. The AAP's focus on local issues worked while the BJP was accused of complacency and of losing touch with the core concerns of the voters since the general election.

A significant distraction had been the pressure for changes to the curriculum in schools to reflect more traditional Hindu values. The RSS was among those urging the government to take 'corrective steps' in order to 'Indianise' the education system. The minister responsible, Smriti Irani, caused further controversy when she announced that Sanskrit, a classical language no longer in common usage, would replace German in some government-run schools. Opposition politicians accused her of wanting to ride roughshod over the country's constitution and impose a 'saffronisation' of education. But she denied she was planning any such thing and promised she would only ever act 'in the spirit of the Constitution.' And yet many academics and professionals working in the arts, publishing and the media detected subtle, and sometimes not so subtle, pressures to avoid promoting anything that might be construed as 'anti-Hindu', or likely to offend Hindu religious sensibilities. The author Salman Rushdie was not alone in worrying that writers and journalists risked being 'bullied' and that some might give in to 'a kind of self-censorship' by which 'people worry that they are going to be bullied and therefore try not to do anything that will attract the wrath of the "Modistas".'

Whatever Modi's personal views on the apparent tension between his development plans and the cultural agenda of some of his supporters, he chose not to express them publicly. Behind closed doors he warned his MPs not to cross the line by making inflammatory statements. There were even unconfirmed reports that he had threatened to leave the RSS if it didn't rein in its own extremists. There was extensive speculation among commentators and analysts about why Modi hadn't spoken out openly. 'Will the real Narendra Modi please speak up?' they asked. Was he keeping silent because he couldn't afford to alienate his more hawkish supporters or because he secretly agreed with them? Whatever his private view, in public he preferred to keep the focus firmly on the positive steps he was taking to show that his manifesto pledges were being kept. And his experience as chief minister of Gujarat had also taught him that delivering real, perceptible changes in people's lives was the surest answer to even the most serious charges of ideological extremism.

As prime minister, Modi said he didn't want to be judged on his first hundred days but on five years in power. But he knew the media would be marking the occasion and his official website, narendramodi.in, was given a makeover with a new banner headline 'Action and Hope'. It declared that 'The wheels of change are fast moving! From quick decision-making to concrete action on the ground level, from improved productivity to India's stature on the world stage increasing, India is truly undergoing phenomenal transformation!' The report card in most of the newspapers was mixed when the 100-day anniversary came around on 3 September, but his cheerleaders could point to some significant achievements to show that he hadn't simply been biding his time. A start had been made on investing in new infrastructure. The Planning Commission, which its critics had likened to a Soviet-style bureaucratic monolith, had been abolished. Important sections of the economy, including defence and the railways, had been opened up to greater foreign investment. An ambitious new scheme to provide bank accounts and accident insurance for the poor was launched.

In September Modi kicked off his 'Clean India' campaign with much fanfare and with the support of celebrities like the cricketing legend Sachin Tendulkar. The PR machine didn't always get it right, however. Some overzealous BJP workers were caught by the cameras scattering leaves on the ground just so one of their leaders could then pose for pictures sweeping them up again. Wielding a broom himself, Modi said he didn't want the scheme to be seen as a political gimmick. 'This is inspired by patriotism not politics. We do not have to do it with an eye on politics. I say that with a clean heart. If we paint this again with a brush of politics, we will again do a disservice to Mother India.'

In October Modi unveiled his promised 'Adopt a Village' campaign. Every member of parliament would be expected to take responsibility for the development of three villages by 2019. He said he didn't expect the scheme to bring about change overnight, but the MPs could be facilitators and 'catalytic agents' whose efforts would have a 'viral effect' across the nation. They were free to choose any villages so long as neither they nor their in-laws lived in them. The initiative was well received, and even Rahul and Sonia Gandhi agreed to take part.

It wasn't just at home that Modi wanted to avoid any distractions caused by rows over ideology. He was much in demand in foreign capitals and there he wanted to spread the message only that India was open for business. After the unassuming Dr Manmohan Singh, India now had a superstar on the world stage. Whether playing ceremonial drums in Tokyo, signing trade agreements in Beijing or shaking hands in Fortaleza with the leaders of Brazil, Russia, China and South Africa [the BRICS nations] to mark the announcement of a new development bank, Modi was making headlines and providing the world's media with a new image for India. He told me he was proud to have been communicating 'what we can do for the world, which is so different to what happened many times when our leaders have communicated what India wants.' He was talking to me in September, shortly after his return from the United States, where he had addressed the United Nations General Assembly, met President Obama and discussed how to fight a successful election with Bill and Hillary Clinton. How had he felt, I wondered, landing in New York after almost ten years in which he'd been barred from the country? 'Regarding the visa issue, it has never bothered me,' he said. 'I really see these as non-issues and do not let them impact on me or my ego.'

The focal point of the trip was the sell-out rally at Madison Square Garden. For the Indian community in America this was bigger than Elvis, Bruce Springsteen or One Direction. On a revolving stage, he applauded the Indian-Americans for their ingenuity and hard work. India had once been regarded as the land of snake charmers, he said, but now they had the world spinning round their finger at the end of a computer mouse. Indians had migrated to every corner of the world, so the country was not just a back office for the globe, but had the capacity to be a world force on its own. With a smile he pointed out that India had just sent a spacecraft to Mars for seven rupees a kilometre when it cost ten rupees a kilometre to cross Ahmedabad in a taxi. The budget for the Mars mission was less than that for the recent Hollywood blockbuster, *Gravity*. It was, said the *Times of India*, 'a mutual love-fest that sharply etched the country's growing power and profile in the minds of Americans.'

The previous day he had made an impromptu appearance in Central Park alongside real-life rock stars including

Beyoncé, Sting and Jay-Z. Clutching the hand of the actor Hugh Jackman above his head, he wooed the crowd with a rousing, 'How are you doing New York? I hope you are having a good time.' The Global Citizen Festival was made up largely of young people. 'You are the future,' he told them. 'What you do today will decide our tomorrow.' They had gathered to demand action to end world poverty and Modi told them, 'You are touching the lives of those who are not fortunate like you. What an admirable act that is.' As he left the stage he added for good measure, 'May the force be with you.'

While in America, Modi was in the middle of the nine-day fast he undertakes every year to mark the Hindu festival of Navratri. At the formal dinner with Barack Obama he sipped only water while the president ate. They discussed their shared passion for technology and exchanged anecdotes about arriving in high office as outsiders. The following morning they travelled together to the Martin Luther King Jr Memorial before sitting down for formal talks in the Oval Office, covering world trade and the need to preserve regional peace and stability. The visit could scarcely have gone better from Modi's point of view. He had put previous disagreements to rest, presented a modern, dynamic vision of India to America and the world, and repaid the many Indians living in the US who had supported his campaign either financially or in more practical ways. Some had even taken time off work to fly to India and vote in person.

Gopal Nadadur had made the trip from New York after watching the election closely on the internet. He's in his late twenties and like many Indians in America he doesn't have much time for extreme Hindu nationalism. He told me he was impressed that Modi was able to push back against it and 'be extremely disciplined about presenting a refreshing, open-minded, and issues-focused image'. He wanted to take part in the voting personally because he had been in the US since attending college there and had never been able to participate before. 'I come from a very patriotic family, and it's embarrassing to see India being so easily surpassed on the global stage by countries like China, Turkey and Brazil. I think a successful Modi tenure will leave India in a much more powerful place on the global stage, with the ability to be a self-confident nation that plays a leadership role in world affairs.' It is sometimes said that Modi never forgives nor forgets, but he had forgiven America for making him a pariah and showed that he hadn't forgotten those Indians living there who had helped make him prime minister.

In November 2014, the Modi road show was on tour again, this time on a four-city visit to Australia. It was the first time an Indian prime minister had been down under in twenty-eight years. The main business on the agenda was the meeting of the G20 group of nations in Brisbane. This time there was no fast to observe, although the welcome barbecue hosted by the prime minister, Tony Abbott, was more to the liking of the carnivores among the guests than the vegetarian Mr Modi. The meeting included discussion of global economic reform, climate change and job creation. And it gave Modi an opportunity to demand action to help open up the global tax havens where so much of the 'black money' he was after was hidden away. Modi used the trip to meet representatives of the Indian community wherever he went and to tell business leaders of the new opportunities for investment his government was committed to providing. The red tape that had strangled so many planned projects in India would be unravelled. 'India has made its policies transparent and we have made the procedures clearly defined and smooth,' he told a business breakfast in Brisbane. 'You will no longer have to reach to opportunities through uncertain and unpredictable pathways, crossing hurdles along the way.'He told the Australian parliament in Canberra that the two countries had many interests in common and that from now on, 'Australia will not be at the periphery of our vision, but at the centre of our thought.'

One thing they had in common was a love of cricket and there was soon another Modi selfie going viral on the internet, this time standing alongside Tony Abbott at Melbourne Cricket Ground. And, once again, Modi was given the rock star treatment when he appeared on stage at Sydney's Allphones Arena. Twenty thousand people had packed into the stadium and the welcome was so rapturous it was as if the election campaign had never really ended. 'This love, this welcome,' he said above the roars, 'I give this to the feet of the children of India.'

Mosiqi Acharya is an Indian journalist who has reported on Modi's rise over the past decade. Now living in Australia, she said she was not surprised by his euphoric reception. 'Modi's election enthused Indians living abroad because they had long felt that India had the potential to be a super-power but lacked the will. Hundreds if not thousands of them travelled from all over Australia to witness him speak. So his visit was not just a huge boost to his image in Australia but has also ignited new interest in India here.'

In the short term at least, Modi had fulfilled his promise to enable India to stand tall in the world again. Turning all that adulation into something his country could bank and use to create jobs would take a lot longer. He didn't waste time trying. In January 2015 the biennial Vibrant Gujarat gathering was effectively turned into a showcase for all of India. Those attending included the UN Secretary General, the Chairman of the World Bank and representatives from every leading industrial economy, including US Secretary of State, John Kerry. In his speech, Modi said he didn't plan incremental changes in India's development. 'We are planning to take a quantum leap.'

By now there were clear signs not merely of a change in the economic mood in the country, but more importantly of growing confidence in India's future prospects based on independent forecasts. In its *World Economic Situation and Prospects* report for 2015, the United Nations predicted steady growth in India's GDP and said it was 'helped by government reforms that encourage consumption and investment'. It added that 'the recovery is partly the result of improved market sentiment after the new administration took office'. The International Monetary Fund (IMF) was similarly upbeat. Its *World Economic Outlook Update*, published towards the end of January, projected that by the year 2016-17 India would become the world's fastest growing major economy, outstripping China. The World Bank, too, anticipated a slow but steady economic recovery while warning that 'Any slackening in the reform momentum could result in a more modest or slower pace of recovery.'

Modi's ambitious plans to try and ensure that many of the poorest in India benefited from greater economic security also appeared to be bearing fruit. The government had given the banks until January 26 to open a hundred million accounts for those previously without one. Even before the deadline the target had been surpassed by more than ten per cent. Well over half the accounts were reported still to have a zero balance, but Modi had the satisfaction of seeing the scheme earn a place in the *Guinness Book of World Records* for the highest number of bank accounts opened in the shortest space of time. Financial security remained a distant dream for millions of Indians, but according to the government, over ninety-nine per cent of households had been enrolled.

Global security was as big a concern at the beginning of 2015 as it had been when Modi first became Gujarat's chief minister within weeks of 9/11. It was one thing for him to tell crowds of idealistic youngsters in New York's Central Park that he shared their belief in world peace, it would be another for India to play its part in reducing the risk of conflict, and in particular the tension on its borders with Pakistan and China. John Kerry had flown to India less to talk about investment opportunities and more to urge Modi to join with America in overcoming decades of distrust in the region. To mark India's Republic Day on January 26, the Pakistani prime minister, Nawaz Sharif, sent a message reaffirming his country's commitment to developing friendly relations with its much larger neighbour on the basis of mutual respect. But since Mr Sharif's invitation to Modi's swearing-in ceremony, those relations had been characterised more by wariness and a lack of meaningful dialogue.

Security issues, both global and regional, remained high on the agenda when Barack Obama arrived in Delhi as the first US president ever to be guest of honour at the Republic Day celebrations. The very fact that he was there was evidence of India's growing significance as a world power. The president said the two countries were natural partners, although he said that partnership would not 'happen overnight'. It would, he said, 'take time to build and some patience', but added that 'deepening ties with India is going to remain a top foreign policy priority for my administration.' Mr Obama ended their joint news conference with a few words in Hindi, '*Chale saath saath*', meaning 'let's walk together'.

The visit was a diplomatic triumph. Cooperation agreements were signed covering a wide range of areas including defence, civil nuclear power, climate change and the development of capital markets. With the signing of the 'India-US Delhi Declaration of Friendship', the relationship between the two countries was reset.

America's reservations about Modi were firmly consigned to history; which is not to say they were entirely forgotten. On his last day in India, the president said both countries had an obligation to uphold religious freedom. 'Every person has the right to practice his faith without any persecution, fear or discrimination,' he said. 'India will succeed so long it is not splintered on religious lines.' The following day, with the presidential party now heading back towards home, Mr Modi addressed a rally of the National Cadet Corps, which he had joined as a teenager. His words were reassuringly inclusive. 'Our country is full of diversities,' he said, 'and unity in diversity is the beauty and strength of our nation.' The message he had been sent was unambiguous and appeared to have been received loud and clear. The opportunities open to India were extensive, but should the country become polarised on religious lines then all that could yet be put at risk.

Away from the high politics, fashion-conscious observers had been treated to yet another demonstration of Modi's sartorial flair. He changed his outfits several times a day and managed even to upstage the famously elegant first lady, Michelle Obama. And for those who detected more than a hint of vanity in the prime minister's choice of outfits, the dark blue jacket he wore when the two men met the media was all the evidence they needed. Closer inspection of the pinstripes showed that Modi's name had been stitched a thousand times into the garment.

That may have looked more than a little egotistical, but the fact is that the previous twelve months had belonged to Modi, both domestically and internationally. He had received plaudits from the very countries who had once shunned him and from business leaders who had not so long ago considered India a bad bet. At the end of 2014 Modi was named 'Asian of the Year' by the *Straits Times* in Singapore. A readers' poll conducted by *Time* magazine had him way out in front as their choice for person of the year, mainly on the strength of votes from India, although the editorial board failed to shortlist him. His Twitter fans were outraged at the snub, pointing out that no Indian had received the honour since Mahatma Gandhi in 1930.

Modi scarcely needed the honour. He could reflect on the previous twelve months with a well-justified sense of satisfaction. When I asked him what stuck in his mind most, it was the tally of over 300 seats won by the BJP and their allies and the reaction of the man who had once doubted whether Modi was the right person to lead India, L. K. Advani. 'Looking back, the best summary was by Advaniji who said following the election win that I had scored a triple century in my very first match.' Looking back is not Modi's favourite pastime, however. The most successful politicians are those who keep their eyes fixed firmly on the future, and that is exactly what Modi has always done. He could now go forward confident that the outside world was willing him to succeed and that, so long as he kept to his promise to govern for all Indians, he would be judged henceforward on what he achieved in office and no longer on events in the past.

CHAPTER TWENTY
THE INDOMITABLE WILL

'Strength,' said Mahatma Gandhi, 'does not come from physical capacity. It comes from an indomitable will.' Time and again, Narendra Modi has demonstrated a will to succeed that has overcome all the hurdles placed in his path. In his long career he has been demonised, shunned, dismissed and condemned. But perhaps the biggest mistake his enemies have made is to underestimate him. He has now earned his place in history. The question that remains is whether that same force of will can bring about a lasting transformation in his party and, more importantly, his country. Has Indian politics really been recast for good?

It is easy after a decisive election victory to say that things will never be the same again, and it is often true. That does not mean, however, that today's landslide winners will not see their own position slide in time. And though the vanquished may look broken and demoralised now, they almost certainly retain the capacity to recover if they too show the requisite determination and a readiness to learn from their mistakes.

In Britain three leaders have secured landslides since the Second World War: Clement Attlee, Margaret Thatcher and Tony Blair. Their majorities in parliament were far larger than Mr Modi's in 2014, but while each left a permanent legacy behind them, none was able to defy the swing of the political pendulum for ever. Indian politics is more fragmented than Britain's; by winning as convincingly as he did, his success at the polls deserves to be compared with theirs. The prospect of going on to bring about lasting change lies well within his grasp, but delivering it remains a formidable challenge.

The 'first past the post' system that our two democracies share favours those parties whose support is concentrated in areas of high population, which therefore return a significant proportion of the MPs. That is why Thatcher and Blair could secure thumping parliamentary majorities with well under 50% of the votes cast. The BJP won an overall majority with less than a third of the votes. It has ambitions to become a truly national party, and it may succeed in doing so, but it isn't there yet. The system also tends to exaggerate a swing in popular opinion. At the previous election in 2009, the Congress Party won just under 29% of the votes and the BJP almost 19%. In 2014 those figures were broadly reversed, with 31% for the BJP and 19% for Congress. While those bald figures take no account of the support for their respective allies among the smaller parties, they do counsel caution in jumping to conclusions about an irreversible shift of loyalties. And as Milan Vaishnav from Columbia University's South Asia Program wrote, 'The decline and fall of the Congress party is a story which has been written many times before, only to be repeatedly torn up and thrown in the wastebasket.'

Part of the legacies of Attlee, Thatcher and Blair was to convince their opponents that the political weather had changed and to force them to change with it. Each of them had a profound and lasting effect on the way in which politics is done in Britain. That in itself is no small achievement. If Congress is to recover, it is likely to do so only if it recognises the reasons why it lost. It wasn't merely anti-incumbency compounded by corruption scandals and rising prices. I have done my best in this book not to pretend to know what is in India's best interests, and I don't intend to start now. What I can say is that Narendra Modi offered the vision of a different kind of politics, in which choices are made on the basis of policies and values, not the accidents of birth or religion. The BJP may not have been willing or able to resist the pull of an uglier kind of politics altogether, but a large number of voters were evidently attracted by the promise of a different way of doing things.

For those people who, like me, set a high store by liberal values of free expression, diversity and religious tolerance, the Modi campaign and the first few months of his government produced ample grounds for concern. I say that not in any way to make a point about Indian politics or even to draw a comparison between east and west. Yes, I happen to count myself lucky to live in a democracy where religion plays relatively little part in the national political discourse. Tony Blair, for whom I worked, was a devout Christian, but whenever the teachings of the church came into conflict with the policies he believed to be right, he followed his political instincts and not the dictates of his religion. And yes, Narendra Modi's religious beliefs clearly do help to shape his political views. But to judge from the first ten months, there has been no evidence since he became prime minister of any impact on policy that is remotely comparable, for example, to the damaging influence of fundamental Christianity on the administration of President George W. Bush.

Where I often part company with many of my fellow liberals, however, is that I can understand the pressures on politicians who want to retain the backing of voters who may think differently to themselves. Sometimes governments have to say or do things to keep intact the broad coalition of support that put them there in the first place. It isn't always terribly edifying but it may be necessary. If Narendra Modi were to jettison completely the Hindu nationalist ideology that he grew up with then he wouldn't last very long. He won't do that and, so far as I can tell, he has no desire to. But if he allows the more extreme elements of Hindutva to influence the way he governs to any significant degree then he risks alienating those at home and abroad who want to believe that his commitment to create a modern, successful and outward-looking India reflects the real Modi. Not all of the mahatma's aphorisms stand the test of time with equal force. 'There goes my people,' he once said, 'I must follow them, for I am their leader.' In Gandhi's case, his people may well have been right, but true leadership also involves being prepared to tell your supporters when they are wrong.

Modi has set a very high bar for himself and for his country. If he can continue to keep his more fundamentalist supporters in check, and if he is able to demonstrate that India's future economic and social development can be advanced both quickly and fairly, without putting the interests of any one community over another, then he will have achieved a great deal.

Mark Tully, the veteran BBC correspondent, has seen Indian prime ministers come and go, many of them offering a new dawn in a country beset by seemingly insurmountable challenges. He has observed the country change and become much more aspirational since the days of Jawaharlal Nehru, Indira Gandhi or Atal Bihari Vajpayee. Today India is looking for a leader who can do more than promise good times ahead. 'You could see Modi as standing on a balloon of hot air,' he said. 'If it gets punctured and the balloon starts to deflate, then Modi could be in for a lot of trouble. He sold himself as the man who will change things at last, and things really need changing in this country. So if he doesn't, the pendulum could swing back the other way.'

Narendra Modi asked for trust in himself and he now has the opportunity to prove that it was not misplaced. His superbly fought and extraordinarily successful election campaign owed much to the hard work of others, but the victory was ultimately his. The way he ran it, just as the way he conducted himself as chief minister of Gujarat, showed one quality above all others. Determination. Not merely a determination to do the best he could in the circumstances, but a determination never to recognise the possibility of failure. There is no reason to believe he will not apply the same indomitable will to the business of government.

Without Modi, India would not now be at such a decisive turning point in its history. The 360-degree campaign was 360 degrees of Modi. Never before has so much trust, whether from the lowly party worker, the successful business executive, or the idealistic young first-time voter, been placed in one man. If expectations have been raised too high, if the image of a leader capable of almost superhuman endeavours has been burnished a little too much, then he has nobody to blame but himself. If he succeeds, or comes even within shouting distance of achieving all that he has promised, then the man who got more votes than any other politician in the universe will have shown that winning was just the beginning.

INDIAN POLITICS: A WHO'S WHO

Adani, Gautam: b. 1962. Self-made business tycoon, chairman and founder of the Adani Group. Personal wealth estimated to be $7.1 billion as of September 2014, according to Forbes. Hails from Modi's native Gujarat state and is known to be very close to the PM.

Advani, L. K.: b. 1927. Deputy prime minister 2002–04; minister of home affairs 1998–2004. Founder member of the BJP. An early mentor of Narendra Modi. He was the unsuccessful prime ministerial candidate for the BJP in the 2009 election and resisted Modi's selection for the role in 2014.

Aiyar, Mani Shankar: b. 1941. Former diplomat and currently a senior politician in the Congress Party. He held various cabinet posts during the Congress-led UPA government of 2004–9 under prime minister Dr Manmohan Singh.

Ambani, Mukesh: b. 1957. Chairman of Reliance Industries with many business ventures in the petrochemicals, manufacturing and wireless sectors. The richest person in India for eight years running according to Forbes, with a net worth of $19.9 billion. A native of Gujarat and one of the industrialists close to Modi.

Banerjee, Mamta: b. 1955. Elected chief minister of West Bengal in 2011. In 1997 she disassociated herself from the Congress Party and formed the All India Trinamool Congress, also known as TMC. The party won a landslide victory in the 2011 legislative assembly elections in West Bengal.

Dikshit, Sheila: b. 1938. Chief minister of Delhi from 1998 to 2013. A member of the Congress Party. Dikshit led the Congress to three consecutive electoral victories in Delhi. She was defeated in the December 2013 Delhi Legislative Assembly elections and was succeeded by Aam Aadmi Party leader Arvind Kejriwal.

Gandhi, Indira: b. 1917; d. 1984. The second longest-serving, and the only female, prime minister of India. She held the post from 1966 to 1977 and from 1980 until her assassination by her Sikh bodyguards in 1984. Daughter of Jawaharlal Nehru, mother of Rajiv Gandhi and grandmother of Rahul Gandhi. She presided over a state of emergency from 1975 to 1977, during which she ruled by decree.

Gandhi, Mohandas Karamchand ('Mahatma'): b. 1869; d. 1948. One of the paramount leaders of the independence movement in British-ruled India. He inspired non-violent movements for civil rights and freedom across the world. As well as demanding self-rule, Gandhi led nationwide campaigns to reduce poverty, expand women's rights, support religious and ethnic understanding and end the discrimination against 'untouchables'. No relation to the Nehru-Gandhi family. He was assassinated in 1948 by Nathuram Godse.

Gandhi, Priyanka: b. 1972. Indian politician and daughter of the late Rajiv Gandhi and his wife, Sonia. Sometimes spoken of as a future Congress Party leader, she was active in the 2014 campaign in support of her brother, Rahul, and her mother.

Gandhi, Rahul: b. 1970. Vice president of the Congress Party since January 2013. Entered politics in the 2004 general election when he won his father's former constituency of Amethi in Uttar Pradesh. He is the eldest of the two children of Rajiv and Sonia Gandhi, the grandson of Indira Gandhi and the great-grandson of Jawaharlal Nehru. He was widely perceived to be the most likely new PM if Congress had won the 2014 election, although the party did not formally announce who would get the post.

Gandhi, Rajiv: b. 1944; d. 1991. Seventh prime minister of India, serving from 1984–89. He took office after the 1984 assassination of his mother, Indira Gandhi, when he became the youngest PM in India's history. He was leader of the Congress Party until his assassination in 1991 by a Tamil suicide bomber.

Gandhi, Sonia: b. 1946. Italian-born politician, who became president of the Congress Party in 1998. MP for Rae Bareli. Leader of the opposition 1998–2004. She decided not to assume the prime ministership when a Congress-led coalition won the 2004 election, preferring to support Dr Manmohan Singh. She is the widow of former prime minister Rajiv Gandhi, and has two children, Rahul and Priyanka.

Godse, Nathuram: b. 1910; d. 1949. Assassin of Mahatma Gandhi, who he shot in the chest three times at point-blank range in January 1948. He was an extreme Hindu nationalist and had been a member of the Rashtriya Swayamsevak Sangh. He left the RSS in the early 1940s to form a more militant organisation, the Hindu Rashtra Dal. Sentenced to death in November 1949 and hanged a week later.

Goyal, Piyush: b. 1964. Appointed minister of power and energy, May 2014. Was treasurer of the BJP during the election campaign and chaired the influential Election Information Campaign Committee, overseeing advertising and social media. A member of the upper house of parliament.

Hazare, Anna: b. 1937. A prominent anti-corruption campaigner. He was a former soldier in the Indian army who became a social activist and led movements to promote rural development, increase government transparency and investigate and punish wrong-doing in public life.

Irani, Smriti: b. 1976. BJP politician and former model, television actress and producer. Appointed minister of human resource development in May 2014. She is a member of the upper house of parliament and unsuccessfully contested the Amethi lower house constituency against Rahul Gandhi in the 2014 election.

Jaitley, Arun: b. 1952. Close supporter of Narendra Modi. Appointed minister of finance and minister of defence in May 2014. He was also a successful Supreme Court lawyer. Member of the BJP national executive since 1991. Former minister in the government of Atal Bihari Vajpayee. Member of the upper house of parliament. He stood for election to the lower house from the Amritsar constituency in 2014 but lost.

Kejriwal, Arvind: b. 1968. Leader of the Aam Aadmi Party (AAP). Former civil servant turned social activist who was an ally of Anna Hazare in the anti-corruption movement. Kejriwal founded the AAP in 2011 and briefly served as chief minister of Delhi from 28 December 2013 to 14 February 2014. Unsuccessfully contested the constituency of Varanasi against Narendra Modi in the 2014 election. Became Delhi chief minister again in February 2015 after the AAP won a spectacular victory in the Assembly polls.

Kumar, Nitish: b. 1951. Chief minister of the state of Bihar from 2005 to 2014. Previously, he was a minister in the national coalition government led by Atal Bihari Vajpayee of the BJP. He belongs to the Janata Dal (United) Party. He opposed the appointment of Narendra Modi as the BJP's prime ministerial candidate and in June 2013 broke the 17-year-old alliance between his party and the BJP.

Madhav, Ram: b. 1965. Appointed vice president and general secretary of the BJP in 2014. Previously he was one of the leaders of the RSS and their official spokesperson. During the 2014 campaign he was in charge of election management for the RSS.

Mayawati: b. 1956. Mayawati Kumari, always known by her first name only, served four terms as chief minister of Uttar Pradesh (UP) between 1995 and 2012. She is leader of the Bahujan Samaj Party (BSP). Her party did very badly in the 2014 election, losing all its seats.

Modi, Narendra: b. 1950. Elected prime minister of India in May 2014. Leader of the BJP and the first politician from outside the Congress Party to win an overall majority in parliament. Modi was chief minister of Gujarat from 2001 to 2014, winning three successive election victories. He was refused a visa to enter the United States in 2005 as a result of the Gujarat riots of 2002, in which over a thousand people died. Modi adopted policies designed to boost the development of Gujarat and established an enthusiastic personal following that enabled him to secure his party's candidature for prime minister in the 2014 elections.

Nehru, Jawaharlal: b. 1889; d.1964. Prime minister 1947–64. India's first PM after independence from Britain. Prominent leader of the Indian National Congress since the 1920s. Established India as a parliamentary democracy and a republic. Father of Indira Gandhi, great-grandfather of Rahul Gandhi.

Patel, Keshubhai: b. 1928. Chief minister of the state of Gujarat in 1995 and 1998–2001. Forced to stand down in 2001 when he was replaced by Narendra Modi. He joined the RSS in 1945 and was a founder member of the BJP in the 1980s. He left the party in 2012 and formed the Gujarat Parivartan Party.

Patel, Sardar Vallabhbhai: b. 1875; d. 1950. A leader of the Indian National Congress and one of the founding fathers of the Republic of India. He organised non-violent civil disobedience movements against the British Raj. After independence he served as deputy prime minister from 1947 to 1950 and minister of home affairs 1948–50. He played a crucial role in uniting the many regions and principalities of the country and became known as the Iron Man of India. A huge statue in his honour is under construction in his native state of Gujarat.

Ramdev, Baba: b. 1965. A spiritual leader and yoga practitioner with a big public following as a result of his TV appearances. He was a supporter of the anti-corruption movement and later publicly supported Narendra Modi's campaign to become prime minister.

Ravishankar, Sri Sri: b. 1956. Spiritual leader and founder of the Art of Living Foundation, which aims to relieve individual stress, societal problems and violence. His organisation conducted a 'happiness survey' during the 2014 elections that was seen to be supporting Narendra Modi's campaign.

Shah, Amit: b. 1964. Appointed president of the BJP in July 2014. Close associate of Narendra Modi. Former home minister of Gujarat. In 2010 he was arrested and accused of involvement in the murder of two suspects. He was banned from Gujarat and allowed to return only in 2012. The charges were dismissed in 2014. In charge of campaigning in Uttar Pradesh in the general election, where the BJP won seventy-three out of eighty seats.

Shourie, Arun: b. 1941. Journalist, author and former BJP minister. He was an economist with the World Bank, a consultant to the Planning Commission of India and editor of both the *Indian Express* and the *Times of India.* He served as minister for telecommunications and information technology from 2002–04.

Singh, Manmohan: b. 1932. Prime minister of India from 2004–14 as head of a coalition led by the Congress Party. He was the first Sikh to hold the office. In 2009 he became the first prime minister since Jawaharlal Nehru to be re-elected after completing a full five-year term. A former economist, he was highly praised for his efforts to liberalise the economy but his reputation later became tarnished by a series of corruption scandals involving his ministers.

Singh, Rajnath: b. 1951. Appointed home minister, May 2014. He was chief minister of Uttar Pradesh from 2000–02 and agriculture minister in the national government of Atal Bihari Vajpayee from 2003-04. President of the BJP 2005–09 and 2013–14. MP for Lucknow and a strong supporter of Narendra Modi.

Swaraj, Sushma: b. 1952. Appointed minister of external affairs, May 2014. Former chief minister of Delhi. She was broadcasting minister for a short period in the government of Atal Bihari Vajpayee. Was an ally of L. K. Advani and resisted the selection of Narendra Modi as prime ministerial candidate but was persuaded to change her mind.

Tata, Ratan: b. 1937. The head of the Tata Sons conglomerate with wide business and manufacturing interests. He has an estimated net worth of over $1 billion. He stepped down as the chairman of Tata Group in December 2012 but continued as the chairman of the group's charitable trusts.

Tata, Sir Ratan: b. 1871; d. 1918. One of the leading Indian industrialists at the beginning of the twentieth century. He gave generous financial backing to Mohandas Gandhi to support his early campaigning on behalf of the Indian community in South Africa. He was the grandfather of Ratan Tata.

Vajpayee, Atal Bihari: b. 1924. Prime minister 1996 (thirteen days) and 1998–2004. The first PM from outside the Congress Party to serve a full five-year term. Seen to be from the more moderate wing of the BJP. He initially sought the resignation of Narendra Modi after the Gujarat riots but later relented, a decision he reportedly came to regret.

Vivekananda, Swami: b. 1863; d. 1902. Hindu monk and chief disciple of the nineteenth-century saint Ramakrishna. He is often quoted by Narendra Modi who regards him as one of the major influences on his life and thinking. He was a key figure in the introduction of the Indian philosophies of Vedanta and yoga to the western world and is credited with raising inter-faith awareness, bringing Hinduism to the status of a major world religion during the late nineteenth century.

Yogi Adityanath, Mahant: b.1972. BJP MP for Gorakhpur in the state of Uttar Pradesh. He became the head priest of the Gorakhnath Mutt, a Hindu temple in his constituency, in September 2014. He is known for his outspoken nationalist views and has been criticised for making alleged hate speeches against other religious communities.

ABBREVIATIONS

AAP: Aam Aadmi Party ('Common Man's Party'), founded in 2012 by Arvind Kejriwal. It formed a short-lived administration in Delhi after the 2013 state legislative elections but performed badly in the general election, securing just four seats. Won a sweeping victory in the Delhi Assembly elections in February 2015 winning sixty-seven out of seventy seats.

AICC: All India Congress Committee. The governing body of the All India Congress Party, or Congress for short, a left-of-centre party that dominated Indian politics under the leadership of the Nehru-Gandhi family for most of the time since Independence. The party came second in the general election but won just forty-four seats.

ASSOCHAM: The Associated Chambers of Commerce and Industry of India.

BJP: Bharatiya Janata Party ('Indian People's Party'), founded in 1980. Winner of the 2014 general election. Under the leadership of Narendra Modi, the party secured 282 seats, giving it an overall majority in parliament. The BJP is a right-wing party with close ideological and organisational links to the Hindu nationalist Rashtriya Swayamsevak Sangh (RSS).

BKS: Bharitya Kisan Sangh ('Indian Farmers Union').

BMS: Bharitya Mazdoor Sangh ('Indian Labourers Union').

BRICS: Brazil, Russia, India, China and South Africa. An association of these five major emerging national economies.

BSP: Bahujan Samaj Party ('Majority People's Party'). Founded in 1984, the BSP has its main base in the state of Uttar Pradesh. Its leader, Mayawati, served four terms as the state's chief minister. Although it came third in the share of the votes cast in the 2014 election it won no seats in parliament.

CAG: Citizens For Accountable Governance. Also Comptroller and Auditor General.

CBI: Central Bureau Of Investigation.

CII: The Confederation of Indian Industry.

DMK: Dravida Munnetra Kazhagam, a party based in the southern states of Tamil Nadu and Puducherry. The party did well in the 2004 elections, winning 40 seats. They were awarded seven ministerial posts in the Congress-led UPA coalition government. In 2014 they failed to win any parliamentary seats.

EC: Election Commission.

EICC: Election Information Campaign Committee. One of the main BJP committees in the run-up to the general election.

HRD: Human Resource and Development. A government department.

JDU: Janata Dal (United), founded in 2003. A centre-left political party based in Bihar and Jharkhand. Previously an important ally of the BJP, the JDU left the alliance in June

2013 to protest against the elevation of Narendra Modi. It won two seats in the general election.

NCC: National Cadet Corps. Founded in 1948, it is a state funded organisation designed to encourage young people to become able leaders and useful citizens. Membership is voluntary and while it is tied to the armed services, there is no obligation to go on active military service.

NDA: National Democratic Alliance. The electoral alliance led by the BJP. It has twenty-nine members. Twelve of them, including the BJP, won seats at the 2014 general election, giving them a total of 336 seats.

NRI: Non-Resident Indians. Citizens of India who are living abroad.

OBC: Other Backward Classes. The Mandal Commission, set up in 1979, grouped together many lower castes as OBCs which it calculated as comprising 52% of the population, although this figure is disputed. It does not include the lowest castes, including Dalits. By virtue of his birth, Narendra Modi is an OBC.

RSS: Rashtriya Swayamsevak Sangh ('National Volunteer Organization'). Founded in 1925, it is a Hindu nationalist organisation whose members focus on charitable, educational and volunteer work. The RSS, often referred to as the Sangh, helped found the BJP in 1980 and many of its leaders are actively involved in BJP politics.

SIT: Special Investigation Team. A team set up by the Supreme Court to inquire into specific allegations, including those against Narendra Modi after the Gujarat riots of 2002.

SP: Samajwadi Party ('Socialist Party') founded in 1992. Based in the state of Uttar Pradesh where it won a landslide victory in the legislative assembly elections of 2012. The party won five seats in the general election.

UP: Uttar Pradesh. India's most highly populated and electorally significant state.

UPA: United Progressive Alliance. The name of the coalition of parties, led by the Congress Party, which governed India from 2004 to 2014. The alliance had ten members at the 2014 election and won a total of fifty-four seats.

CHRONOLOGY

1947

August 15: Indian Independence from British rule. Partition of the country into the Dominions of India and Pakistan.

1948

January 30: Assassination of Mahatma Gandhi by Nathuram Godse.
February 4: RSS banned following Gandhi's assassination.

1949

July 11: Ban on RSS lifted 'unconditionally'.

1950

September 17: Modi born in Vadnagar in the north of what is now the state of Gujarat.

1951-52

Oct 51 – Feb 52: India's first general election. Jawaharlal Nehru, leader of the Congress Party, became PM with a huge majority.

1957

Feb – March: Second general election. Jawaharlal Nehru won a second term after another landslide.

1962

February: Third general election. Jawaharlal Nehru re-elected with a slightly reduced majority.

1967

February:	Fourth general election. The Congress Party won comfortably under the leadership of Nehru's daughter, Indira Gandhi.

1971

March:	Fifth general election. Indira Gandhi re-elected with a big majority.

1975

June 25:	Emergency rule declared by Indira Gandhi following political unrest. It gave her the authority to rule by decree and lasted twenty-one months.

1977

March:	Sixth general election. The Congress Party was defeated for the first time. A Bhartiya Lok Dal/Janta Party coalition took office under Morarji Desai as prime minster.
March 23:	Emergency lifted and all arrested leaders released from jail.

1980

January:	Seventh general election. The Congress Party under Indira Gandhi returned to power with a huge majority.
April 6:	The Bharatiya Janata Party (BJP) founded with the support of the leadership of the Hindu nationalist RSS.

1984

October 31:	Assassination of Indira Gandhi by two of her bodyguards in the aftermath of Operation Blue Star against the Sikh Golden Temple in Amritsar.
December:	Eighth general election. A landslide victory for Indira Gandhi's son, Rajiv.

1989

November: Ninth general election. No party had a majority. The Congress Party went into opposition and V.P. Singh became prime minister at the head of a National Front alliance that was supported by the BJP.

1990

February: Gujarat state assembly election. The Congress Party was defeated after a decade in power. The new government included both the Janata Dal Party and the BJP.

1991

May - June: Tenth general election. Again no party could get a majority. A minority government was formed under P.V. Narasimha Rao of the Congress Party.

May 21: Assassination of Rajiv Gandhi, by Tamil militants while campaigning for elections near Chennai, Tamil Nadu.

1992

December 6: Babri Masjid mosque in Aodyha destroyed by Hindu extremists.

1995

March 14: Keshubhai Patel of the BJP became Gujarat chief minister after a landslide victory in the state assembly election. Modi had returned to Gujarat to work in the campaign.

1996

April – May: Eleventh general election. A hung parliament resulted in an unstable government and three prime ministers in two years.

May 16: BJP leader Atal Bihari Vajpayee took office as prime minister but lasted just thirteen days. On 1 June he was replaced by H.D. Deve Gowda from the Janata Dal Party.

1998

February: Twelfth general election. No party had a majority. The BJP leader, Atal Bihari Vajpayee, took office at the head of an unstable coalition.

March 4: Keshubhai Patel of the BJP returned as Gujarat chief minister after the party's victory in the state assembly election. Modi had returned to Gujarat again to help organise the campaign.

May 19: Modi promoted to become the party's general secretary in charge of organisation.

1999

Sep-Oct: Thirteenth general election. Atal Bihari Vajpayee of the BJP formed a stable coalition at the head of the National Democratic Alliance (NDA).

2001

October 4: Modi appointed leader of the Gujarat party and interim chief minister of Gujarat after Keshubhai Patel was forced to resign.

2002

February 27: Train carrying over two thousand Hindu pilgrims attacked at Godhra railway station. Fifty-nine people killed.

February 28: Riots erupted in Gujarat. Over the next three days at least 1000 people were killed, the majority of them Muslims.

April 30: Report by Human Rights Watch entitled *We Have No Orders to Save You* published. It claimed the riots were planned in advance and implicated both the police and officials from the BJP.

December 22: Narendra Modi sworn in as chief minister again after winning his first Gujarat state assembly election as leader with a big majority.

2003

August 17: Modi speech at the Wembley Conference Centre in London during a visit to the UK.

September 28: First 'Vibrant Gujarat' Global Investors' Summit held.

2004

April-May: Fourteenth general election. The BJP lost office and the Congress Party-led United Progressive Alliance (UPA) formed a government. Sonia Gandhi announced she would not take the post of prime minister which went to Dr Manmohan Singh.

2005

March 19: US government visa ban on Narendra Modi announced under the Immigration and Nationality Act which included the power to exclude anybody believed to have been 'responsible for, or directly carried out, at any time, particularly severe violations of religious freedom'.

2007

February 27: Narendra Modi's second victory in the Gujarat state assembly election with a big majority.

October 19: Modi walked out of a TV interview with Karan Thapar for CNN-IBN when questioned about Godhra riots.

2008

January 21: Prince Charles speech on the environment delivered by hologram to a conference in Abu Dhabi.

October 3: Tata Motors announced it would shift production of its Nano car to Gujarat from West Bengal, praising Modi's pro-business policies.

2009

February 1:	Modi's first 'tweet' on Twitter.
May 5:	Modi Facebook account opened.
April-May:	Fifteenth general election. The Congress Party-led United Progressive Alliance formed a government for a second time under Dr Manmohan Singh.

2010

March 27-28	Modi gave testimony for nine hours before the Supreme Court appointed Special Investigation Team (SIT), into the 2002 riots.
August 12:	Reports published linking the Congress-led government to alleged corruption in contracts for the 2010 Commonwealth Games in Delhi.
October 20:	Facebook article on Modi posted under the heading 'Narendra Modi as Prime Minister? Why Not?'
November 10:	Corruption story broke implicating ministers in the sale of 2G mobile phone spectrum licenses.

2011

April 5:	Anti-corruption movement launched by social activist Anna Hazare.
June 1:	Yoga guru and anti-corruption campaigner Baba Ramdev met at Delhi airport by four government ministers.

2012

Feb – March:	Uttar Pradesh state assembly elections, Samajwadi Party (SP) led by Akhilesh Yadav won a majority.
February 28:	'Clean chit' reported to have been given to Modi by the Special Investigation Team (SIT) on Godhra riots.
March 1:	Modi blog said the events of 2002 'pained me deeply'.
March 16:	Modi appeared on the front cover of *Time* magazine in Asia.
August 17:	Report by Comptroller and Auditor General claimed

	billions of rupees lost to the public purse in the allocation of coal reserves.
October 22:	Meeting between Modi and Sir James Bevan, British High Commissioner, lifting the ban by UK Government.
November 18:	First 3D hologram rallies staged by Modi during the Gujarat elections.
December 12:	Second round of 3D rallies reached 53 locations, earning Modi a place in the *Guinness Book of Records.*
December 20:	Results of Gujarat elections declared. Modi elected as chief minister for the third time. During his victory speech the crowd shouted 'PM, PM' and 'Delhi, Delhi'.

2013

January 7:	Modi welcomed by EU ambassadors in Delhi.
March 31:	Modi appointed to BJP's top decision making body, the parliamentary board.
June 9:	BJP parliamentary board declared Modi chairman of the General Election Campaign Committee.
June 12:	Amit Shah arrived in Lucknow, capital of Uttar Pradesh, to start preparations for the general election campaign after being appointed by Modi.
June 16:	Nitish Kumar, leader of the Janata Dal United Party (JDU), broke its 17-year old alliance with the BJP.
July 14:	Modi speech at Fergusson College in Pune, Maharashtra. First use of crowd-sourcing ideas for his speeches through social media.
August 27:	Murder of a Muslim and two Hindu youths in Muzaffarnagar in eastern Uttar Pradesh. More than 60 people were killed in the ensuing riots.
September 13:	Modi chosen as prime ministerial candidate by the BJP Parliamentary Board.
September 15:	Modi's first rally after being declared PM candidate in Rewari, Haryana, where he addressed ex-servicemen.
September 18:	Court in Muzaffarnagar, Uttar Pradesh, ordered the arrest of 16 politicians and community leaders for inciting violence.
October 27:	In Patna, in the state of Bihar, bombs exploded in and around the site of a Modi rally killing six people.

October 31:	Foundation stone laid for the Statue of Unity by Modi and L.K. Advani.
November 15:	Testimonial match for Indian cricketer, Sachin Tendulkar. The crowd chanted Modi's name when Rahul Gandhi walked into the stadium.
November 15:	'Snoopgate' story appeared on two news websites.
December 4:	Assembly elections held in New Delhi, the BJP got the most seats followed by the Aam Aadmi Party (AAP). No party had a majority. BJP declined to form a government.
December 15:	'Run for Unity' organised simultaneously across 1,100 locations.
December 17:	Lokpal Act passed creating anti-corruption ombudsmen.
December 28:	AAP leader Arvind Kejriwal sworn in as Delhi chief minister.

2014

January 8:	Dr Manmohan Singh statement, 'yes, we are facing bad days but the good days will be coming soon.'
January 14:	New BJP slogan unveiled by Modi 'Good Days Are Coming'.
January 17:	Rahul Gandhi speech to All India Congress Committee (AICC) meeting.
January 17:	'*Chai wala*' remark by Congress MP Mani Shankar Aiyar.
January 27:	Rahul Gandhi's much criticised interview with Arnab Goswami for the *Times Now* TV channel.
February 12:	First round of *'Chai pe Charcha'* tea stall chats at more than 1,000 locations.
February 13:	US ambassador Nancy Powell met Modi.
February 14:	Arvind Kejriwal resigned as Delhi chief minister after forty-nine days.
March 5:	Dates for the general election announced. Model Code of Conduct imposed by the Election Commission of India.
March 8:	Second round of *'Chai pe Charcha'* across 1,500 locations in India and transmitted live to thirty foreign countries.

April 4:	Amit Shah accused of giving a hate speech in Shamli, Uttar Pradesh.
April 7:	BJP Manifesto unveiled. Polling day in the first phase of the general election.
April 9:	Polling day in second phase of the general election.
April 10:	Polling day in third phase of the general election.
April 11:	Attempt to overturn Modi's 'clean chit' over the Gujarat riots rejected by the Supreme Court.
April 11:	Amit Shah banned from holding further public rallies by the Election Commission for alleged hate speech.
April 11:	Modi 3D rallies launched across 100 locations at one time.
April 12:	Modi's first appearance on a national TV interview on India TV's *'Aap Ki Adalat'*.
April 12:	Polling day in fourth phase of the general election.
April 17:	Polling day in the fifth phase of the general election.
April 24:	Modi filed his nomination papers in Varanasi.
April 24:	Polling day in sixth phase of the general election.
April 30:	Modi posed for a 'selfie' with the BJP symbol, the lotus flower, in breach of election rules.
April 30:	Polling day in seventh phase of the general election.
May 5:	Controversy over Modi's rallies in Faizabad and Amethi, the constituency of Rahul Gandhi.
May 7:	Polling day in eighth phase of the general election.
May 8:	Modi's procession to BJP party headquarters in Varansai after he is forced to cancel a rally.
May 8:	Modi met Muslim war veteran, Col. Nizamuddin and kissed his feet.
May 8:	Modi's final TV interview of the campaign, with *Times Now,* broadcast.
May 10:	Last day of election campaigning.
May 12:	Polling day in the ninth and final phase of the general election.
May 16:	Declaration of the general election results. The BJP won with 282 seats, giving it a parliamentary majority. Narendra Modi tweets *'India has won'*.
May 26:	Modi sworn in as the fifteenth prime minister of India.
May 26:	Modi's first cabinet announced.
July 10:	Finance minister Arun Jaitley presented his first budget.
July 13:	Modi arrived in Brazil to attend the BRICS summit.

August 15:	Modi's first Independence Day Address at the Red Fort, Delhi.
August 28:	Plan to provide banks accounts and accident insurance for the poor unveiled.
August 30:	Start of Modi visit to Japan.
September 3:	End of Modi's first 100 days.
September 13:	Uttar Pradesh by-elections held in 11 assembly seats. Samajwadi Party (SP) won eight seats and the BJP won three seats.
September 26:	Modi departure for the US.
September 27:	Modi address to the United Nations General Assembly.
September 27:	Modi appearance at Central Park rally.
September 28:	Modi speech at Madison Square Garden.
October 2:	'Clean India' project launched.
October 11:	'Adopt a Village' scheme launched.
October 15:	Haryana state assembly elections. BJP won a majority for the first time.
October 15:	Maharashtra state assembly election. BJP won the largest number of seats and formed a coalition government.
November 14:	Modi departure for Australia to attend the G-20 summit.
November 18:	'Selfie' with Tony Abbott at Melbourne Cricket Ground.
November 18:	Modi address to the Australian parliament in Canberra.
November 25:	Modi visit to Nepal.
November 11:	Modi announced new ministers in enlarged government.
December 30:	Charges against Amit Shah while Gujarat home affairs minister dismissed.

2015

January 11:	Vibrant Gujarat summit opened with many world leaders attending.
January 26:	Republic Day. President Obama guest of honour in Delhi.
February 10:	AAP wins landslide victory in Delhi Assembly elections taking 67 seats to 3 for the BJP.

NOTES

CHAPTER ONE: THE OUTSIDER

Page 5 'secularism and communalism . . . have significantly different meanings.' 'Secular' in India isn't the opposite of 'religious' or 'spiritual'. It signifies support for an inclusive approach to all religions, often with special help for those that are in a minority. 'Communal' has nothing to do with something 'shared' or held in common. It means owing allegiance to your own community, usually your religion, caste or ethnic group.

Page 6 'It is not hard to find people who readily define Modi as an extremist . . . a fascist.' *Financial Times* (14 March 2014) headlined a commentary by its South Asia Correspondent, Victor Mallett, *India elections – the return of Hitler.* Mallett was remarking on how readily Hitler's name is bandied about in Indian politics. Rahul Gandhi had just likened Modi to Hitler, saying 'Hitler was the biggest arrogant who thought people had no wisdom and there was no need to listen to them. He thought he had all the knowledge himself. Similarly, there is a leader today in India who says "I have done this, I have done that" and behaves arrogantly. A leader should not be arrogant." As Mallett pointed out, Gandhi's grandmother, Indira, had been likened to Hitler by a leading BJP politician, Arun Jaitley, who became Modi's finance minister in 2014.

Page 6 'the diary of my time in Downing Street'. *The Spin Doctor's Diary*, Lance Price, (Hodder & Stoughton 2006).

Page 6 'my second book'. *Where Power Lies*, Lance Price, (Simon & Schuster 2010).

Page 7 'in Mandela's case he was more than happy'. *The Spin Doctor's Diary,* Lance Price, (Hodder & Stoughton 2006), p. 256.

Page 7 'Fifty-six inches is a very cleverly crafted tool'. Nilanjan

Mukhopadhyay, *Narendra Modi, the Man, the Times* (Tranquebar Press 2013), p. 279.

Page 11 'former President Herbert Hoover . . . I could do better without it'. *newslaundy.com*, 12 November 2012.

Page 12 'I am an outsider . . . elite class of this place.' The text of all Modi's major speeches can be found on his website *narendramodi.in*.

Page 14 'An absolutely model campaign . . . even they hadn't dreamed of.' Interview with the author.

Page 14 'Half the people . . . nothing on earth.' Patrick French, *India – A Portrait* (Penguin 2012), p. 67.

Page 15 'Candidates running under the colours of the BJP secured 31%'. All figures from the *Election Commission of India*. Full election statistics are published on their website *eci.nic.in*.

Page 15 'The greatest show on earth'. *New York Times*, 2 June 2009.

Page 15 'Gold standard'. Hillary Clinton speech, 20 July 2011, Chennai.

Page 16 'Eligible electorate in India'. The United Nations World Population Prospects, 2012 revision, as quoted by S.Y. Quraishi, *The Making of the Great Indian Election* (Rupa Publications 2014), pp. 63-64.

Page 17 'You campaign in poetry, you govern in prose.' *The New Republic*, 4 April 1985.

CHAPTER TWO: CHAI WALA

Page 19 'I am a person . . . becoming anything.' Narendra Modi, *Aap Ki Adalat*, India TV, 12 April 2014.

Page 20 'In all corners of the country . . . wanted to see him win.' Interview with the author.

Page 20 'Past elections have shown . . . trusted name not a party name.' Interview with the author.

Page 21 'He would help his father sell tea'. *Aap Ki Adalat*, India TV, 12 April 2014.

Page 22 'I was in the train compartment . . . and take the money.' Andy Marino, *Narendra Modi, A Political Biography* (Harper Collins 2014), p. 9.

Page 22 'While Gandhi was born into a comfortably off family'. Mohandas Gandhi was born into the Bania caste, an occupational community of money-lenders, merchants, bankers and traders. 'Mahatma' is an honorary title meaning 'venerable'. India's caste system has traditionally separated everybody into rigid social groups and persists to this day, although social mobility has increased considerably since independence.

Page 22 'OBC's are classified as socially and educationally backward.' The Constitution of India details the Scheduled Castes and Scheduled Tribes of the country, prohibits discrimination on grounds of caste, creed or birth and empowers the state to make special provisions for the advancement of any socially and educationally backward classes.

Page 22 '*Childhood Stories of Narendra Modi.*' The Modi cartoon book followed the huge success of a strand of comics that told fictionalised stories of mythological heroes as children. They became a rage and spawned a TV series.

Page 23 'Narendrabhai would also read our palms'. *Times of India*, 9 April 2014.

Page 24 'I was brave not naughty . . . teachers were very upset.' *Aap Ki Adalat*, India TV, 12 April 2014.

Page 24 'only an average student '. *The Caravan*, 1 March 2013.

Page 24 'Narendra always wanted to do something different'. *The Caravan*, 1 March 2013.

Page 24 'Modi would later join the National Cadet Corps'. The NCC is a military cadet organisation open to students from the age of 13. It is similar to the British Combined Cadet Force. Modi said on the campaign trail that he had wanted to join the army but his parents couldn't afford it.

Page 25 'A unique phenomenon in the history of Bharat [India]'. Bharat is derived from the Sanskrit name for the Indian subcontinent, Bharatra.

Page 25 'Sangh's sphere of influence has been spreading far and wide'. *rss.org*.

Page 25 'second largest political movement . . . Chinese Communist Party.' Edward Luce, *In Spite of the Gods* (Abacus 2011) p. 144.

Page 26 'open admiration for Hitler'. Marzia Casolari, an Italian scholar who studied Indian politics, once wrote of RSS' connections with European fascism: 'The existence of direct contacts between the representatives of the [Italian] Fascist regime, including Mussolini, and Hindu nationalists demonstrates that Hindu nationalism had much more than an abstract interest in the ideology and practice of fascism. The interest of Indian Hindu nationalists in fascism and Mussolini must not be considered as dictated by an occasional curiosity, confined to a few individuals; rather, it should be considered as the culminating result of the attention that Hindu nationalists… focused on Italian dictatorship and its leader. To them, fascism appeared to be an example of conservative revolution.' Quoted in *International Business News,* 6 March 2012.

Page 26 'closely modelled on that worn by Mussolini's Blackshirts'. Edward Luce, *In Spite of the Gods* (Abacus 2011), p. 152.

Page 27 'The RSS is at best an effort to protect Hinduism.' Email from Swaminathan Gurumurthy.

Page 28 'There are several senior leaders . . . less fond.' Nilanjan Mukhopadhyay, *Narendra Modi, the Man, the Times* (Tranquebar Press 2013), p. 304.

Page 28 'There is no Mussolini in the RSS . . . away with the show.' Interview with the author.

Page 29 'Anyone who has read the basic texts of Hindu nationalism . . . not their *punyabhumi* (holyland)'. *Indian Express*, 27 March 2014.

Page 30 'It is a way of life in India . . . so there is no issue.' Interview with the author.

Page 30 'Muslims and Christians in the country are descendants of converts from Hinduism'. Edward Luce, *In Spite of the Gods* (Abacus 2011), p.154.

Page 30 'one nation, one people and one culture.' Preface to the 2014 BJP Manifesto, *Ek Bharat Shreshtha Bharat,* ('One India, Excellent India').

Page 30 'to improve their status by embracing Islam or Christianity.' Edward Luce, *In Spite of the Gods* (Abacus 2011), p.154.

Page 31 'Modi's marriage was never consummated'. *The Times*, 10 April 2014.

Page 31 'We had no idea where he had disappeared to . . . turned up one day.' *The Caravan*, 1 March 2013.

Page 32 'I could fit all . . . begging for food.' *Aap Ki Adalat*, India TV, 12 April 2014.

Page 33 'Until 1978 I was behind . . . how to plan.' Interview with the author.

Page 33 'I was a 25-year old . . . brutally trampled over.' Modi's blog, *narendramodi.in,* 26 June 2013.

Page 33 'I was lucky . . . a different world.' Andy Marino, *Narendra Modi, A Political Biography* (Harper Collins 2014), pp. 44–45.

CHAPTER THREE: CHIEF MINISTER

Page 35 'By refusing to put Muslim fears to rest. . . nurtures it.' *The Economist*, 4 April 2014.

Page 35 'India is a country with multiple religions . . . many of its people.' *New York Times*, 16 October 2013.

Page 36 'It might have lasted longer'. Kingshuk Nag, *The Saffron Tide – the Rise of the BJP* (Rupa Publications 2014), p. 197.

Page 37 'Modi should be allowed to return'. Andy Marino, *Narendra Modi, A Political Biography* (Harper Collins 2014), p. 86.

Page 38 'Many Hindus believe Ayodhya was the birthplace of the Hindu god Ram'. Edward Luce, *In Spite of the Gods* (Abacus 2011), p.158.

Page 39 'the allegation resurfaced intermittently'. For example by party spokesperson Shaktisinh Gohil, who asked, "If you don't call him *maut ka saudagar* (merchant of death), how else can you describe him," *Indian Express*, 21 March 2014.

Page 39 'accusing Sonia Gandhi and her party of besmirching'. *The Hindu*, 13 December 2007.

Page 39 'Human Rights Watch's findings . . . state government.' Human Rights Watch report Vol.14, No.3[c], 'We have No Orders To Save You – State participation and Complicity in Communal Violence in Gujarat', 30 April 2002.

Page 40 'We are aware . . . when he's here.' Home Office statement. *The Guardian*, 18 August 2003.

Page 41 'We were under intense . . . a reasonable compromise.' Interview with the author.

Page 42 'no criminal case is made out against Narendra Modi'. *ibnlive.com,* 11 May 2012.

Page 42 'most of the domestic media . . . "a clean chit"'. *The Hindu,* 10 February 2012.

Page 42 'pulled every trick in the book'. Sundeep Dougal writing in *Outlook*, 3 February 2011.

Page 42 'the events of 2002 . . . "pained me deeply"'. Andy Marino, *Narendra Modi, A Political Biography* (Harper Collins 2014), pp. 240-1.

Page 43 'tweeted simply "God is great"'. *The Hindu*, 12 September 2012.

Page 43 '*No Full Stops in India*'. By Mark Tully, (Penguin 1992).

Page 43 'Rahul Gandhi called the ruling . . . "too premature"'. *India Today*, 11 April 2014.

Page 44 'If Narendra Modi . . . answer for them.' Sudesh Verma, *Narendra Modi – the Game Changer* (Vitasta 2014), p. 354.

Page 44 'The impact of . . . the incident.' Kingshuk Nag, *The Saffron Tide – the Rise of the BJP* (Rupa Publications 2014), p.197.

Page 45 'Gujarat's economy grew at 10.1 per cent'. *India Today*, 4 April 2014.

Page 45 'contributes around 16 per cent of country's industrial production'. Nilanjan Mukhopadhyay, *Narendra Modi, the Man, the Times* (Tranquebar Press 2013), p. 363.

Page 46 'declared Ahmedabad 'the best of India's mega-cities'. *Times of India*, 11 December 2011.

Page 46 'Gujarat is not yet the perfect state'. *India Today*, 4 April 2014.

Page 47 'Mr. Modi's performance as chief minister. . . make it happen.' *The Economist*, 4 April 2014.

Page 47 'I believe it will . . . our work.' Interview with the author.

Page 48 'People would . . . Modi has provided electricity.' *Aap Ki Adalat*, India TV, 12 April 2014.

Page 48 'fast to the death unless Modi resigned'. *Times of India*, 12 December 2004.

Page 48 'I was twenty-seven . . . public perception.' Interview with the author.

Page 49 'Since 2002 . . . state of Gujarat.' Interview with the author.

Page 50 'points with pride to the constituency of Jamnagar'. *India Today*, 16 March 2013.

Page 50 'Look at the records . . . Godhra is wrong.' Nilanjan Mukhopadhyay, *Narendra Modi, the Man, the Times*, (Tranquebar Press 2013), p. 347.

CHAPTER FOUR: BEHIND THE MASK

Page 51 'Narendra Modi as Prime Minister? Why Not?', *facebook.com/notes/india/narendra-modi-as-prime-minister-why-not-please-comment-on-it-/168519983161043.*

Page 52 'Across digital media . . . to do something.' Interview with the author.

Page 54 'The Modi spin machine . . . accountability.' *Truth versus Hype*, social.ndtv.com. 16 December 2012.

Page 55 'After Obama's election . . . use them.' Interview with the author.

Page 56 'Congress alleged that Modi was wearing a "pseudo mask of development".' *Economic Times*, 22 April 2014.

Page 57 'the same accusation was made against Atal Bihari Vajpayee'. The description was made by a man who himself came from that hard-line tradition, K.N. Govindacharya, a veteran RSS ideologue who was close to L.K. Advani. Govindacharya, who was the BJP general secretary at the time, had a bit of a reputation for making unguarded comments so while he denied a report in a Hindi daily newspaper that he had told three British diplomats that Vajpayee's role was "akin to that of a mask in a play", while "Advani is the real power in the BJP", the damage was done. *India Today*, 21 August 2014.

Page 59 'his team were delighted to see their man on the cover of *Time* magazine'. *Time*, 26 March 2012.

Page 60 'Several leading industrialists had spoken out against him'. *The Caravan*, 1 March 2012.

Page 60 'something close to the businessman's darling'. Nilanjan Mukhopadhyay, *Narendra Modi, the Man, the Times* (Trandquebar Press 2013), p. 340.

Page 60 'no-frills Nano car project'. Andy Marino, *Narendra Modi, A Political Biography* (Harper Collins 2014), p. 211.

Page 60 'Gujarat had emerged as the most preferred investment destination'. *Business Standard*, 1 August 2012.

Page 60 'time to bring the chief minister's pariah status to an end'. *The Guardian*, 22 October 2012.

Page 61 'Personally I don't think he was culpable'. Interview with the author.

Page 62 'We are now in a new phase'. *Hindustan Times*, 9 February 2013.

Page 62 'It would take US ambassador Nancy Powell . . . United States was also ready to end its boycott'. *Times of India*, 13 February 2014.

Page 62 'development and Modi's approach to leadership'. *indiatvnews.com*, 28 September 2012.

Page 63 'paradigm shift in the way technology was perceived and utilised'. *narendramodi.in*, 14 March 2013.

Page 63 'Prince Charles, used a system based on Pepper's Ghost'. *Daily Telegraph*, 22 January 2008.

Page 64 'I had no idea what he was like . . . down to work.' *rediff.com*, 5 May 2014.

Page 65 'he swore everybody to secrecy'. Interview for this book given on the condition of anonymity.

Page 65 '"morally reprehensible" to spend so much money on a 3D speech'. *newslaundry.com*, 22 November 2012.

Page 65 'pointed to as many as 125 seats for the BJP in a state assembly of 182'. Nilanjan Mukhopadhyay, *Narendra Modi, the Man, the Times* (Trandquebar Press 2013), p. 378.

Page 66 'By serving Gujarat I serve India. . . what is wrong.' *CNN-IBN*, 21 December 2012.

CHAPTER FIVE: THE BIG MO

Page 69 'People wanted the Congress out.' Interview with the author.

Page 69 'By far the biggest and most blatant exercise in corruption in independent India's history.' *Times of India*, 29 August 2010.

Page 70 'Even with somebody else leading the BJP'. Interview with the author.

Page 71 'Andimuthu Raja, was from one of the Congress Party's coalition partners, the DMK'. Dravida Munnetra Kazhagam, a party based in the southern states of Tamil Nadu and Puducherry. The party did well in the 2004 elections, winning 40 seats. They were awarded seven ministerial posts in the Congress-led UPA coalition government. In 2014 they failed to win any parliamentary seats.

Page 71 'He was accused not only of misallocating the licences . . . sent to jail.' *Times of India,* 25 April 2014.

Page 71 'The "2G scam" became emblematic of a perceived flaw in the UPA arrangement'. Harish Khare, *How Modi Won It,* (Hachette India 2014), p. 23.

Page 71 'Coalgate had the potential to inflict even greater political damage'. *dnaindia.com,* 3 September 2012.

Page 73 'Hazare started another fast-unto-death that he called India's second struggle for independence'. *Times of India,* 28 July 2012.

Page 73 'in December 2013, the Lokpal Bill was passed into law.' *Times of India* 18 December 2013.

Page 73 ''I am going on the path of agitations and he has formed a political party'. *dnaindia.com,* 16 December 2013.

Page 74 'India's most famous yoga guru, known as Baba Ramdev'. *The Hindu,* 2 June 2011.

Page 75 'Sri Sri Ravi Shankar led the vast Art of Living Foundation'. *artofliving.org.*

Page 75 'His campaign was spiritual not political'. *Times of India,* 31 October 2011.

Page 76 'Had she . . . assumed the top job, the controversy would have been massive'. *firstpost.com,* 1 August 2014.

Page 77 'Singh . . . "swallows everything, doesn't spit anything out."' Sanjaya Baru, *The Accidental Prime Minister* (Viking 2014), quoted in *The Economist,* 3 May 2014.

Page 78 'Manmohan Singh was the chief election agent'. Interview with the author.

Page 78 'These are people who held Modi's hand to make him walk'. *Aap Ki Adalat,* India TV, 12 April 2014.

Page 79 'I believe we need an experienced hand as PM.' *Headlines Today,* 3 March 2013.

Page 79 'Gujarat model of economic development . . . had already been successful. ' *Times of India,* 2 June 2013.

Page 80 'The head of the RSS Mohan Bhagwat, asked him to reconsider'. Kingshuk Nag, *The Saffron Tide – the Rise of the BJP* (Rupa Publications 2014), p. 224.

Page 80 'Janata Dal United . . . brought to an end its seventeen-year old electoral alliance'. *Indian Express,* 16 June 2013.

Page 81 'RSS called on the party to get on with it and threw its support behind Modi'. *Times of India*, 3 August 2013.

Page 81 'Advani was . . . worried . . . an early announcement would shift attention from the weakness of Congress and onto Modi's controversial personality'. *Times of India*, 12 September 2013.

Page 81 'disappointment over your style of functioning.' *Times of India*, 13 September 2013.

Page 81 'It was Mr Rajnath Singh who called me first.' Interview with the author.

Page 82 'You didn't have to be the Indian equivalent of a Kremlinologist' *The Hindu*, 17 September 2013.

CHAPTER SIX: THE MODI OPERANDI

Page 83 'The lamp of assembly-based democracy . . . became common.' John Keane, *The Life and Death of Democracy* (Simon & Schuster 2009), p. xi.

Page 83 'The DNA of democracy . . . makes India.' Interview with the author.

Page 89 'never go to the BJP office, don't hold the BJP flag.' *The Caravan*, 11 May 2014.

Page 89 'He became a sort . . . development man.' Interview with the author.

Page 90 'There are a lot of misnomers . . . work for him.' Interview with the author.

Page 92 'I used to coordinate . . . stand of the party.' Interview with the author.

Page 93 'I told him . . . presidential campaign.' Interview with the author.

Page 94 'When a group of . . . coffee table.' *indiancag.org.*

Page 94 'Meet the most trusted strategist in the Narendra Modi organisation.' *Times of India*, 7 October 2013.

Page 95 'We would like . . . Modi's team.' Interview with the author.

Page 95 'changing minds to change people's votes'. *nitidigital.com/aboutus.*

Page 96 'switch focus from maximising allies to maximising seats'. Rajesh Jain, Project 275 for 2014, May 2011.

Page 96 'Back to the Nineties . . . bring change.' Interview with the author.

Page 98 'governing style has never been so distant from what people want'. *modibharosa.com/aboutus.*

CHAPTER SEVEN: I, MODI

Page 99 'BJP parliamentary board had unanimously chosen Narendra Modi'. *NDTV.com,* 11 September 2013.

Page 100 'I was still . . . political scenarios.' Interview with the author.

Page 100 'This was the first . . . bandwagon.' Interview with the author.

Page 103 'Rahul Gandhi failed to connect with the crowd the way Modi did'. *India Today,* 18 September 2013.

Page 104 'lacuna at the heart of the Congress strategy . . . on a sitting duck.' Harish Khare, *How Modi Won It,* (Hachette India 2014), p. 51.

Page 104 'the use of Muslim names has long been part of his demagogic repertoire'. Harish Khare, *How Modi Won It,* (Hachette India 2014), p. 40.

Page 104 'Congress protested that the use of the word was "undignified".' *India Today,* 26 October 2013.

Page 105 'Rahul Gandhi went to see . . . new leader.' Interview with the author.

Page 105 'For most part there seemed to be genuine enthusiasm for Modi'. *firstpost.com,* 28 October 2013.

Page 106 'announcements over the speaker system referring only to "tyre blasts and fire crackers"'. *India Today,* 27 October 2013.

Page 107 'raised concerns about security in writing with the state government'. *NDTV,* 28 October 2013.

Page 107 'necessary arrangements were not made. This is criminal negligence.' Rajdeep Sardesai, *2014: The Election That Changed India* (Penguin Books 2014), p. 258.

Page 107 'very few Muslims in the crowd'. *India Today,* 27 October 2013.

Page 107 'Ten people were charged in connection with the bombings'. *Times of India,* 23 August 2014.

Page 109 '"Sahib" (sir), which was claimed to be a reference to his boss, Narendra Modi'. *Business Standard,* 23 November 2013.

Page 109 'The tapes indicate that . . . relaying it to his Saheb.' *gulail.com/the-stalkers.*

Page 110 'I would like to ask the women . . . yet to answer for Snoopgate.' *Times of India,* 25 March 2014.

Page 110 'Any further investigation, she said, would invade her privacy'. *Hindustan Times,* 6 May 2014.

CHAPTER EIGHT: IRON MAN 2

Page 112 'It will be a unique memorial . . . close to Sardar's heart.' *dnaindia.com,* 7 October 2010.

Page 112 'Modi slapped him down, saying the statue was for everyone'. *Indian Express,* 31 October 2013.

Page 113 'through pamphlets in regional languages . . . to involve the youth.' *Sunday Standard,* 20 October 2013.

Page 114 'largest mass run of its kind in the world'. *statueofunitymovement.com,* 14 December 2013.

Page 114 'Sardar Patel devoted his life to . . . the nation.' *Times of India,* 15 December 2014.

Page 114 'Sheila Dikshit, duly resigned'. *ndtv.com,* 8 December 2013.

Page 115 'The BJP response was to accuse Kejriwal of trying to find excuses'. *The Hindu,* 17 December 2013.

Page 115 'For Kejriwal . . . will depend on how wisely he runs Delhi.' *Times of India,* 29 December 2013.

Page 115 'chief minister and his cabinet colleagues taking to the streets'. *Times of India,* 18 January 2014.

Page 115 'Arvind Kejriwal quits.' *Times of India,* 15 February 2014.

Page 117 'the Arajak Aadmi Party.' *India Today,* 26 January 2014.

Page 117 'money . . . improperly used to fund political campaigning'. *Times of India,* 24 April 2014.

Page 118 'Ramdev "contributed significantly to the formation of the Narendra Modi government"'. *ndtv.com,* 14 September 2014.

Page 118 'It's like giving keys to a driver with a learner's licence' *Economic Times,* 17 January 2014.

Page 118 'Lakshmi always rides on the lotus'. *Indian Express,* 20 March 2014.

Page 119 'Lata Mangeshkar . . . prayed to God that Modi would become PM'. *Hindustan Times,* 1 November 2013.

Page 120 'demanded that Lata Mangeshkar should be stripped of her "Bharat Ratna"'. *NDTV,* 12 November 2013.

Page 120 'he wouldn't serve a third term as PM'. *Times of India,* 3 January 2014.

Page 121 'BJP campaign song, written by Bollywood composer Prasoon Joshi'. *youtube.com/watch?v=XMEBFw-lhh8.*

Page 121 'Gujarat model of development was a "toffee model"'. *Times of India,* 29 March 2014.

Page 122 'speech on the "Idea of India"'. *Times of India,* 20 January 2014.

Page 122 'The speech added weight and substance'. *narendramodi.in/full-speech-shri-narendra-modi-at-the-bjp-national-council-meet-delhi.*

Page 123 'I convert these stones into a ladder'. Sudesh Verma, *Narendra Modi – the Game Changer* (Vitasta 2014), p. 175.

CHAPTER NINE: TEA BREAK

Page 124 'They are the ones who will sell combs to the bald'. *Times of India,* 24 January 2014.

Page 124 'I never sold combs'. *Aap Ki Adalat,* India TV, 12 April 2014.

Page 126 'We aren't helping our campaign by mocking him.' *ibnlive.in.com,* 17 January 2014.

Page 126 'not a tea vendor but he was a canteen contractor.' *Press Trust of India,* 15 February 2014.

Page 126 'Someone rising from a tea shop can never have a national perspective'. *Daily Mail,* 13 December 2014.

Page 128 'By the time . . . tea stall.' Interview with the author.

Page 128 'Modi's campaign priorities and events had proved highly popular'. *Indian Express,* 6 December 2013.

Page 130 'Finally after three . . . in India.' Interview with the author.

Page 130 'Any kind of allurement . . . is not permissible'. *Hindustan Times,* 16 March 2013.

Page 131 'Modi is focusing on . . . 3D technology.' *Times of India,* 20 April 2014.

Page 131 'The questions had been carefully vetted'. Rajdeep

Sardesai, *2014: The Election That Changed India* (Penguin Books 2014), p. 267.

Page 131 'the rallies had been cancelled . . . at all one hundred locations.' Interview with Gaurav Bhatele for this book.

Page 132 'The poll rallies . . . postponed due to a technical reason.' *Times of India,* 7 April 2014.

Page 133 'I just opened one of the stuck bolts and these people went crazy'. Interview with Gaurav Bhatele for this book.

Page 133 'We reached fifty-three places at one time and made it to the *Guinness Book of World Records*'. *oneindia.com,* 11 April 2014.

Page 134 'I would chose a colour that would suit the 3D hologram and he would wear that.' *rediff.com,* 5 May 2014.

Page 135 'These village people are saying they will not let me go'. Interview with Gaurav Bhatele for this book.

Page 135 'In Hindu mythology . . . rural areas.' Interview with the author.

Page 135 'The 3D technology has been a huge asset for the Modi campaign.' *Times of India,* 8 May 2014.

Page 136 'In my head . . . these activities.' Interview with the author.

CHAPTER TEN: IMODI

Page 138 'It was our . . . Facebook likes.' Interview with the author.

Page 138 'I said you . . . much higher.' Interview with the author.

Page 140 'over 240 million people were on-line by the middle of 2014'. Figures from the Internet and Mobile Association of India, *ndtv.com,* 29 January 2014.

Page 140 'need money for Pappu's brain transplant'. *zeenews.india.com,* 24 August 2014.

Page 142 'spread the colours of peace, prosperity and happiness'. *Financial Times,* 18 March 2014.

Page 144 'There's a history . . . be hostile.' Interview with the author.

Page 145 'I said where . . . job as well.' Interview with the author.

Page 145 'he pulled out of a "Facebook Talks Live" debate'. *ibnlive.in,* 3 March 2014.

Page 146 'Mr Modi then decided to cancel. He is best placed to state the reasons.' *newslaundry.com,* 3 March 2014.

Page 146 ‘By building a large and devout Twitter following . . . news priorities.’ Rajdeep Sardesai, *2014: The Election That Changed India* (Penguin Books 2014) pp. 242-3.

Page 147 ‘Can women of this country trust a man . . . who deprives his wife of her right.’ *The Times,* 10 April 2014.

CHAPTER ELEVEN: ‘SUPERSTAR’

Page 149 ‘constant feeling inside Downing Street that they were out to get him’. Lance Price, *The Spin Doctor’s Diary*, (Hodder & Stoughton 2006), pp. 188, 194.

Page 149 ‘Gordon Brown and John Major . . . driven literally to distraction by what was said and written about them’. Lance Price, *Where Power Lies* (Simon & Schuster 2010), chapters 10 and 12.

Page 150 ‘It was certainly a watershed moment for the Indian news media.’ *Hindustan Times,* 17 August 2014.

Page 151 ‘I think media . . . corporate sector.’ Interview with the author.

Page 155 ‘no conditions had been set in advance’. *The Telegraph,* 21 October 2007.

Pagc 156 ‘we just didn’t know how badly Rahul would end up looking’. Rajdeep Sardesai, *2014: The Election That Changed India* (Penguin Books 2014), p. 225.

Page 157 ‘Rajat Sharma, a friend of Modi’s for over forty years’. Rajdeep Sardesai, *2014: The Election That Changed India* (Penguin Books 2014), p. 227.

Page 157 ‘The programme received the highest TV ratings in India’s history’. *Economic Times,* 17 April 2014.

Page 158 ‘nobody could claim that difficult issues hadn’t been raised’. *India TV,* 12 April 2014.

Page 158 ‘Qamar Waheed Naqvi . . . had gone because he thought the show had been “fixed”’. *Indian Express,* 15 April 2014.

Page 158 ‘The entire programme was part of the Modi propaganda machine’. Rajdeep Sardesai, *2014: The Election That Changed India* (Penguin Books 2014), p. 229.

Page 158 ‘Such reasons are baseless, and we condemn the effort being made to use it for political gains’. *Indian Express,* 15 April 2014.

Page 159 'Modi, it seems, still hadn't forgiven or forgotten the reporting done by the NDTV channels'. Rajdeep Sardesai, *2014: The Election That Changed India* (Penguin Books 2014), p. 231.

Page 159 'There are people . . . can't stand.' Interview with the author.

Page 160 'In recent years corruption within the media . . . or broadcasting information.' S.Y. Quraishi, *The Making of the Great Indian Election* (Rupa Publications 2014), p. 325.

Page 160 'the Indian media has been discharging its responsibility with spectacular effect.' S.Y. Quraishi, *The Making of the Great Indian Election* (Rupa Publications 2014), p. 346.

CHAPTER TWELVE: VOTE LOTUS

Page 165 'Whether or not the BJP was pulling a fast one . . . delay had been caused by logistical problems'. *Hindustan Times*, 3 April 2014.

Page 165 'In the age of 140-character Twitter messages'. *Economic Times*, 3 April 2014.

Page 165 'The RSS was said to be demanding that it appeal more forcefully to Hindu nationalists'. *ndtv.com*, 4 April, 2014.

Page 165 'one man who had held up publication was . . . Narendra Modi'. *ibnlive.in.com*, 3 April, 2014.

Page 167 'every family will have a *pucca* house'. *The Hindu,* 8 December 2013.

Page 169 'Modi is the manifesto. Modi is the vision.' *India Tribune*, 3 April 2014.

Page 169 'he was permitted to stand in two constituencies'. Modi chose to represent Varanasi and a by-election was held in Vadodara, which the BJP won comfortably. In Britain in the nineteenth century leading candidates often stood in more than one place. In fact it was only in the 1983 Representation of the People's Act that candidates were required to attest that they wouldn't stand in more than one seat.

Page 169 'Nobody was . . . vote for.' Interview with the author.

Page 173 'After that . . . big time.' Interview with the author.

Page 174 'if you want to know about the importance of going after every vote, just ask Mukhtar Abbas Naqvi'. *The Hindu*, 18 May 2014.

Page 177 'this time nothing can save the mother-son government'. *The Guardian*, 30 April, 2014.

Page 177 'it was in the nature of political speech intended and calculated to influence and affect the result of elections'. *Indian Express*, 1 May 2014.

Page 177 'he was starting an investigation against chief minister Narendra Modi . . . under Section 126'. *Indian Express*, 1 May 2014. Section 126 of the Representation of the People Act, 1951, prohibits, 'public meetings during a period of 48 hours ending with the hour fixed for conclusion of polling. Section 126 (1) (a) states that no person shall convene, hold or attend, join or address any public meeting or procession in connection with an election. Section 126 (1) (b) says no person shall display to the public any election matter by means of cinematograph, television or other similar apparatus. Any violation of these provisions are punishable with imprisonment of up to two years or fine or both.'

Page 177 'no charges were ever brought and the case was closed in August after Modi had become PM'. *The Hindu*, 22 August 2014.

CHAPTER THIRTEEN: BRAND MODI

Page 179 'Mr Modi stands out literally and strategically.' *New York Times 'On the runway'*, 3 June 2014.

Page 179 'when Tony Blair realised for the first time that he needed glasses'. Lance Price, *The Spin Doctor's Diary* (Hodder & Stoughton 2006), p. 143.

Page 179 'his glasses are from Bvlgari, his watch is a Movado'. *Indian Express*, 28 May 2014.

Page 179 'I had to wash my own clothes . . . happy to hear that I dress well.' *Aap Ki Adalat,* India TV, 12 April 2014.

Page 180 'Modi's fashionable tastes are said to be one reason that some traditionalists in the RSS . . . became suspicious of him' *Narendra Modi, the Man, the Times,* Nilanjan Mukhopadhyay, (Trandquebar Press 2013), p. 279.

Page 180 'If you see the scenario two years back . . . in Modi.' Interview with the author.

Page 181 'We showed him various things like cups . . . he said, "Go ahead and do it".' Interview with the author.

Page 183 'How many times do we get a product so easy to sell?' Interview with the author.

Page 183 'Mr Modi had far more equity . . . starting point for us.' Interview with Gaurav Bhatele for this book.

CHAPTER FOURTEEN- MOTHER GANGES

Page 191 '*I come to you as a child to his mother . . . giver of sacred rest.*' Quoted on *exoticindiaart.com/article/ganga.*

Page 192 'I feel Mother Ganga has called me to Varanasi.' *Times of India*, 24 April 2014.

Page 193 'We knew that if we created a mega television event . . . voting was on.' Rajdeep Sardesai, *2014: The Election That Changed India* (Penguin Books 2014), p. 306.

Page 193 'The election has not banned the filing of nominations'. *ndtv.com*, 25 April 2014.

Page 193 'Modi was going to win so victory was not a target . . . like defeat.' Interview with the author.

Page 194 'It was mainly cleanliness and unemployment . . . for people.' Interview with Geetika Sehmay for this book.

Page 194 'Eggs were thrown at Mr Arvind Kejriwal . . . religious beliefs of people.' Interview with the author.

Page 195 'He is convinced that he is the epitome of manhood. . . love all that about him.' Interview with the author.

Page 197 'the intelligence bureau had warned of a security threat'. *Economic Times*, 9 May 2014.

Page 197 'This is not a banana republic'. *Hindustan Times*, 7 May 2014.

Page 198 'Timid men can dwarf high offices'. *Times of India*, 8 May 2014.

Page 198 'leaders to use proper discourse . . . like the EC.' *New Indian Express*, 9 May 2014.

Page 198 'India is not under British rule . . . on the roads.' *rediff.com*, 8 May 2014.

Page 198 'As his convoy arrived . . . security cordon.' *The Hindu*, 9 May 2014.

Page 199 'The message was to be around "we will not stop, whatever happens".' Interview with the author.

Page 199 'We are unstoppable . . . this is a storm of change.' *Roke nahi ruk payenge, yeh jwala nahin rukne wali, prem bhara yeh jan sailab, is janta ko pranam, yeh badlav ki andhi hai*".

CHAPTER FIFTEEN: THE ONLY WAY IS UP

Page 201 'Shah . . . was out on bail facing serious criminal charges'. On 25 July 2010 Shah was arrested and charged with the murder, extortion and kidnapping among other offences. He was exiled from the state of Gujarat until 2012. Shah maintains that the charges were politically motivated and false.

Page 201 'The charges against him were dropped'. *Hindustan Times,* 30 December 2014.

Page 204 'Politics is greatly influenced by the primordial affiliations of caste and religion'. *hardnewsmedia.com*, 7 April 2014.

Page 204 'You have to concentrate on the booths . . . fall into place' *The Caravan,* 1 April 2014.

Page 204 'Laxmikant Vajpayee, agreed to adopt a booth'. *The Caravan,* 1 April 2014.

Page 206 'Normally, party workers turn up . . . will be futile.' *dnaindia.com* 12 March 2014.

Page 206 'There was a huge craze for caps . . . order more supplies' Interview with Geetika Sehmay for the book.

Page 207 'OBCs make up over 40% of the population of UP'. 2011 census figures.

Page 209 'Rajesh Verma, a journalist working for the IBN7 TV channel, died after being shot in the chest.' *India Today*, 7 September 2013.

Page 209 'Murky politics are already at work . . . fire up Hindu supporters.' *The Economist*, 21 September 2013.

Page 210 'The BJP even went so far as to announce that three politicians who had been officially accused of fanning violence would be among their candidates'. *The Caravan,* 1 April 2014.

Page 210 'This is not just another election . . . insult meted out to our community.' *Times of India*, 5 April 2014.

Page 211 'The BJP called it a "monstrosity of judgment"'. *ndtv.com,* 12 April 2014.

Page 211 'further evidence of the BJP's communal and anti-Muslim politics'. *Financial Express,* 5 May 2014.

Page 211 'the BJP said he had been referring to the lack of development'. *Economic Times,* 5 May 2014.

Page 211 'You can insult Modi . . . But do not insult the lower caste'. Patna rally, 27 October 2013.

Page 211 'I have never seen Gandhi . . . show disrespect to other's caps.' *India TV,* 12 April 2014.

Page 212 'The strategy was to show that Mr Modi is a nationalist . . . even if they are Muslims'. Interview with the author.

Page 212 'How long will these evils continue . . . we have done nothing.' New Delhi, 15 August 2014.

CHAPTER SIXTEEN: RALLY DRIVER

Page 213 'a 360 degree campaign'. Arvind Gupta. Interview with the author.

Page 215 'They must go back . . . of their livelihood.' *in.reuters.com,* 4 May 2014.

Page 216 'accusing him of seeking votes in the name of religion and trying to spread communal disharmony'. *CNN-IBN.* 5 May 2014.

Page 217 'Only the poor will understand the pain of being poor'. *dnaindia.com,* 5 May 2014.

Page 219 'We need you . . . we will make it up to you.' Interview with the author.

Page 220 'quoting a Hindi saying, "*Aap ke muh mein ghee-shakkar*" (May your words come true)'. *inblive.com,* 5 May 2015.

Page 220 'The backdrop featured a huge picture of Lord Ram'. *inblive.com,* 5 May 2015.

Page 220 'This is the land of Lord Ram . . . broke their promises?' *Times of India,* 5 May 2014.

Page 221 'The decision of having the Lord Ram . . . central party headquarters.' Interview with Gaurav Bhatele for this book.

Page 221 'It's the heart of the Gandhi family . . . they wanted Modi.' Interview with the author.

Page 221 'I'll tell them who Smriti Irani is . . . my younger sister.' *ndtv.com*, 5 May 2014.

CHAPTER SEVENTEEN: GOTV

Page 225 'Booth level kits were prepared . . . two days before polling.' Interview by Gaurav Bhatele for this book.

Page 226 'It may sound amusing . . . islands and coastal areas.' S.Y. Quraishi, *The Making of the Great Indian Election* (Rupa Publications 2014), p. 3.

Page 227 'What miserable luck I have . . . somebody has to do it.' *New York Times*, 12 May 2014.

Page 227 'I am confident . . . fair and unifying government.' *aljazeera.com*, 12 May 2014.

Page 228 'The AAP berated the television networks'. *aamaadmiparty.org/complaint-to-ec-against-tv-channels.*

Page 228 'The insanely huge and complex exercise known as the Indian election.' *Time*, 5 March 2014.

Page 229 'the TV channels started to flash up their own exit polls'. *indianexpress.com*, 12 May 2014.

Page 229 'Apart from the Chanakya survey which did predict an overall majority'. *2014-elections-in-india.blogspot.co.uk/2014/05/todays-chanakya-exit-poll-2014-for.html* 12 May 2014.

Page 229 'the Election Commission raised questions about how honest all the parties . . . when submitting their election expenses'. *indianexpress.com*, 12 May 2014.

Page 230 'People asked how come the BJP spent so much money . . . good for them.' Interview with the author.

Page 230 '"Is it Modi's money?" asked Rahul Gandhi.' *Economic Times*, 3 May 2014.

Page 230 'The AAP . . . accused Modi of being their "property dealer"'. *Times of India*, 8 March 2014.

Page 230 'Crony capitalism should not be there.' *in.reuters.com*, 11 April 2014.

Page 231 'I have never received any special treatment . . . not the BJP's ATM machine.' *CNN-IBN*, 28 April 2014.

Page 231 'India's richest businessmen have long been a major source of funds'. *thehundubusinessline.com* 8 January 2014. See also *adrindia.org*.

Page 231 'Mahatma Gandhi described himself as "a friend of the capitalists"'. *rediff.com* 16 August 2004.

Page 233 'a wedding celebration . . . was one massive exercise in bribery'. S.Y. Quraishi, *The Making of the Great Indian Election* (Rupa Publications 2014), pp. 263-4.

Page 233 '2014 election . . . the most transparent and free'. *The Statesman*, 11 August 2014.

Page 233 'the authorities still seized three billion rupees in cash (over thirty million pounds), some 22 million litres of alcohol and 30,000 kilogrammes of illegal drugs.'. S.Y. Quraishi. Interview with the author.

Page 234 'names were missing from the electoral register . . . The BJP suspected political interference'. *dnaindia.com,* 25 April 2014.

CHAPTER EIGHTEEN: INDIA RECAST

Page 236 'Modi was said to be watching television'. *NDTV*, 16 May 2014.

Page 238 'After filing my nomination . . . you gave me 570,000 votes.' *livemint.com* 16 May 2014.

Page 239 'Modi promised the moon and the stars to the people.' *The Independent*, 16 May 2014.

Page 239 'The Congress Party . . . set up an internal inquiry into why it had done so badly'. *India Today*, 15 August 2014.

Page 240 'Some of Modi's party elders . . . offered positions as mentors instead'. *India Today,* 26 August 2014.

Page 240 'The biggest contribution was from our opposition . . . result would not have come.' *India Today,* 26 August 2014.

Page 240 'pariah to prime minister'. *Open Magazine*, 16 May 2014.

Page 240 'great to be talking to someone who just got more votes than any other politician anywhere in the universe.' *Economic Times*, 10 July 2014.

Page 241 'President Obama, began to look more and more like the kid who was picked last for teams during recess'. *New York Times*, 19 May 2014.

Page 241 'those aged 18 – 22, had preferred the BJP'. By age group, the percentage of the votes were split between the BJP and Congress as follows: 18-22: 36/17; 23-25: 33/20; 26-35: 33/20; 36-45: 30/18; 46-55: 30/20; 56+: 27/20. Source: *National Election Studies, Centre for Study of Developing Societies.*

Page 241 'Muslim voters had preferred Congress candidates by almost four to one'. In 'bipolar' contests between the BJP and Congress, Muslims voted 73% for Congress and 19% for the BJP. In 'multipolar' states, where regional and other parties were in contention, the figures were Congress 37%, BJP 7% and Others 56%. Source: *National Election Studies, Centre for Study of Developing Societies.*

Page 242 'the BJP did not nominate a single Muslim candidate in UP'. *How Modi Won It,* Harish Khare, 2014, Hachette India, p. 196.

Page 242 'for the first time ever the BJP had outpolled its rivals among those at the bottom of the caste system'. 24% of Dalits voted BJP in 2014 compared to 19% for Congress. In the previous general election of 2009 the figures had been 12% and 27% respectively. Under Modi 38% of tribal votes went to the BJP against 28% for Congress. Five years earlier it had been 24% BJP and 38% Congress. Source: *National Election Studies, Centre for Study of Developing Societies.*

CHAPTER NINETEEN: FROM PARIAH TO PM

Page 244 'His first priority was India's nearest neighbours'. *The Hindu*, 27 June 2013.

Page 245 'Ashoka . . . came in search of Buddha to tread the path of peace'. *Niti Central*, 3 August 2014.

Page 245 'Modi had warned the country that it would need to take a "bitter pill" in order to restore the nation's finances.' Speech in Goa. *narendramodi.in*. 14 June 2014.

Page 245 'it was a Congress budget "with saffron lipstick added"'. *Economic Times*, 11 July 2014.

Page 245 'price inflation . . . fell to a five-year low'. *Economic Times*, 8 November 2014.

Page 245 'many economists said the new government could not claim full credit'. *firstbiz.com*, 30 August 2014.

Page 245 'Investment was especially weak. Credit growth has been feeble.' *The Economist*, 6 December 2014.

Page 246 'He's not anti-golf or anything, but just pro-work.' *Daily Telegraph*, 2 June 2014.

Page 246 'Modi even went so far as to introduce biometric clocking-in devices'. *dnaindia.com*, 7 October 2014.

Page 247 'hadn't turned up for duty once since going on leave twenty-four years previously.' *The Guardian,* 9 January 2015.

Page 247 'He asked them to identify eight to ten regulations in their ministries that could be done away with.' *Hindustan Times*, 4 October 2014.

Page 247 'Even our secretaries and advisers are imposed on us.' *Outlook*, 1 September 2014.

Page 247 'He gives us some freedom . . . have the courage to take decisions.' *Times of India*, 2 September 2014.

Page 247 'telling him to go home and change into something befitting his job'. *Outlook,* 1 September 2014.

Page 248 'Modi had made much of his intention to bring back so-called "black money"…Some of his senior ministers . . . quoted as saying . . . within his first 100 days'. Rajnath Singh was the most senior minister to make the 100 day promise. *Economic Times,* 17 April 2014.

Page 248 'Jaitley . . . government would "not rest until the last account is identified".' *Times of India,* 26 November 2014.

Page 248 'In his first broadcast, he urged all Indian to shed their despondency'. *Times of India*, 3 October 2014.

Page 248 'As far as black money is concerned . . . should come back.' *ibnlive.in*, 3 November 2014.

Page 248 'Corruption is the enemy of the nation . . . unwarranted persons as ministers.' *The Guardian*, 27 August 2014.

Page 249 'these are cases arising out of criminal accusations, not cases out of a crime.' *in.reuters.com*, 10 November 2014.

Page 249 'The Election Commission . . . proposed banning candidates facing serious criminal charges'. S.Y. Quraishi, *The Making of the Great Indian Election* (Rupa Publications 2014), p. 414.

Page 249 '34% of the total number of MPs elected in May had been charged with a serious offence'. *Times of India*, 9 December 2014.

Page 249 'a draft bill . . . was shelved . . . for lack of consensus among leading political parties'. *Economic Times*, 9 December 2014.

Page 249 'At the end of the year a judge dismissed the charges against Amit Shah'. *Hindustan Times,* 30 December 2014.

Page 250 'Nationalists in the state raised the spectre of a "love jihad".' *Times of India*, 5 September 2014.

Page 250 'These are cases of love marriages and not love jihad' *Times of India*, 5 September 2014.

Page 250 'Love jihad is a media creation . . . not true that we have started some big campaign on the issue.' *Economic Times*, 11 September 2014.

Page 250 'other comments by BJP figures were seen as evidence that below the shiny surface of Modi's modernisation and development agenda lay the same extremist Hindutva ideology'. *Indian Express*, 3 December 2014.

Page 251 'Mahanth Yogi Adityanath, was . . . condemned by the Election Commission for allegedly promoting religious hatred.' *Times of India* 11 September 2014.

Page 251 'In Maharashtra the BJP's share of the vote rose . . . and in Haryana the figures were even more remarkable, *elections.in/maharashtra/.*

Page 251 'Shah launched a membership drive . . . where the BJP had performed less well'. *Business Standard*, 29 November 2014.

Page 251 'pressure for changes to the curriculum in schools to reflect more traditional Hindu values. The RSS was among those urging the government to take 'corrective steps'. *Indian Express*, 26 July 2014.

Page 252 'RSS was among those . . . to "Indianise" the education system.' *scroll.in,* 2 August 2014.

Page 252 'The AAP's focus on local issues worked while the BJP was accused of complacency and of losing touch with the core concerns of the voters since the general election.' In its assessment of the results, the *Times of India* concluded that 'The 7–0 scoreline in the Lok Sabha elections made the BJP complacent about the Delhi assembly polls. Delhi had fallen off its radar. It allowed the AAP and Kejriwal to regroup and recover . . . The party was relying too much on Narendra Modi's appeal and Amit Shah's organising abilities. By the time BJP became serious, Kejriwal and

AAP had taken a lead and were setting the agenda.' *Times of India*, 10 February 2014.

Page 252 'Smriti Irani . . . announced that Sanskrit would replace German'. *Times of India*, 14 November 2014.

Page 252 'she would only ever act "in the spirit of constitution".' *Asian Age*, 2 December 2014.

Page 252 'many academics and professionals . . . detected subtle . . . pressures to avoid promoting anything that might be construed as "anti-Hindu"'. There was controversy, for example, over the film 'PK', which was criticised for hurting Hindu sentiments. *firstpost.com,* 3 January 2015.

Page 252 'Salman Rushdie, was not alone in worrying that writers and journalists risked being "bullied"'. *ndtv.com* 6 May 2014.

Page 252 'Behind closed doors he warned his MPs not to cross the line by making inflammatory statements'. *ibnlive.in.com*, 16 December 2014.

Page 252 'unconfirmed reports that . . . he had threatened to leave the RSS'. *firstpost.com*, 20 December 2014.

Page 253 'Will the real Narendra Modi please speak up?' *firstpost.com,* 24 December 2014.

Page 253 'his official website, narendramodi.in, was given a makeover with a new banner headline "Action and Hope".' *actionandhope.narendramodi.in.*

Page 254 'Some overzealous BJP workers were caught by the cameras scattering leaves on the ground'. *ndtv.com*, 18 November 2014.

Page 254 'If we paint this again with a brush of politics, we will again do a disservice to Mother India.' *zeenews.india.com*, 26 November 2014.

Page 254 'Modi unveiled his promised "Adopt a Village" campaign'. *Times of India,* 11 October 2014.

Page 254 'even Rahul and Sonia Gandhi agreed to take part'. *Times of India*, 14 November 2014.

Page 255 'a mutual love-fest that sharply etched the country's growing power and profile in the minds of Americans'. *Times of India,* 28 September 2014.

Page 256 'How are you doing New York?' *ndtv.com*, 28 September 2014.

Page 256 'Gopal Nadadur had made the trip from New York . . . "it's embarrassing to see India being so easily surpassed on the global stage".' Interview for this book.

Page 257 'You will no longer have to reach to opportunities through uncertain and unpredictable pathways'. *ibnlive.com*, 17 November 2014.

Page 258 'Australia will not be at the periphery of our vision'. *ibnlive.com*, 18 November 2014.

Page 258 'I give this to the feet of the children of India.' *ndtv.com*, 17 November 2014.

Page 258 'Modi's election enthused Indians living abroad . . . new interest in India here.' Interview with Geetika Sehmay for this book.

Page 259 'We are planning to take a quantum leap.' *busineworld.in* 11 January 2015.

Page 259 'the United Nations predicted steady growth in India's GDP'. *thehindubusinessline.com,* 20 January 2015.

Page 259 'The International Monetary Fund (IMF) was similarly upbeat . . . The Word Bank . . . anticipated a slow but steady economic recovery'. *livemint.com* 20 January 2015.

Page 259 'the highest number of bank accounts opened in the shortest space of time.' *zeenews.india.com* 21 January 2015.

Page 259 'over 99 per cent of households had been enrolled.' According to the Financial Services Secretary, Jan Dhan Yojana, the figure was 99.74%. *zeenews.india.com* 21 January 2015.

Page 260 'John Kerry had flown to India . . . to urge Modi to join with America in overcoming decades of distrust in the region.' *Bloomberg News,* 13 January 2015.

Page 260 'Nawaz Sharif, sent a message reaffirming his country's commitment to developing friendly relations'. *zeenews,india.com* 26 January 2015.

Page 260 'relations had been characterised more by wariness and a lack of meaningful dialogue'. There had been a war of words between the two countries in August when Modi had ordered the cancellation of talks at foreign minister level, blaming a meeting between a Pakistani envoy and separatist rebels in Kashmir. *The Diplomat* 15 January 2015.

Page 260 'The president said the two countries were natural partners . . . "a top foreign policy priority for my administration".' *New York Times,* 25 January 2015.

Page 260 'Mr Obama ended their joint news conference . . . "let's walk together".' *thehindu.com* 25 January 2015.

Page 260 'With the signing of the 'India-US Delhi Declaration of Friendship', the relationship between the two countries was reset'. The agreement included more regular summit meetings, a hot-line between the two capitals, and enhanced cooperation in a range of fields. It said, 'Each step we take to strengthen the relationship is a step towards shaping international security, regional and global peace, prosperity and stability for years to come.' *whitehouse.gov*.

Page 261 'the president said both countries had an obligation to uphold religious freedom.' Quoting from the Indian constitution, Obama added, 'Your Article 25 says all people are equally entitled to the freedom of conscience and have right to freely profess and practise and propagate religion. In both our countries, in all countries upholding with freedom of religion is the utmost responsibility of the government but also the responsibility of every person'. *Times of India* 27 January 2015.

Page 261 'Modi addressed a rally of the National Cadet Corps . . . His words were reassuringly inclusive. *pmindia.gov.in*.

Page 261 'The dark blue jacket he wore . . . had his own name stitched a thousand times'. *indiatoday.in* 26 January 2014.

Page 261 'A readers' poll conducted by *Time* magazine had him way out in front as their choice for person of the year'. *time.com* 19 November 2014.

CHAPTER TWENTY: THE INDOMITABLE WILL

Page 264 'The decline and fall of the Congress . . . thrown in the wastebasket.' *bbc.com,* 17 May 2014.

Page 266 'There goes my people . . . I must follow them, for I am their leader.' *Advance Study on the History of Modern India (Volume 3, 1920-1947),* G.S. Chhabra, 2005, Lotus Press, p. 49

Page 266 'You could see Modi as standing on a balloon of hot air.' Interview with the author.

ACKNOWLEDGEMENTS

The prospect of getting so deeply immersed in Indian politics over a relatively short space of time was a daunting one. I'm relieved to say that it turned out to be both rewarding and enjoyable. All the same, I feel I should move the rather clichéd author's line – 'the responsibility for any remaining errors is entirely mine' – right up here to the top. I had a lot to learn but, thankfully, I had the support of some outstanding people who were patient in the face of my constant questions and skilful in helping me navigate the intricacies of Indian traditions and culture. My two researchers, Gaurav Bhatele and Geetika Sehmay, were hardworking, well informed in their respective fields of expertise – politics and the media – and great fun. Vinesh Chandel did some valuable digging into the detail of the campaign and Alex Cisneros helped me make sense of Indian and British constitutional law. Jaskirat Singh Bawa kindly allowed us to use his excellent unpublished photographs from the campaign trail. Unusually, I had two editors and they were two of the best. It was a huge pleasure to be reunited with Rupert Lancaster at Hodder & Stoughton in London. He knew what to expect as we'd worked together unpicking another towering political figure a decade ago in *The Spin Doctor's Diary.* Thomas Abraham at Hachette India in Delhi provided just the level of guidance I needed, egging me on and reining me in where appropriate. The other members of the team in both offices were a model of professionalism and efficiency. My agent, Broo Doherty at the DHH

Literary Agency, looked after me with all the good sense and good humour that I have come to depend upon. I am fortunate in having many good Indian friends here in Britain who were able to help me make sense of the country they all love, despite, or perhaps that should be including, all its idiosyncrasies and frustrations. Special mention should go to Harjeet Johal, Kapil Gupta and Siddo Deva. This book would not have been possible without the help and cooperation of Narendra Modi himself and members of his staff at the prime minister's office, in particular Dr Hiren Joshi, Nirav Shah and Yash Gandhi. And it benefitted enormously from the contributions of all those who agreed to be interviewed – ministers, party workers, campaign volunteers and professional advisers, as well as journalists, academics and others. Where appropriate they have been named in the text. In some cases they felt the need to help me anonymously, but I am equally grateful to all. My partner, James Proctor, and my family, put up as usual with my long absences and with the fact that my head was so often in India while my feet were in Europe. Narendra Modi is a seemingly indefatigable workaholic. What sometimes felt like long and tiring days for me were as nothing compared to his schedule. I hope I have done justice to his achievements without ever overlooking the downsides. I come from a very different cultural and political background, but while there are very many things on which I doubt we would ever agree, we both admire democracy and thrive on the excitement of elections. That, above all, is what this book is about.

INDEX

NM in the index indicates Narendra Modi

PICTURE ACKNOWLEDGEMENTS

Most of the photographs are from the Narendra Modi official website, reproduced by permission.

Additional sources:
AFP/Sebastian D'Souza/Getty Images: 2 above right.
AP/Press Association Images: 14 below left.
Jaskivat Singh Bawa: 1 middle left, 4 above and below right, 8 above and below, 9 below, 10 above and below, 11 above and below, 14 middle right.
BJPGujarat.org: 2 middle right.
BJP.org: 6 middle right.
EPA/Jagadeesh Nv/Alamy: 9 above right.
NaMo Gujarat YouTube: 6 above left.
Lance Price: 7 below right, 16 below.
Reuters/Corbis: 14 above left/photo Adnan Abidi.
14 middle left/photo B. Mathur, 15 photo Amit Dave.
REX/ddp USA: 12 above.
Vibrant Gujarat: 2 below.